The America-China Divide

The Race to Control the World

Daniel Wagner

Country Risk Solutions
Connecticut, USA

Cover photo: Pixabay

Cover design: Anna Zayco - aniazayco@gmail.com

Also by Daniel Wagner

- *The Chinese Vortex*

- *China Vision*

- *AI Supremacy*

- *Virtual Terror*

- *Global Risk Agility and Decision-making*

- *Managing Country Risk*

- *Political Risk Insurance Guide*

A repository of his published work (including more than 700 articles on current affairs and risk management) may be found at: www.countryrisksolutions.com.

This book is dedicated to everyone on planet Earth. May America and China possess the wisdom to work together to make it a better place.

Acknowledgements

I am grateful to the following individuals for agreeing to review this book: Dinny McMahon (Fellow at the Paulson Institute's MacroPolo), Joshua Meltzer (Senior Fellow in Global Economy and Development at the Brookings Institution), Scott Moore (Director of the Penn Global China Program), Mixin Pei (Tom and Margot Pritzker '72 Professor of Government and George R. Roberts Fellow at Claremont McKenna College), and Frans-Paul Van Der Putten (Senior Fellow, Clingendael Institute). And a special thanks to Anna Zayco, once again, for her great design work on the book cover and to Raymond Gray for again using his fabulous voice to produce the audio book.

CONTENTS

About the Author

Daniel Wagner is the founder and CEO of Country Risk Solutions and has three decades of experience managing cross-border risk in the private and public sectors.

Daniel began his career at AIG in New York and subsequently spent five years as Guarantee Officer for the Asia Region at the World Bank Group's Multilateral Investment Guarantee Agency in Washington, DC. During that time, he was responsible for underwriting political risk insurance for projects in a dozen Asian countries. After serving as Regional Manager for Political Risks for Southeast Asia and Greater China for AIG in Singapore, Daniel moved to Manila, Philippines, where he served in a variety of capacities in the Asian Development Bank's Office of Co-financing Operations, including as Senior Guarantees and Syndications Specialist. He then became Senior Vice President of Country Risk at GE Energy Financial Services.

Daniel has published more than 700 articles on current affairs and risk management and is a regular contributor to the *South China Morning Post*, *Sunday Guardian*, and many others. His editorials have also been published in such notable newspapers as the *New York Times* and the *Wall Street Journal*. He is also the author of seven previous books: *The Chinese Vortex*, *China Vision*, *AI Supremacy*, *Virtual Terror*, *Global Risk Agility and Decision-Making*, *Managing Country Risk*, and *Political Risk Insurance Guide*.

He holds master's degrees in International Relations from the University of Chicago and in International Management from the Thunderbird School of Global Management, in Phoenix. Daniel received his bachelor's degree in Political Science from Richmond College, in London.

daniel.wagner@countryrisksolutions.com

linkedin.com/in/danielwagnercrs / twitter.com/countryriskmgmt

Praise for *The America-China Divide*

Daniel Wagner has written a comprehensive and clear-eyed view on what a rising China means for the US and the world more broadly. He does an excellent job identifying how China has managed to benefit from the US-led international system, but as it has grown more powerful now presents the US and its allies with a series of increasingly difficult challenges, ranging from international trade through to security. This book is a must-read for policy makers, business leaders, academics and anyone interested in understanding how the US-China relationship might develop and the implications for the world.

Joshua Meltzer, Senior Fellow, Global Economy and Development Program, Brookings Institution

It is often argued the China's relationship with the US will define the global order for decades to come, but never has anyone surveyed that relationship – in all its complexity, and in such an accessible way – as Daniel Wagner has here. *The American-China Divide* addresses everything from trade and tech wars to aid, diplomacy, and other parts of the relationship that get less attention but are nonetheless evolving in ways that headlines fail to capture. It's an incredibly engaging work that delivers a holistic outlook on the relationship, one that will be of value to the layperson and China expert alike. As a China analyst, I was surprised by just how much I learned.

Dinny McMahon, Fellow, The Paulson Institute's MacroPolo

Great power competition between the US and China is quickly emerging as the dominant theme in global affairs. In

The America-China Divide, Daniel Wagner explains why this is so in a sharp analysis of a highly complicated relationship. He identifies both sides' main perceptions, interests, and aims, as well as their most important strengths and weaknesses. Daniel makes a convincing case that the scale and scope of the Sino-US power struggle surpasses any previous instance of geopolitical rivalry, and that we are probably only at the start of a prolonged phase of uncertainty and instability. In his view, a military conflict between the US and China, while not impossible, is not the most likely outcome. Rather, global companies and advanced technologies have become the key strategic national assets, which have propelled America and China into a race to control the world.

Dr. Frans-Paul van der Putten, Senior Research Fellow at the Clingendael Institute and Coordinator of the Clingendael China Center

Daniel Wagner sketches a vision of a future divided essentially into two Cold War-esque blocs, one led by China and the other by the US. He rightly draws attention to several phenomena that are important but little-noted by other observers, such as Beijing's support for think tanks, which aim to shape policymaking and discourse around the globe, and China's increasingly close ties to countries like Saudi Arabia. Wagner is also careful to call for the US to respond to these challenges not by antagonizing China but rather by equipping itself to compete more effectively. Much of the book is a collection of sober analytical observations and similarly sensible recommendations. So much so, in fact, that it creates a certain fundamental tension: how do serious observers of China attempt to shape policy and discourse in a time when it seems that so much of the discussion, in Washington at least, is fundamentally absurd? Part of the answer may be found in important points recounted in the book. If, as Wagner suggests, such chasms can be bridged, perhaps the America-China Divide may yet shrink instead of grow inexorably wider.

Professor Scott Moore, Director, Penn Global China Program

Abbreviations

A2/AD	anti-access/area denial
AI	Artificial Intelligence
AIIB	Asian Infrastructure Investment Bank
America	United States of America
ASAT	anti-satellite
ASEAN	Association of Southeast Asian Nations
BRI	Belt and Road Initiative
BSL-2	Biosafety level-2
BSL-4	Biosafety level-4
BWC	Biological Weapons Convention
CCP	Chinese Communist Party
CDC	Center for Disease Control
CDB	China Development Bank
CFIUS	Committee on Foreign Investment in the United States
COVID-19	SARS-CoV-2 virus
CRISPR	clustered regularly interspaced short palindromic repeats

DAMO	Discovery, Adventure, Momentum, and Outlook
DF	Dong Feng
DL	Deep Learning
DOD	US Department of Defense
ESG	Environmental, Social, Governance
EU	European Union
EXIM	Export-Import Bank
FDA	US Food and Drug Administration
FDI	Foreign Direct Investment
FIRRMA	Foreign Investment Risk Review Modernization Act
GDP	Gross Domestic Product
GII	Global Innovation Index
GPS	global positioning system
GSD	PLA's General Staff Department
HEU	highly enriched uranium
HIPC	Highly Indebted Poor Country
HPM	high-power microwave
INF	Intermediate-Range Nuclear Forces Treaty
IP	Intellectual Property
ISR	intelligence, surveillance, and reconnaissance
MDBs	Multilateral Development Banks
MEP	Ministry of Environmental Protection
MFA	China's Ministry of Foreign Affairs
MNEs	Multinational Enterprises

NASA	US National Aeronautics and Space Administration
NATO	North Atlantic Treaty Organization
NGO	Non-governmental organization
NIH	US National Institutes of Health
NIRR-1	Nigerian Research Reactor 1
NSF	National Science Foundation
OFDI	Outward Foreign Direct Investment
OTH	over-the-horizon
PLA	People's Liberation Army
REMs	rare earth minerals
RT	Russia Today
SARS	Severe Acute Respiratory Syndrome
SIPG	Shanghai International Port Group
SOEs	state-owned enterprises
SSF	Strategic Support Force
TPP	Trans-Pacific Partnership
TTP	Thousand Talents Program
UN	United Nations
UNCLOS	United Nations Convention on the Law of the Sea
UK	United Kingdom
US	United States of America
WCO	World Cybersecurity Organization
WHO	World Health Organization
WTO	World Trade Organization

UN   United Nations

Preface

Over the course of my life, whenever I have lived overseas, I have gained valuable insight and perspective about a great many things, including the state of the world and my own country, the United States (US). This was true in 2019 when I lived in Abidjan, Cote D'Ivoire, and from where I wrote this book. What better perch than Africa to contemplate the book's topic, given that China has had such a profound impact on the continent over the past decade. Of course, it is not just Africa that will continue to be greatly impacted by the divide that is growing between America and China, but the stakes are probably higher in Africa than anywhere else in the world.

That is because Africa, and the world, face a stark choice – to pivot in the direction of the US for the remainder of this century, to pivot instead toward China, or to have divided loyalties between the two. For some governments, businesses, and individuals, that will be an easy choice. For others, it will be rather difficult, acknowledging that there are pluses and minuses associated with going in either direction. At the heart of the matter is not only whether a nation or people fundamentally believes in what either option implies on a whole range of issues, but also, what is likely to be in their long-term collective interests in the future.

Not long ago, there was really no choice for most countries. America was the land of the free, home of the brave, a bastion of capitalism, and a shining beacon for the world's poor and disenfranchised. In the second decade of the 21st century, many would argue that this is no longer the case. Torn apart by divisiveness politically, economically, socially, and on moral issues of the day, America is increasingly being perceived by many around the world to be a declining power that is fractious and filled with inherent contradictions. It is no longer the place it *used* to be, many will argue, and since no power stays on top indefinitely, many would say it is China's turn to lead the world. If not China, then perhaps a grouping of nations (the G7 or the

BRICS, for example), but they, too, suffer from profound disagreements and divisiveness, which prevent them from carving a path forward on a host of issues.

While many may disagree about what China is today – some would say, an authoritarian communist state where the supremacy of the Chinese Communist Party (CCP) reigns supreme at the cost of individual liberty – few can object to the incredible economic miracle that China has become, or the many hugely significant achievements it has made in science, technology, and the eradication of poverty among the vast majority of its 1.4 billion people. A lot of non-Chinese may find the CCP's tactics objectionable, but hundreds of millions of people in China would disagree, noting that they live a far better life today than their parents did, and it is equally likely that their own children will live a more prosperous life than them. The CCP's tactics (and I am making a clear distinction here between the Chinese government versus its people) are highly objectionable on a whole range of issues but, it is getting the job done, many would argue, and people throughout the world recognize that.

This multifaceted landscape is the subject of this book. There is indeed a choice to be made, and every nation, international business, and person on the planet will in some way be making that choice – either now or at some point in this decade, when China becomes the world's largest economy and its power grows exponentially from what it is today. Governments will make the choice by the company they keep. Businesses will make that choice by where they choose to operate and sell their products. And individuals will make that choice by the products they buy. The America-China divide is really all about shaping our future, and the stakes could not be higher.

I readily acknowledge that my perspective on this subject is that of a proud American. However, anyone who knows me will tell you that I am also a proud citizen of the world who is intellectually honest and attempts to be levelheaded and fair in my written work. In this book you will easily note my own biases, but also, I hope, my attempt to praise and criticize both America and China, since both countries are clearly deserving of praise and criticism. In this book I tackle a lot of sub-topics and cover a lot of ground. I do not claim to have all the answers to the many questions posed throughout the book, but I hope that by making at attempt to tackle these issues I will have succeeded in raising the profile of the topic and contributed meaningfully to the ongoing debate about the America-China divide.

Chapter 1: An Ideological Choice

The world is in a state of disruption on a variety of levels–politically, economically, technologically, socioculturally, and in terms of the environment. No one really knows how this state of disruption will manifest itself in the coming decades, but our world is already being pulled in two important directions: one that remains dominated by America and an alternate version that will be dominated by China. The potential for a paradigm shift away from America is a source of great concern to some who have derived great comfort (and security and prosperity) from the post-war liberal order largely designed by the United States of America (the "US" or "America"). The fact that the prospect of such a dramatic change is happening during a time of relative peace (with no major cross-border wars, no new global terrorist movement or imminent threats on the horizon) makes it all the more important.

It will not be lost to some readers that China's incredible rise as a global power over the past 30 years has really only been possible *because* of the liberal world order that America helped create, which it used to its maximum advantage. China has embedded itself into the world order economically, diplomatically, technologically, in business, and in so many other ways as a net *beneficiary* of that order. In that regard, globalization was the best thing ever to happen to China, enabling it to become the manufacturing powerhouse of the world. Of course, it had a little help from thousands of foreign companies which chose to establish their manufacturing operations in China, lured by its vast population and the potential for decades of future profitability as a result of operating there.

As many of those businesses can attest, that is not necessarily the way it ended up. Many of them experienced legal, judicial, regulatory, partnership, and other issues which made operating in China a real challenge. Many of the contracts they agreed to allowed only for Chinese court jurisdiction, and foreign businesses must generate their own foreign exchange in order to make cross-border currency transfers; they cannot utilize the Chinese Central Bank's foreign exchange reserves to make that happen. China's currency, the yuan, is still not convertible on the capital account – an important precursor to becoming a global currency. Yet, Beijing sits atop the world's most fantastic aggregation of foreign exchange, which reached as high as $4 trillion in 2014,[1] almost 29 times greater than that of America's at that time (approximately $140 billion[2]). Beijing may not like the fact that it did not create the post-war order, but it has certainly made the most of it.

If you did not already know it, China likes to play by its own set of rules. And not just in China. My previous book on China – *China Vision* – describes how Beijing is in the process of creating an alternative world order based in its own image. A Chinese world order is one in which Beijing sets the parameters and calls the shots. If you are a citizen of a poor developing country and your government needs money to build infrastructure, China may well provide it – but with a strict set of conditions that can include onerous repayment terms (sometimes much higher than that of the multilateral development banks (MDBs)) – and when your government defaults on that debt (which it inevitably will, since Beijing is lending the money knowing there is a high likelihood it will never be repaid), it will then seize the asset it built and own it, in your own country, while your government labors under tens of billions of dollars of debt. This has happened numerous times, especially in Africa. It is called debt trap diplomacy.

Although many analysts would say China has abused the privileged position it sits in as a result of its population size, economic strength, growing wealth, and power, let us give credit where credit is due. The CCP has lifted hundreds of millions of its citizens out of poverty over the past 40 years and it deserves a lot of credit for having done so. It greatly enhanced the socioeconomic status of the vast majority of its citizens during the same period. Although China consumes a significant percentage of the world's natural resources, in doing so it is supporting exporting economies around the world. It is also in the process of transforming itself from being one of the most polluted (and polluting) countries in the world to becoming a major supporter of green energy. It is clearly one of the most influential countries in the corridors of global power and a leading provider of foreign aid (even if some strings may be attached). And it is also a leader in a number of areas of technology, including Artificial Intelligence (AI). So, kudos to the people of China and the CCP for all that they have accomplished in a very short period of time.

How does the US stack up? In spite of the impact of the Trump presidency, which, many would argue has significantly diminished America's standing and influence in the world, the US remains the world's most important political, economic, scientific, and military power and, as everyone knows, has accomplished a great many fantastic things over the past 100 years. That said, no great power stays on top indefinitely, as countless historical examples have demonstrated, and many people think that America's days as the world's leader in so many areas are slowly coming to an end. While that ultimately may prove to be true, for now, it remains on top. Even if it is eventually replaced by China in some areas, it may take decades for that to occur.

Or perhaps not. China could well become the world's leading economic power in *this* decade. It is very likely also to become the world leader in AI in this decade. Were the yuan to become fully convertible, it could well become an alternative reserve currency in this decade. It is not hard to imagine China giving the US a run for the top title in any number of other categories – in this decade. That is how fast China's position as a world power is progressing. So many of the predictions of learned experts in terms of how quickly China will rise to assume the top ranking in so many areas have proven to be wrong (i.e. they have projected too far out into the future), largely because they have failed to take into account how China is allocating resources in pursuit of its objectives, and how quickly the pace of change is occurring. So, if you think it may be too soon to consider China supplanting the US as the world's leading power, I would argue that you are wrong.

Assuming that my supposition is correct, what does this imply for the world? That is the central question that will be addressed in this book. Although we currently live in a multipolar, G-zero world, and although that is unlikely to change in the near term, eventually, a new dominant global power *will* emerge. That power is likely to be China. The writing is on the wall. The signs are everywhere. We are already in the middle of that transition, but most people either do not realize it or do not think of it in those terms. They may simply think of it more as a choice, between an iPhone or a Huawei phone, between Chase or the China Industrial and Commercial Bank of China, or between Amazon or Alibaba. American and Chinese products exist and are readily available everywhere in the world, so for consumers, it often boils down to a choice of brands.

It may well be the world's consumers who decide which country reigns supreme. Or it may be the degree to which either China or the US is stronger in the corridors of global power, or on the high seas, or in cyberspace. It may end up being the result of a combination of such variables. What seems clear is that the world's consumers, businesses, and governments have a choice to make. That choice, which is increasingly between the products, brands, influence, and policies of two great nations – China and the US – will increasingly define how the world transitions from an American led past and present to what could very well could become a Chinese-led future.

What does the world actually think of China and the US, and does it matter?

So, just what does the world actually think about China and the US? The Pew Research Center conducted a survey[3] across the world in 2018 to find out. The Center surveyed more than 26,000 people from 25 countries.[4] The results were, in some respects predictable, but also, at least a little surprising. More citizens of countries around the world still view the US as the world's leading economic power, rather than China. This was particularly true in Latin America and the Asia-Pacific region, but by slimmer margin than most might have expected: 39% named the US as the top global economy, but 34% said it was China. In fact, the majority of people surveyed in nearly every participating country said they believed that the future would be better if the US were the world's leading power than if China were. 63% said they preferred a world in which the US was the leading power; only 19% would favor a world led by China.

At the same time, favorable views of the US remained at historic lows in many of the countries polled, during the second year of the Trump presidency. Among possible sources of resentment was the widespread perception that the US does not consider the interests of other countries when making foreign policy decisions, and some respondents viewed the US as not being sufficiently engaged in resolving international problems. As for China, 34% of those surveyed had confidence in President Xi, while 56% lacked confidence in him. But there was a widespread sense in the countries surveyed that China plays a more important role in the world than it did in 2008. In all but two nations, half or more said that China's power had increased. Of the 25 country populations participating in the study, 16 voted in favor of the US by at least 50%; by contrast, only one country clearly felt China would be a better leading power by that margin. Across the countries surveyed, a median of 45% had a favorable view of China, while 43% held an unfavorable view. Majorities or pluralities in 12 countries gave China positive marks; positive views of China were most prevalent in Africa, the Middle East, and parts of Asia.

More than 60% in Tunisia, Kenya, and Nigeria viewed China favorably, as did roughly half or more of the numbers surveyed in South Africa and Israel. More than half of those surveyed in Russia, Indonesia, and the Philippines also had positive opinions of China. Economic ties spurred by China's Belt and Road Initiative (BRI), including the fact that these three nations are among the top three recipient countries of Chinese contracts, may partly explain the sanguine attitudes toward Beijing. A median of 66% of people surveyed across the 25 countries thought the Chinese government did not respect the personal freedoms of its people. The respondents that said China ignores the rights of its people tended to have more unfavorable views of China, while publics less critical of China's human rights record also showed lower unfavorable opinions of China overall.

What this appears to imply is that there is an acknowledgement from people around the world that China is a rising power, has great influence in a great many places, and is receiving the respect that it deserves in many quarters. But most of the respondents placed great value on democracy and respect for human rights. If the Chinese government were to become more democratic and place greater emphasis on the rights of its citizens, this survey implies that more of the world's people may be more favorably inclined to welcome Chinese leadership in the future. However, since that is extremely unlikely to occur in the next decade, we should expect that a clear preference for US leadership will remain steadfast among the world's population for some time to come.

On the other hand, the pendulum that forms public opinion is in a state of flux. The world is slowly transitioning from a liberal world order to a more authoritarian one, with populations throughout the world choosing more conservative rule via *democratic* elections. Trump in America, Bolsonaro in Brazil, Orban in Hungary, Duterte in the Philippines, and Erdogan in Turkey – these are all examples of populations that have said they are tired of liberalism and desire a path toward core values and law and order. Many of them see the liberalism that has dominated the global landscape for decades as having resulted in tremendous public sector debt, with little to show for it. This trend will surely continue well into the current decade.

Could China's model be well ahead of its time? It is worth noting that the CCP has made a pact with the Chinese people, in essence saying it will give them a better life than their parents had in return for a tacit understanding that they accept the prevailing order and will not cause any trouble. This model has worked very well for decades, but many people in the West naturally project their own experience and set of values into the picture and presume that living under a Chinese-style dictatorship would result in constant misery. For them, perhaps it would. But the average Chinese citizen appears to be content with the arrangement. The government delivers the goods and most citizens do not challenge the system.

One could easily argue that this approach to governing has been central to enabling China to become the economic powerhouse that it is today. That is because the CCP has been able to keep the plates spinning all these years. The 2019 official growth rate of approximately 6% per annum was roughly half of what it had been in 2010[5] (and gross domestic product (GDP) growth has been sliding ever since then). The trade war with the US, declining global consumption, and a hyper-competitive global economy have all taken their toll on China's economy. The CCP must be wondering how it can continue to keep the plates spinning.

That is part of the beauty of being an authoritarian power. The CCP does not need to ask permission to do anything; it just does it. Have you ever wondered why the Chinese economy rarely seems to have a hard landing, a soft landing, or no landing at all? That is because the government is able to manipulate official statistics, quickly shift resources around, and declare that there really is no housing bubble or non-performing loan crisis – everything is just fine and no one can prove otherwise.

How is that different than Western stock markets brushing off bad news, continuing to break record after record, declaring that inverted yield curves don't mean a thing, and that there really is no long overdue recession lurking around the corner? In a way, that is its own form of authoritarian rule, with the Western media lapping it all right up and consumers not appearing to know the difference. The Chinese people have been made numb by CCP propaganda and Westerners have been made equally numb by the one percenters saying that night is day and black is white. Quelle est la différence ?

The rollout of China's social credit system has shocked many observers in the West. The system is designed to identify those the government deems "desirable" versus those it deems "undesirable", based on individual behavior. In essence, if you pay your bills on time, do what you're told, don't ask too many questions, and mind your own business, you get a good score. If you don't pay your alimony, abuse your spouse, act poorly at work, ask a lot of questions, and challenge the government, you get a bad score. In the West, this would be deemed unwarranted action on the part of a government, overly intrusive, and even illegal. But in China, it is all part of the grand plan. The CCP argues that it is designed to maintain law and order and root out the bad apples from the good ones. And it will probably achieve those objectives, so the average Chinese person is likely to ask, what's the problem? – bearing in mind that he/she is not likely to be judged as a bad actor, so it is unlikely to make any real net difference to most Chinese citizens in the long run.

That, of course, remains to be seen. No one really knows how the social credit system will manifest itself over the long-term. It could turn out to be a dystopian nightmare, but it is a great way for a government to keep tabs on its people and is being replicated by governments around the world, courtesy of the CCP. Here again, one could argue that the US government has been doing something similar for years. The Snowden revelations certainly painted a dark picture of what the government had been doing in terms of snooping on American citizens and learning a lot about how they spend their time, what they talk about, and who they associate with – all in the name of the global War on Terror.

The central point being, China and US are often perceived as being worlds apart on a wide range of issues but, depending on one's experience and perspective, they may not necessarily be all that different in a lot of ways. Does the Kenyan farmer, Bolivian miner, or Bangladeshi textile worker know, or necessarily care, about the nuances of great power rivalry and domination? No. Will whoever rules the world make much difference to their nation, or in their lives or those of their family members? Probably not, over the long haul. Most "average" people know very little about the ideological battle between China and the US, and they probably do not care, either. What matters more is what happens in the global corridors of power.

China Likes to Play by a Different Set of Rules

Although China is the world's second largest economy and has begun to assume a high profile and flex its muscles on the global economic stage over the past decade, it has been doing so politically and diplomatically in the global corridors of power for some 20 years. China is well represented in most international organizations, and although its shareholding in the MDBs is generally much smaller than that of the US, its influence in the decision-making process far exceeds its shareholding percentages. In some of these institutions, little gets done without the wink and nod of China.

As China increases the level of its cross-border investments around the world and amasses great wealth, it continues to reap benefits from the MDBs intended to accrue to the world's truly needy nations. By all rights, *China should be strictly a donor nation to MDBs, not a recipient of aid.* That China continues to be one of the development banks' largest recipients of funds (sometimes, its largest) really is scandalous, coming at the cost of the poorest of the poor nations, which truly need the resources. *At what point does China's absolute strength count for more than its per capita development, and why do donor countries allow this double standard to continue to occur?*

The truth is, the MDBs need China to continue to absorb billions of dollars of loans, grants, and technical assistance they provide each year because many of the smaller and poorer countries do not have the capacity to absorb them. Without China, lending amounts would decline, which would call into question how these banks operate. That is a subject few in the management of these institutions are inclined to tackle seriously, even though doing so is long overdue.

For Beijing to continue to receive development assistance, given the strength and prominence of its economy, makes even less sense since it has taken specific action to assume a more substantial role in lending to developing countries through the Chinese-led Asian Infrastructure Investment Bank (AIIB) and in its participation as a founding member of the New Development Bank. Beijing formed the AIIB to counter the absence of a more pronounced leadership role in other MDBs at the time, as well as to help pick up the slack in infrastructure investment lending in Asia. *Why does it, and the other MDBs, not recognize the incongruity in taking a prominent leadership role in infrastructure-related lending institutions while continuing to accept development assistance on a grand scale from the MDBs it is now competing with?*

China is naturally capable of getting to its desired finish line any way it wishes to do so, but *it would ultimately be far preferable if it were to become the global power that it strives to be as a member of the community of nations that demonstrates that it acknowledges and plays by internationally accepted rules, standards, and norms.* It remains to be seen whether President Xi can transform China into a country that recognizes the longer-term benefits of playing on the same field, by the same rules, as most of the world's other nations.[6] If he *were* to become successful in doing so, China's importance to the global economy would only grow.

But China has not exactly had difficulty projecting its power within the existing system of international organizations. A Chinese national is now in charge of 4 of the 15 specialized agencies of the United Nations (UN): the Food and Agriculture Organization, the International Civil Aviation Organization, the UN Industrial Development Organization, and the International Telecommunication Union. By comparison, a French national leads two specialized agencies (the International Monetary Fund and the UN Educational, Scientific and Cultural Organization), the United Kingdom (UK) leads one (the International Labor Organization), and the US leads the World Bank, UN Children's Fund, and the World Food Program.

The US contributed between 22% and 28% of the UN's various agency budgets in 2018.[7] By contrast, China contributed just 8% of the UN's regular budget from 2016-2018 (which will rise to approximately 12% by 2021[8]). So why does China have more leadership roles and receive more recognition for its smaller contributions? Unlike China, US contributions have been large, consistent, and taken for granted by other member states. Unlike the US, China rarely demands budgetary restraint or reforms that inconvenience the UN or member states, which may account for at least part of its appeal.

It is also worth noting that China has also not hesitated to use its veto power at the UN, even on issues that other nations find particularly sensitive. China has used its veto to block a Security Council resolution 12 times since 1971. All but three of those vetoes have occurred since 2007 and served to prevent Security Council action against such states as Myanmar, Syria, Venezuela, and Zimbabwe.[9] Since 2013, China has become increasingly assertive in UN human rights institutions, promoting its own interpretation of international norms and mechanisms.[10] At the UN, that has translated into a violation of Article 100 of the UN Charter, which states: "In the performance of their duties the Secretary-General and the staff shall not seek or receive instructions from any government or from any other authority external to the Organization. Each Member of the UN undertakes to respect the exclusively international character of the responsibilities of the Secretary-General and the staff and not to seek to influence them in the discharge of their responsibilities."[11]

All UN employees take an oath of office confirming that they will honor the UN Charter, but the more confident employees believe that their actions are unlikely to result in some form of punishment – either by the UN or their home governments – the more likely they are to act either independently or against the grain of what their government desires. As a result, UN employees from Western nations regularly act either independently of, or counter to, the wishes of their governments.

The same is not true of authoritarian governments. As was noted in a 1985 US Senate Report,[12] the UN Secretariat employees from the Soviet Union were deliberately sent there to collect information on UN activities, recruit agents, support intelligence operations, and collect scientific and technological information of value to the Soviet Union. Today, China closely mirrors the Soviet Union in terms of the loyalty it expects of its citizens at the UN. In a 2019 interview, Wu Hongbo, former UN Under-Secretary-General in charge of UN Department of Economic and Social Affairs, admitted that he was required to act in the interests of China as a UN civil servant.[13] China therefore appears to be interested in expanding its influence within the UN, not because it supports the organization's founding principles, but rather to alter the programs and policies of the UN in ways that will benefit Chinese priorities in the future.[14]

This is a theme that will be explored throughout this book. For now, suffice it to say that part of China's playbook is to stretch the boundaries of acceptable behavior to its limits, within the theoretical confines of existing international rule of law and world order. By stepping past that line and retrenching, then doing the same again and again, it succeeds in establishing a new normal that has been defined by China. Unless a nation or organization formally objects *and* does something to prevent the breach of behavior from happening again (which is critical since, most of the time, such objection and corrective action does *not* occur), China will continue to act in such a manner.

Such behavior has been exhibited by China in numerous instances, the most notable of which in recent years was in the South China Sea where, despite a formal ruling from The Hague[15] specifically noting that China's claims to territorial sovereignty over the Sea are not consistent with international law, Beijing claimed the Spratly and Paracel Islands as Chinese territory and built military outposts on them anyway. The international community (most notably, the US) stood by, watched it happen, and did nothing to stop it.

<u>Does China's governance model have broad appeal</u>?

When considering whether to be drawn closer to China or the US, some nations, businesses, and consumers might be concerned about such behavior and draw their own line on ideological grounds, choosing not to associate with China. However, that is not really how the world works, and China knows it. There are not many governments or businesses that will simply brush China and its 1.4 billion citizens off because they disagree with how Beijing gets things done. And so much of the world's supply chains run through China that, if a consumer wanted to avoid purchasing Chinese-made products, that could be difficult to do. Even China's more ardent ideological opponents would not recommend simply ignoring China and refusing to engage with it. The world knows that it *must* engage and do business with China.

Many people and governments around the world are inclined to believe that China is merely acting in its own interest, as any other government tends to do, and they would be right to believe that. As Lord Palmerston noted in the British House of Commons in 1848, states have no eternal allies, and no perpetual enemies. Their *interests* are eternal and perpetual, and it is a nation's duty to follow those interests.[16] Certainly, all the great powers throughout history, including the US, of course, do the same thing. The issue is *how* interests are pursued and the lengths to which a nation will go to protect its interests.

As China has risen over the past three decades to once again become a great power (China had been a great power from about 1100 to 1800 AD[17]), those in favor of the Western democracies, and Liberalism more generally, derived comfort from three basic arguments. First, China has generated an average growth rate of nearly 10% over the past four decades by embracing economic liberalization rather than by doubling down on central planning. Second, there was the belief that China's economic modernization would eventually result in political modernization. And third, there was also the belief that direct exposure to the US by a growing number of Chinese students, businesses, tourists, and government officials would generate admiration of the American model, and a desire to emulate it.[18]

These arguments are less applicable today than they were just a few years ago, however. Since becoming China's President in 2012, Xi Jinping has actually *reduced* the pace of market reforms and *enhanced* support for state-owned enterprises, imposed greater state intervention in the economy, added restrictions on foreign investment, and enhanced the CCP's influence over private companies in China. The Chinese economic system is no longer on a path toward possible convergence with American-style capitalism; rather, it is producing its own hybrid model of socialism and capitalism (with Chinese characteristics, of course). Doing so has coincided with reduced GDP growth which, as noted earlier, is attributable to a number of variables, but the idea that China would continue liberalizing its economy without deviating on that path was never realistic. Nor was the notion that economic liberalization would naturally result in political liberalization. That would have implied that the CCP supported working itself out of a job, which was never going to happen.

The third area in which comfort was previously derived presumed that any Chinese person who came into direct contact with America would not only love it but want to be just like it, which was also a fallacious assumption. Beijing has not hesitated to criticize any number of things about America, from the inequities inherent in its economic model to its history of slavery and the state of race, as well as its relations to the country's pervasive gun violence. While China has been busy building bridges (literally and figuratively) to the rest of the world, under President Trump, America has been busy withdrawing from the world and many of the commitments it made to the world. While Trump was *removing* America from some of the previous commitments it had made to the rest of the world – such as the Paris Climate Accord, the Trans-Pacific Partnership, the Iran nuclear agreement, and the Intermediate-Range Nuclear Forces Treaty (INF) – Xi was *affirming* China's commitment to free trade, the climate, and international security.

The truth is that fewer people are seeking inspiration from the US these days. The US government is no longer commenting with the same regularity or degree of specificity about human rights abuses around the world and is, instead, being criticized for its own human rights abuses with respect to its immigration crisis. The moral high ground that had been a hallmark of American supremacy over decades has largely disappeared during the Trump years. That high ground can now be claimed, at least on paper, by Beijing. China has become the world leader in providing foreign aid[19] and is the second largest contributor to the UN's peace keeping budget[20] (after the US). If perception matters, then China has scored well in terms of the moral high ground, while the US has been floundering on that front in recent years.

As noted in the Pew study, that does not mean that the populations of most countries surveyed necessarily seek to emulate China as an alternative model. The question is, how much more can the US drop in the court of global public opinion and can China rise before Beijing's approach to governance may be seen as a viable, alternative model? Here again, that will depend on who you ask. Few Americans are likely to drop America's version of democracy and capitalism in favor of China's authoritarian model of state-dominated socialism. But that might not sound like a bad idea to hundreds of millions of people around the world who may be benefitting from Chinese aid, jobs, and infrastructure projects.

In fact, in Africa, where the Chinese government has been actively (even aggressively) investing in infrastructure, manufacturing, and other projects in earnest for the better part of a decade, there are plenty of examples of investments gone wrong but also of knowledge sharing, skill development, and mutually beneficial success. Africans tend to think of China in mixed terms, but surprisingly positively in a general sense. While some of the allegations made against China in Africa are indisputable – such as that Chinese investment exacerbates corruption and that many governments fall into a debt trap as a result of Beijing's approach to funding and lending –others are simply not true.

Among them is an oft-repeated criticism that Chinese companies employ primarily Chinese workers. China actually creates more jobs in Africa than any other foreign investor, and surveys of employment on Chinese projects there have repeatedly found that three-quarters or more of workers are locals. While early-stage projects, particularly in countries where China has had little experience, tend to be staffed primarily by Chinese employees, that pattern has tended to be reversed over time.

And while, on an individual country basis, Chinese foreign direct investment has accounted for a significant portion of national debt in Africa, it is worth noting that, from 2000 to 2016, despite tens of billions of dollars-worth of lending throughout the continent, Chinese loans only accounted for 1.8% of Africa's foreign debts, and most of that had been invested in infrastructure.[21] Some Chinese loans contain onerous terms, but many others tend to either be competitive with, or at a lower interest rate, than most of the MDBs. Some of the debt is eventually written off, since it cannot be repaid, but the 2018 Forum on China-Africa Cooperation included $15 billion of grants, interest-free loans, and concessional loans from China to African nations.

Although there are numerous allegations that China is in the process of sending millions of peasants to Africa in order to grow food for China, and that Beijing is grabbing land there, there is no evidence to support these claims. According to the UN Commodity Trade database, China has been *sending* food to Africa. While this will eventually change with the passage of time, the only significant food exports sent from Africa to China as of 2018 were sesame seeds and cocoa, produced by African farmers.[22]

In 2015, Afrobarometer issued some surprising results in its survey of 54,000 people in 36 African countries. China ranked number two in terms of favorable views, following the US. In three of five regions of the continent, China either matched or surpassed the US in popularity vis-à-vis its approach to development. Public perceptions not only confirmed China's perceived economic and political importance to Africa but also generally portrayed its influence as beneficial.[23] China's debt trap diplomacy is creating some distinct casualties, but Chinese loans are also powering a vibrant Africa. While the jury will be out for some time about whether China's experiment with Africa was a net-plus or minus, its impact on African business and society is casting a wide net, and much of it is positive.

So, it is reasonable to conclude that, while at least some of China's methods of doing things in the international arena might be considered objectionable to different people for different reasons, China has been successful in getting a great many things done, in places that some Western governments (notably, the US) are either in the process of ignoring or are doing an inadequate job of supporting. China is lending money to African (and other) governments, knowing it is unlikely to be fully repaid, by virtue of the volume of funding and the terms under which it is being lent. There are several interpretations about why China may be doing this. Among them are that this is Beijing's way of establishing and/or deepening its relationship with developing economies; it is generating enhanced influence over them in the process; it is ensuring the continued delivery of natural resources from them; or it is simply helping them to develop.

Say what you will about *how* China is doing this, and that it is resulting, in some instances, in highly indebted poor country (HIPC) status for some countries that had actually previously graduated from the HIPC designation (such as the Democratic Republic of Congo and Zambia[24]). The point is that China is heavily engaged in Africa at a time when the continent really needs such engagement and existing sources of aid are grossly inefficient to meet Africa's growing infrastructure and other needs. Beijing has a habit of actually doing things while other countries may only talk about doing so. Its tactics may be objectionable on many levels, and the net result of some of its actions may prove to be largely negative over time, but it has stepped up to the plate when action was needed. Hundreds of millions of people around the world will not forget that and may even say that they would like their governments to be more like China as a result.

<u>Beijing's expanding global influence</u>

Beyond the disbursement for foreign aid and cross-border investment, Beijing is expanding its soft power influence in a range of ways, none more important than its growing influence in the Western press. As part of its attempt to exert influence in foreign affairs, Chinese state-run media companies are expanding their integration with Western news outlets. The CCP has rapidly expanded its efforts to influence discussion about China beyond its borders to attempt to suppress criticism of the Chinese government and mold international media to refer to China in a positive light. In 2018, Xinhua, China's largest state-run news agency, announced that it was expanding cooperation with the US news service The Associated Press (AP), having declared that the two news agencies had established broad cooperation in such areas as new media, economic information, and the application of AI.

At the time, the US-China Economic and Security Review Commission warned that Xinhua was rapidly expanding globally in an effort to discredit Western media outlets. The AP maintained, in response to a Congressional inquiry on the scope of the agreement between AP and Xinhua, that Xinhua would not influence its reporting or have access to sensitive information in AP's possession. In the wake of Russia's interference in the 2016 US presidential election, no US media outlet would subsequently agree to partner with Russia Today (RT) or Sputnik. Some US members of Congress were of the view that Beijing's influence operations inside the US represented a similar threat.[25]

Like other powerful countries (including, first and foremost, of course, the US), China utilizes aid, cultural programming, and the media to boost its global image. But for Beijing, the current influence offensive is on a much greater scale. Beijing can more easily shape global narratives through state media, which reaches hundreds of millions of people around the world. It is pouring money into such outlets as the China Global Television Network, turning them into major global media players, as Russia did with RT and Sputnik. Chinese social media and messaging platforms have also spread globally, making it easier for Beijing to push Xinhua and other state-run platforms on to more social media users outside China.

Beijing is, in addition, seeking to shape media coverage of China by using state-owned media to train foreign journalists, especially from developing countries, inviting reporters from Southeast Asia to Latin America to visit China to participate in workshops and courses that offer an officially sanctioned view of Chinese foreign and economic policies. Purchases of local media outlets in South Africa, for example, by pro-China business tycoons are providing Beijing with direct access to target markets.

Pro-China business owners are also donating funds to influence research institutes, universities, and think tanks abroad. China's Confucius Institute project, run by the Ministry of Education, helps set up Chinese language and culture studies programs at universities around the world, including many in the US. While the project has been successful in some countries, there has been a backlash against it in other countries, where such programs are seen as an attempt to enhance the influence of the CCP.[26] Where they have been successful, some of the Institutes have not only promoted the Chinese language and cultural studies but have created a climate of self-censorship at some universities around issues deemed sensitive to Beijing. A 2017 report from the National Association of Scholars concluded that the arrival of more than 100 Confucius Institutes in the US had led schools to self-censor programming about Taiwan, Tibet, and the 1989 Tiananmen crackdown.[27]

More pro-Beijing think tanks are also being created all over the world, some directly funded by the government and others endowed by pro-Beijing businesses. Nowhere has China been more successful in swaying research institutions and business organizations than in Southeast Asia. In Thailand, for example, the Chinese Embassy has established close links to several prominent business and cultural organizations that, over the past decade, have become regular mouthpieces for Beijing's policy objectives in the kingdom and around the region. The German government levied that charge against China in 2017, claiming that Beijing had used LinkedIn and other social media to target more than 10,000 of its citizens, including lawmakers and other government employees, posing as leaders of think tanks and headhunters and offering all-expense-paid trips to China and meetings with influential clients.

Many countries spend money projecting soft power in a similar manner. The challenge is to differentiate between benign types of cultural and political promotion versus more direct and potentially meddlesome influence-peddling and interference. While many Western intelligence agencies are focused on Russia's information warfare, comparatively few of them are presumably devoting a similar scale of resources to understand China's influence operations and how the country is projecting its soft power abroad.[28] One could easily argue that Beijing's influence operations are far more important, given that this is China's century.

In addition to punching above its weight in influence peddling, Beijing is also punching above its weight in science. Success in modern science requires institutions of higher education, capable researchers, and a lot of money. Since China has all the necessary ingredients, it is rapidly climbing the rankings of scientific achievement. Apart from its impressive landing on the dark side of the moon in 2019, Beijing has spent many billions of dollars to detect dark matter, make great advances in quantum communications, and become a leader in renewable energy and advanced materials.

In 2018, Nikkei and Elsevier found that more scientific papers originated from China than from any other country in 23 of the 30 most active fields of study. While the quality of American research has been consistently higher, China is rapidly advancing in terms of the scale, scope, and quality of its scientific research.

The looming prospect of a dominant China in science alarms Western governments not only because of the new weaponry Beijing is in the process of developing but because of the implications for how else it may be used – whether for repression at home, AI development, or purposes of spying. Science may end up changing China, and the world, in ways no one is anticipating,[29] but for China to be all it can be in the scientific realm implies granting its scientists an unprecedented degree of freedom to be all that they can be. That implies that President Xi and the CCP will need to ease up on the reins of the scientific community in China. Are they capable of actually doing that?[30]

That remains to be seen, but Xi has already proven himself to be masterful at adapting when needed to accommodate new realities and keep his vision of an omnipotent China on course. Based on his deft projection of China's soft power to date, there is little reason to believe that he will not be successful in doing so in the future.[31]. That should alarm Western governments only to the extent that they do not believe they have a better story to tell, or a better way to tell it.

A World with Chinese Characteristics

Today, English remains the world's predominant language, the US is the world's largest economy, the dollar remains its reserve currency, Google is the world's primary search engine, and Facebook is its largest social media platform. Fast forward 30 years and things are likely to look very different. Once the BRI is completed, Beijing's ability to project its soft and hard power will be greatly enhanced, China will have become the world's largest economy, and parents around the world will ensure that their children speak Mandarin (many already do).

Once the Chinese government makes the yuan fully convertible, it could well become the world's reserve currency and, given the growth in the number of Chinese speakers, Baidu may well become the world's predominant search engine and Weibo may supplant Facebook as the world's largest social media platform. The growth in the Chinese middle class, already larger than the US and EU populations combined, by some estimates, will help ensure that China weens itself of overdependence on exports to sustain growth and becomes increasingly self-reliant for economic growth.

If Xi has his way, there will be no distinct center of gravity. More likely, China, India, the EU, and the US will compete for supremacy but, much as is the case in the race for AI supremacy, there may be no single victor, and any country that may hold the top spot in politics, economics, technology, or as a military power may not stay there for long. As the US continues its downward trajectory and China maintains its inexorable rise, world order will continue to be multipolar.

Yet, the coming Chinese world order is likely to be devoid of the kinds of checks and balances the world has come to take for granted in the postwar order. Rather, it is more likely to be akin to a transaction-driven landscape where the strongest party rules and the weak are considered collateral damage. The Chinese order will likely see a break with the Western model by moving decisively away from the Enlightenment ideal of transparency in exchange for the opacity of power.

This transformation has already begun and, as it is occurring, the US and many other countries are essentially asleep at the wheel. As domestic crisis upon crisis piles up, the world's leading Western economies continue to turn their attention inward, preoccupied with political and economic crises at home and functioning with unipolar blinders on. Many of the world's leaders fail to appreciate the implications that a world with Chinese characteristics may have on the future.

Not since the modern liberal order was born in the 1940s has the world had to grapple with the possibility of its demise, and at the hand of a rising China. Just at a time when the world is in need of the stability and governance it has had the luxury of relying upon for decades, it must contemplate transitioning to a world order not of the West's choosing. Clearly, the era of US hegemony is coming to an end. Will the global institutions it was so instrumental in creating become less relevant or forceful with time? Will Beijing be successful in crafting new institutions derived from a Chinese footprint? If so, will good governance and rule of law be consistent with such organizations? Only time will tell, of course.

What is certain is that Beijing's realization of the Chinese century is sure to be infused with precepts and applications that are uniquely Chinese. The world has yet to fully contemplate all that this portends but Xi wants to ensure that his vision of world order achieves, at a minimum, the perpetuation of the CCP, its continued domination over the Chinese people, and a pathway that guarantees the supremacy of China throughout this century and beyond.

If the Chinese government is to be encouraged to modify the manner in which it engages with the rest of the world, it is up to the world's nations to enhance the manner in which they challenge Beijing, for the CCP is unlikely to become incentivized to do so without some externally-derived inspiration. The US government has taken an important first step by not only strenuously objecting to Beijing's incessant theft of intellectual property (IP) on an institutionalized basis but by being willing to endure some pain on a sustained basis in order to focus minds in Beijing. But any leveling of the playing field will have only limited appeal, impact a small percentage of the world's countries, or be likely to endure for a limited period of time before Beijing finds other ways to create yet another uneven playing field somewhere in the global economic system.

It is also not only America's battle to fight, though there are plenty of other nations around the world who are only too happy for Washington to lead the charge and endure much of the pain of seeking change in how the Chinese government interacts with the rest of the world, without themselves either joining the battle or enduring the pain. All of the world's nations – rich, poor, developed, developing, and middle income alike –should join hands to take collective action to help ensure that the rising goliath that is China adheres to the letter and spirit of international and domestic law in the future.

This is China's century, but that does not mean it should be able to thwart the law, create its own set of rules, or avoid sanction when it acts in a manner contrary to established norms. Beijing's vision of the future *could* become a force for good and generally mutual benefit. It is entirely within China's power to make that a reality. If it were to do so, that would make choosing a side in the China-America divide a much more difficult process. Either way, Beijing is going to continue to expand its influence in every corner of the world, and

Washington will continue to remind the world that it is a viable alternative to China. Will the balance truly be tipped in Beijing's favor and against the US? If so, when?

Chapter 2: Sino-US Relations

The modern bilateral relationship between Beijing and Washington has experienced diplomatic triumph, great collaborative success, and more recently, economic calamity. Mostly, however, it has been a marriage of mutual economic convenience that worked rather well for both countries for several decades. What is commonly referred to as "Chimerica", wherein China produces products and purchases American treasury bonds, and the US purchases Chinese products and derives fiscal stability as a result of Beijing's purchase of a large percentage of those bonds, has resulted in shared prosperity and strength.

That came to an abrupt end during the Trump era, of course. Instead of being defined by collaboration, the relationship between China and America can now more rightly be called tempestuous. There are many reasons for this, ranging from China's cunning and daring approach to international relations and business to America's failure to take Beijing to task for some of its behavior, while simultaneously prioritizing the pursuit of profit over a fair and equal trading relationship. No dance between two nations occurs in a vacuum and these two goliaths both bear responsibility for the current state of affairs between them.

This is a complicated, intricate, multifaceted tale, and anything but black and white. The two countries did not create the world's most important economic relationship easily or quickly – it was the result of painstaking diplomacy, a decision to proceed on the basis of mutual trust, and a willingness to take a chance on each other. The objective of this chapter is to understand just what is at stake in that relationship – for China, for America, and for the world.

At issue is a blurring of the lines between commercial and national interest, subsidies and protectionism, dual use technologies, foreign policy, deal making, political ideology, morality, and either disdain for or an embrace of the international rules-based order. The outcome of this pivot point in the two countries' relationship will set the stage for which of them will dominate parts of the global economic and political landscape in the decades to come.

Could the trade war be the best thing that ever happened to China?

Not since Herbert Hoover enacted the Smoot-Hawley Tariff Act has a US president so openly embraced trade protectionism. In 1930, the Act raised tariffs on approximately 20,000 goods and is widely acknowledged by economists to have helped exacerbate the impacts of the Great Depression. Many economists have noted that tariffs generally do not achieve their objective because the recipient nation often imposes counter-tariffs and consumers (on both sides) end up paying the bill. In Trump's world, up is down and black is white; he initially insisted that American consumers did not pay more for Chinese goods.

In some ways, Trump's election was a gift to the Chinese. This may sound completely counter-intuitive but consider, for example, that, by withdrawing America from the Trans-Pacific Partnership (TPP) in 2017, Trump opened the door for China to expand its trade relationship with the remaining TPP members – which it did. Similarly, the imposition of trade tariffs forced China to modify its supply chains and consumption patterns, find alternative markets for some of its goods, modify some of its own tariffs being applied to other countries, and reevaluate its trading relationships more generally. From a long-term perspective, that was a good thing for Beijing.

Within two years of having first imposed the tariff increases in 2018, Trump increased the average tariff on Chinese goods to 24%, from an average of 3% before he began imposing the tariffs. The net effect was not only a dramatic decline in foreign direct investment (FDI) into the US but a suppression of job and wage growth and a disruption of international supply chains that had significant knock on effects for the entire global economy.[1] As the US economy slowed in 2019, the US Federal

Reserve began to lower interest rates for the first time since the Great Recession, despite low unemployment and what would otherwise have been considered an acceptable growth rate (around 2% per annum). At the time, China posted its lowest growth rate in 27 years and began devaluing the yuan, prompting the US Treasury Department to name it a currency manipulator.

The trade conflict distorted global supply chains, with some winners and losers. For instance, Vietnam became a net beneficiary as US companies began to relocate there from China. The US imported 40% more from Vietnam in 2019 than in 2018, the country ran a $40 billion trade surplus with the US, and the Vietnamese economy grew at approximately 7% that year. As a result, Trump said Vietnam had abusive trade practices and ordered the country to take steps to reduce the surplus which he had caused!

As another example, the economy of the European Union (EU) relies heavily on trade for its economic growth. Germany produces nearly the same value of exports as the US, despite having only a quarter of the population size. More than a quarter of all German jobs are derived from its export market, and although the US is its largest export market, China became Germany's most important growth market. Germany's trade with China increased more than 1,000% between 2000 and 2019. Germany remains concerned about the long-term impacts on its ability to export, as it has for the past two decades, to a slowing China.[2]

As the trade war continued into 2019, an anti-China consensus rose in the US, among Democrats and Republicans in both houses of the US Congress, among the business community, and among individuals of all political persuasions. The US is terribly divided among a great many topics – immigration, race relations, gun laws, and climate change, to name just a few – but on the subject of China's alleged theft of IP, its cyber intrusions, and its unbalanced trade relationship with the US, there was a high degree of agreement. A survey of 1,500 Americans, by the Pew Research Center,[3] in 2019, revealed that negative views of China had reached a 14-year high, with some 60% of Americans having an unfavorable opinion of China, up from 47% in 2018. Americans also increasingly saw China as a threat, with 24% naming China as the country that posed the greatest threat to the US – twice as many as said the same in 2007. And, 81% of Americans believed that China's growing military power was bad for the US.

Although any former US president over the past 20 years could have taken action against China for its exploits, it was Donald Trump who actually did it. Whatever his true motivations were – whether pandering to his political base, wanting to arrive at a genuine solution to the problem, or just wanting to pick a fight – Trump has earned the credit and the blame. It is too soon to tell what the lasting impact of this anti-China consensus will be. Only time will be the ultimate arbiter, but 40 years of convergence has begun to unravel in a rather unpleasant way.

America's official policy of focusing on the mutual benefits of a "win-win" relationship for so long has come at a steep price. China has become so strong that it threatens America's status in the world. It almost would not matter if America had adopted a more isolationist approach to the world during the Obama and Trump administrations – China would have been strongly ascending either way. Becoming more isolationist merely made China's rise that much easier to achieve. Let us not forget that the US has been turning a blind eye toward China for at least three decades now. It is the US that has winked and nodded as China gradually stepped on to the world stage – pausing occasionally as distasteful events have blown over, such as Tiananmen Square in 1989, the Taiwan Strait crisis of 1996, and the spy plane standoff in 2001. *America has been complicit in nurturing China's rise and only has itself to blame for waiting until 2018 to say "enough".*

Given its wealth and achievements in various realms, China is well-positioned to transition from an economy that imports critical inputs (such as aviation technology, microchips, and robots) to manufacturing these itself. Its middle class is so large (by some estimates, larger than the populations of America and Europe combined[4] by the middle of this decade) that the country can cater to its increasingly prosperous population and meet many of its own needs. That does not mean, of course, that it will stop importing vast amounts of natural resources, agricultural products, and other economic inputs, but as China's economy continues to mature, it has the luxury of relying less and less on the rest of the world for things that it can produce for itself. That is spurring innovation on an unprecedented scale there and propelling the country even further from a competitive perspective.

One could even argue that the trade war is the best thing that could have happened to China. In essence, *it got away with its IP theft, cyber intrusions, and grossly unbalanced trading relationship with the US (and a great many other countries) for a couple of decades – enough time to build itself into an economic powerhouse and give most of its citizens time to graduate to middle class status, so that it could transition from being a poor nation that copied other countries' technologies to a wealthier nation that is quickly becoming capable of beating much of the rest of the world at its own game.*

Certainly, that is what it did with globalization. Could it all have been part of a grand plan among the Chinese leadership that was hatched decades ago? Who can say with certainty that it wasn't? China's leadership probably cannot believe that the West allowed it to get away with what it was doing for so long. Indeed, many in the West cannot believe it, either! If the trade war forces China to make some long-delayed choices – about supply chains, sourcing, production methods, investment versus consumption, and other issues critical to the country's long-term future – then it may well turn out to have been a blessing in disguise. China is well positioned to take on the US on the global stage, but it still has a way to go before that boxing match can be considered a match between equals.

A battle at least a decade in the making

Beijing did not exactly make its ambition to challenge the US in Asia and elsewhere a secret. Following the Great Recession of 2008, it saw an opportunity to take advantage of a wounded America by enhancing its presence in multilateral institutions, militarizing the South China Sea, becoming a leading provider of foreign aid, and investing heavily overseas. The US was seriously preoccupied with its own recovery until at least 2012, which gave Beijing a good five years to focus on its objectives – while America was sleeping. Once Xi became China's president, in 2012, its global ambitions coalesced into a long-term plan, coinciding with a crackdown on reform and dissent. The progress that had been made since the 1990s on market liberalization was abruptly stopped.

Beijing began to lose any real friend that it had in the US establishment, in essence, systematically alienating them one by one. The combination of China's crackdown at home, its assertiveness in foreign policy, military adventurism, and espionage activities made congressional lawmakers wonder why the US was maintaining friendly relations with Beijing. Eventually, the US business community became alarmed and, ultimately, alienated by the reversals of what most observers saw as genuine progress. As a result, the foreign policy hawks in the US began to have their way, culminating in the Trump presidency, a willingness to call a spade a spade, and the beginning of an inevitable backlash that was a decade in the making.

Now that the genie is out of the bottle, centrifugal forces have taken over. The trade war reached a feverish pitch, insults flew across the Pacific, China was again called a currency manipulator, business executives from both sides began to curtail travel, cross-border investment declined dramatically, consumers began to pay more for goods imported from both nations and began to change their purchasing habits. Similarly, exporters from both sides started looking for alternative markets, American manufacturers slowly began to find different locations for production, and the great experiment between the two countries gradually began to come apart.

Plenty of innocent victims on both sides have been caught in the crossfire: small businesses, farmers, students, cultural performers, researchers, professors, and scientists. Although cooler heads will eventually rule the day, the net result is likely to be a permanent fissure between the world's two largest economies. This might have been avoidable if China had not been so blatant in its actions and if previous US presidents had not hesitated to put a stop to it as soon as it started – but neither scenario was really very realistic. Although there will not be a complete disentanglement between the two economies, cross-border trade, investment, and lending is likely to end up a fraction of what it was at its peak. A price will be paid by everyone.

Another result is the rise in economic nationalism. Trump and Xi have already used the conflict to whip up nationalist sentiment. That does not simply disappear once a revised trade agreement is signed. American and Chinese citizens have long memories. Trust has been permanently eroded, as has a desire to return to what were once routine practices. China will be able to rely on the BRI to make up for some of the slack. America will eventually repair its frayed alliances and replace some of the business lost to China with new bilateral trade agreements. The world will look different at the end of this decade than it did at the beginning. But both China and America will benefit in the long-term; they had both gotten into some bad habits, which are coming to an end.

Time for a new way of thinking

Are either a tight embrace or war the only two options for America and China? The way some thought leaders on both sides of the Pacific spoke in the wake of the start of the trade war, one would have thought that war was actually a possibility, even though no one wanted it. Then, as now, it was easy for the US to slip back into a simplistic and outdated "black or white" mentality. As recently as 2001, the world had been divided by George W. Bush into nations that were either with the US in its (then new) Global War on Terror or with the terrorists.[5] Many Americans had spent so much time thinking about the world in Cold War-esque terms for so long that reverting back to such an outmoded manner of thinking seemed perfectly natural. This time is it is not the Soviet Union or Al Qaeda but China that is the bad actor in their minds.

China's rise need not necessarily imply America's fall, but it does imply the need to adopt a strategy for competing with China that matches Beijing's own forward-looking orientation. While the US is busy focusing on the next quarter for business, the next year from an accounting or tax perspective, the next two years in anticipation of the coming state or national election, or the next four years for a presidential election, China is busy thinking about the next five, ten, or even thirty years down the road. Its "Made in China 2025" strategy was created in 2015, its "New Generation Artificial Intelligence Development Plan" (targeting 2030) was launched in 2017, and Xi's plan to make China a superpower by 2050 was announced in 2019. To China's credit, it has had a forward-looking orientation for many decades, and it has paid off.

It would help if more Americans knew more about China. A lot of Americans lack a natural curiosity about the world, and a large percentage of Americans have never even left the US. In 1990, just 4% of Americans even had a passport. As a result of heightened levels of immigration since then, that figure stood at 42% in 2017[6] – which means, by definition, that, at that time, some 58% of Americans had never even left the country. Of those that had, the majority had visited either Canada, Mexico, or Europe[7]. Not exactly what one would call indicative of a broad orientation to the rest of the world.

According to the China National Tourism Administration,[8] 1.7 million Americans visited China between January and September 2016, when tourist numbers between both countries were at their peak. If that sounds like a lot, consider that, according to Mexico's National Tourism Office,[9] more than 31 million Americans visited Mexico that same year (nearly 10% of the entire US population at the time[10]). Tourism numbers between China and the US have naturally dropped considerably since the trade war started.

Apart from the fact that the vast majority of Americans had never visited China, most Americans also had absolutely no idea what a powerhouse China was turning into, starting in the 1990s. It was almost as if their stereotypical view of China as a backward, poor, primarily agricultural society was a myth, and they had been kept in the dark by America's leadership about what China was becoming. The truth is, regardless of how much tourism has grown between the two countries, tourist numbers remain a tiny fraction of the population of either country. Most Americans still know very little about China and vice versa. That is not very helpful when judging the wisdom of either country's lawmakers' policy choices toward the other country. Perhaps both sets of lawmakers want it that way, since it is easier to manipulate lesser informed populations.

There are many lessons that America can learn from China, none more important than how China reacted to and recovered from successive challenges from the West. In 1840, following the breakdown in negotiations with the Qing Dynasty over the trade of opium on Chinese territory, a large British military force captured the city of Canton (now Guangzhou) before entering central China at the Yangtze River delta. Within two years, Great Britain had overwhelmed China and, through the subsequent peace treaty, extracted significant concessions, such as control of Hong Kong (in perpetuity), the expansion of trade in new ports, and extraterritoriality for British subjects in

China-a status then obtained by the American and French governments soon afterwards.

These events comprised the First Opium War, a defeat which began an era known in China as the Century of Humiliation. It lasted until 1949, when Mao Zedong proclaimed the founding of the People's Republic of China.[11] The Chinese have not, and will not, forget this painful period in their history. Indeed, Chinese history books are filled with references to this period. The Chinese government wants to make sure such a humiliation will never happen again, and it has helped define Beijing's orientation to foreign policy since that time.

China's rise will remain the greatest challenge to America for decades to come. The US cannot prepare for it, or counter it, by remaining static and presuming that its current state of supremacy will enable it to remain on top. What is needed is an open and honest dialogue between the American people and their future presidents, legislators, and businesses. China is not going anywhere, so it is important to manage the task ahead in a manner similar to what the Chinese did to overcome their humiliation at the hands of foreigners. Chinese leaders spent a lot of time thinking about the mistakes they made and the weaknesses they exhibited, then determined what they needed to do to ensure that such events never occur again.

Just as the Chinese recognized they had a hand in their own demise (as a result of poor planning, a weak foreign policy, and impotent armed forces), the US would be well advised to consider what it might have done differently to avoid the need for a trade war, having its IP stolen, or being successfully targeted by cyber intrusions by China. Trump's incessant focus on America's trade deficit with China is not a solution to the problem and diverts attention from the country's own underlying weaknesses.

The Trump administration (and future administrations) would be well advised to do something meaningful about its chronic budget deficits, crumbling infrastructure, out of control defense spending, excessive legislative partisanship, deteriorating student performance, and standing in the world. These subjects are, ultimately, a greater threat to America's ability to successfully compete than China's rise. China's rise would be less of a concern if these issues had been addressed a couple of decades ago.

Despite what ordinary citizens of both countries might be inclined to believe, America and China need not be adversaries. Both have benefitted by engaging one another and jointly participating in common objectives since the formal establishment of bilateral relations in 1979. Some examples are the successful containment of the USSR (which led to its disintegration), participating in a negotiated peace in Korea and Vietnam, a common understanding regarding Taiwan, and China's stimulus package in the wake of the Great Recession (which helped keep America and the global economy afloat).

It is, of course, in both countries' interests to find a way to make the bilateral relationship work again. The potential business impacts of a permanent fissure between Beijing and Washington are massive. Two-way trade between the two was $660 billion in 2018.[12] Chinese FDI into the US reached an annual peak of $47 billion in 2016,[13] while annual US FDI into China peaked at $117 billion in 2018.[14] There is a lot at stake – so much so that various actors within the bilateral relationship want nothing to do with the enduring battle at the national government level. Businesses just want to do business, US state governors want all that Chinese FDI to continue, and American universities want the significant flow of Chinese students to their institutions to continue. Chinese students form the largest contingent of foreign students in the US, with more than 130,000 graduate students and 148,000 undergraduates enrolled in 2017-2018.[15] An astounding 21% of all students at Harvard came from China in 2019[16]. Their ability to pay full freight helps to keep many of America's colleges and universities afloat financially.

That said, we have reached a critical juncture. The gloves have finally been removed by both countries, so why not broaden the list of grievances America has with China to include all the other issues that remain simmering beneath the surface? If the goal is healthy and successful competition, that should extend to all realms of society – not just trade. What the US is seeking via the imposition of such sweeping trade tariffs is fair and equal treatment – no more and no less. That should include access to the Chinese market more generally. Plenty of US companies – technology companies in particular – have either been barred or severely constrained from operating in China. America should apply the same restrictions to Chinese firms. *Wherever restrictions have been placed on American firms, reciprocal treatment should be applied to Chinese firms in America.*

American universities should restrict foreign student access to classified research, and any Confucius Institutes that operate contrary to the principles of academic freedom should be prohibited from operating on campuses. University administrators should make clear that, if foreign students exercise free speech on campuses under the control or guidance of foreign governments, or with the objectives of suppressing the rights of others on campus, they will be disciplined. As things stand, there are few or no penalties applied toward such behavior.

China should also be held to the same standard that members of all international organizations are held to – whether it is at the World Trade Organization, the UN, or the MDBs – no ifs, ands, or buts. When China is caught using entities at the UN to promote Chinese government objectives, or that otherwise violate the UN Charter, it should be called out for it and held accountable. That is the only way that lasting progress toward an equitable bilateral relationship can be achieved. China has already amply demonstrated that it does not respond well to simply saying "please". President Obama tried that in 2015 when he urged Xi to stop the cyberattacks against the US government, businesses, and citizens. Xi said China would stop. Shortly thereafter, the attacks resumed.

An America that is open, prosperous, and true to its values has little to fear from Chinese competition.[17] So let China understand that America did not ascend to its numerous and immeasurable heights by being timid or bashful in asserting itself. While doing so has not always ended so well (as the wars in Korea, Vietnam, and Afghanistan illustrate), it has stood for liberty and righteousness and freedom, even if its tactics were later judged to be wrong. America is still the world's largest economy (for now) with its largest and most powerful military, its reserve currency, its superior research and technological competencies, and a whole host of capabilities that remain unmatched. If ever there was a time to take China on – in every way – it is now, because that window of opportunity is slowly closing.

Strategic Competition

On one hand, America is holding a lot of cards by virtue of being either the biggest or the best at so many things. On the other hand, from a foreign policy perspective, it is tripping over itself and making it much easier for China to try to gain an upper hand. The Trump administration's America First set of policies has alienated many American allies and raised questions among a host of other countries that might be inclined to either become or remain American allies about whether that is a good or bad idea.

In Africa, for example, where China has acquired great influence as a result of engaging so many countries on the continent, investing so much money, and devoting so many resources to establishing long-term bilateral relationships, it is well positioned to be far more influential than America at this particular juncture. The US, more generally, hasn't done Africa a lot of favors since Trump became president. The Trump administration requested $5.2 billion in foreign aid to Africa for fiscal year 2018, a 35% decrease from 2015 aid levels,[18] saying that America was choosing to focus on the countries with the most strategic value to the US. That same year, Xi pledged to give $60 billion to African countries, with no political strings attached (apparently), to focus on infrastructure development.[19]

That ability to influence countries extends around the globe. Where Trump has slapped restrictions on countries, insulted their leaders, or raised question about the sanctity of friendship with America, China was right there, cozying up to them or trying to strengthen its relationship with them. Here are just a few examples. While America was busy lambasting Mohammad bin Salman of Saudi Arabia over the brutal killing of the journalist Jamal Khashoggi at the Saudi consulate in Istanbul in 2018, China was busy becoming Saudi Arabia's largest purchaser of oil – a title America had once held. US imports of Saudi crude dropped from a high of 2.3 million barrels per day in 2003 to less than half a million barrels per day in 2019,[20] the result of American self-reliance via domestic oil and gas production. By contrast, China imported approximately 1.8 million barrels per day of Saudi crude by the summer of 2019[21] – an all-time high. Its strategy was to keep buying more Saudi crude to strengthen the bilateral relationship.

So China is clearly making significant strides in improving its ability to impact the global economy but, according to the World Economic Forum's Global Competitiveness Index, which measures the microeconomic and macroeconomic foundations of national competitiveness (defined as the set of institutions, policies, and factors that determine the level of productivity of a country), in 2018 the US was ranked first while China was ranked 28th.[22] The competitiveness rankings are based on measures of a country's enabling environment, human capital, the robustness of its markets, and its innovation ecosystem.

The traits that contribute toward competitiveness cannot simply be acquired or constructed overnight. China will continue to lag in its enabling environment and the extent to which it fosters innovation because its governing system and internal security protocols inhibit some of the very qualities which make an economy competitive. America can count on maintaining that status for a while, but perhaps for a shorter period of time than it may imagine, since China is an extremely worthy competitor.

Strategic competition has become a central tenet of US security strategy toward China, and indeed toward the rest of the world, under the Trump administration. To strengthen America's ability to compete, the administration wants Americans to "out-think, out-maneuver, out-partner, and out-innovate" its rivals. As noted in the Africa example, one way the Trump administration is doing so is by prioritizing what nations, companies, and strategies best serve US interests.

That may not be compatible with outdoing China, however. To out-think Beijing, it will need to adopt the same type of long-term, forward leaning, visionary planning that the CCP does on a routine basis. To out-maneuver and out-partner Beijing, it will need to strengthen and, in some cases, rebuild its alliances (presumably after Trump leaves office). As it continues to strengthen and modernize its military, the US will need to revisit the extent to which it is willing – and actually able – to deliver on its security guarantees around the world. To out-partner Beijing, the US will need to do a much better job at maintaining its existing alliances and begin to re-engage in cooperative action on a mass scale. And to out-innovate Beijing, the US must determine a sensible, realistic policy direction, identify what is required to achieve it, and devote the resources necessary to move swiftly.[23]

Part of the problem is that US foreign policy is a bit like an oil tanker – it can gradually shift course, but it takes a long time and great effort to actually move it in the desired direction (once it has been determined where it actually wants to go). American foreign policy's shift away from China has been years in the making; the change in course is only now becoming visible. The notion that China represents an existential threat to the US and the international order has become mainstream. One of the impediments that will prevent the anti-China foreign policy hawks from succeeding in gaining the American people's agreement to engage China in a generational struggle is that Americans are tired of generational struggles – against communists, against authoritarian governments, and against terrorists.

Most of those previous battles have eventually been won, in one form or another, but having spent thousands of lives and trillions of dollars on the wars in Vietnam, Afghanistan, and Iraq, and having ultimately lost those military battles, Americans certainly do not want more wars. Nor do they want protracted battles in other spheres. What they can stomach, and what many Americans would actually like, is to compete on the global stage and win fair battles. That is why Trump's economic war with China has gained so much support. Americans know that China has not been playing fair pool and they want to level the playing field. But most of America's allies have refused to join the fight. They remain afraid of damaging their lucrative relationships with China and instead prefer to sign on to and benefit from the BRI.

China's threats to US national security are both direct and indirect. No one believes there will be a war with China, and no one wants there to be one (including the American and Chinese people), but China does indeed pose a direct threat to US national security through its incessant theft of US IP, as a result of its ongoing cyberattacks, and because of its aggressive strengthening of its military capabilities (many people do not realize it, but China already has the world's largest navy). The BRI, China's diplomatic overtures toward nations throughout the world, and its stature in multilateral organizations all pose indirect threats to the US.

Part of what makes China so much of a threat is its ability to successfully launch a multi-pronged strategy to challenge or work within the existing international order and change it from within. It is, at times, a stealth strategy, wherein, as noted earlier in the UN example, China becomes a member of an institution and then presses up against existing boundaries often enough, and with enough success, that it creates a new boundary before anyone knows the boundaries were even under threat of being changed.

Beijing realizes also that all the effort it has put into engagement with the US has not been wasted. For one thing, this engagement allowed China to enter the Western-designed corridors of power and achieve all that it has *without* being perceived as changing the system from within. It also enabled Beijing to create and lead multilateral institutions of its own to compete with that system (vis-à-vis the AIIB and New Development Bank, for example). And, while it may not generally be perceived as a responsible stakeholder in the system, China has demonstrated a willingness and ability to contribute meaningfully and responsibly to international initiatives (whether global peacekeeping or rescue operations or climate change diplomacy) where mutual interests converge. It is, if you will, a form of *competitive cooperation*. That is not to say that China does not directly challenge the international order, as its trade practices or its territorial claims in the South China Sea amply demonstrate.

The biggest difference between the current global regime and the Cold War is that, today, few countries are willing to pick sides. The US has found it very difficult to get even some of its staunchest allies to agree to reject Huawei's 5G technology. It is the latest sign that the growing strategic competition between the US and China will probably not result in a definitive winner or loser. The US should not hesitate to embrace this competition, not to contain China but to raise America's own stakes in the game.[24] Actively engaging and competing with China is the only way America is going to come out on top.

Adrift without an anchor

If one were to make an analogy to characterize the current state of Sino-US relations, it would be to say that the bilateral relationship is a ship that is adrift without an anchor. That ship is in the middle of the ocean, wandering aimlessly toward rocks, shoals, and disputed island chains, devoid of direction and with no destination. The ocean is big, it could take years to determine a direction, and there will be dangerous obstacles that will inhibit it from reaching a destination, once it becomes clear. The ship is also taking on water and it may sink. What should be done?

Since neither country knows where their relationship is headed, and since the relationship has done nothing but get worse since 2018, neither side really has an incentive to engage in confidence building measures to try to make it better. But Trump only "negotiates" from a "winner takes all" perspective, and both sides have so much at stake and are guilty of using the trade issue to whip up nationalistic fervor among their respective populations as if it were emblazoned on their national flags, that the ideas of accommodation and restraint are anathema to both.

With every month and year that passes, as the stakes and degree of tension between them rise, the chance that a miscalculation or misreading of a situation could lead to some sort of political or military conflict can only rise. Once all the economic measures against one another have been implemented, either side may see value in turning up the heat by doing something that it otherwise would not do. For example, China might decide to further militarize the Spratly and Paracel Islands, increase the number of Chinese ships that navigate the South China Sea or Straits of Malacca, or deliberately antagonize American allies such as Japan or South Korea. The US could decide to begin monthly visits from US warships to Taiwan or publicly renounce the One China policy.

It does not help that the US is extremely divided politically, more insecure, and less confident than it was during the Cold War, or that China's economy is slowly stalling, confidence in Xi is waning, and the challenge to the CCP posed by the protestors in Hong Kong in 2019 has raised questions about whether something like that could happen on the mainland. In a military engagement, China could easily overestimate its fighting capabilities, particularly if a conflict occurred in Asia.

By the same token, the US could do the same, in the belief that, with a majority of its navy dedicated to Asia as a result of the Pivot to Asia under Obama, it could defeat the Chinese navy. However, as of 2019, only the Seventh Fleet was forward deployed, with only 57 (out of a total of 170) warships (the remainder of the Pacific Fleet is located in California, Hawaii, and Washington state[25]). Also, China has made great advances in creating weaponry that can deter the US navy from a great distance.

Were a military conflict to actually erupt, it could easily have global consequences, ranging from plunging stock markets to divided allegiances, with the potential to turn into a much large conflagration as a result. Surely, the leadership and military planners on both sides *must* realize that neither side can win a military confrontation and that, ultimately, they must come to some acknowledgement that neither side is going anywhere, both are strong, highly capable and worthy opponents, and they stand to gain so much more by figuring out a way to coexist peacefully than by being permanent sparring partners.

If we assume that Xi and the CCP intend to deploy the tactics of Sun Tzu from *The Art of War*, this will be a long and protracted battle, filled with deception. That would, in theory, at least, give the Chinese the upper hand in any form of conflict. Then again, US and other Western military planners and strategists have become familiar with Tzu's tactics and will presumably anticipate and plan accordingly. As we will see in Chapter 6, both sides possess comparative advantages in the military realm.

Realistic Expectations

Deng Xiaoping once said that, "the China-US relationship can never be too good or too bad" because it is too important. In other words, the leaders and people of both countries should be realistic about how close their bilateral relationship can be at any given point in time, and they should never let their disagreements get so out of hand that their general peace and prosperity are threatened. Although China recognizes America's unique position as the world's sole superpower (for the time being, at least), its political orientation and national pride dictate that it pursues its own political and developmental path. It has also pursued an independent foreign policy that it believes (and would like the rest of the world to believe) is ultimately aimed at achieving peace in Asia and elsewhere. Many countries in Asia, and the world, are highly skeptical about this so-called "peaceful development", pointing to China's unilateral actions in the South China Sea as directly contrary to that objective.

China views itself and the US as "different, but not distant" because Confucian philosophy advocates "accommodating divergent views". Xi has repeatedly said that the Pacific Ocean is vast enough to accommodate both China and the US. He has proposed a new model of international relations aimed at avoiding confrontation and conflict, and respecting one another's political systems and national interests, while pursuing joint win-win cooperation. That all sounds good on paper. The question becomes whether and how Confucian philosophy may become more consistent with current international law, whether both sides can reach an understanding about how China's rise may coincide with America's gradual decline as a global power, and how China's neighbors will view ongoing territorial disputes in the future. Much will depend on how far all sides are willing to reach across the table and genuinely compromise.

China's dual strategy of claiming to want to pursue diplomatic negotiations on the South China Sea dispute, while simultaneously continuing its unilateral construction activities on its islands, creates an environment that is not conducive to honest and meaningful negotiation. Maintaining equilibrium – between China and its neighbors, as well as China and the US – will remain of paramount importance. Sino-US relations will remain the world's most important bilateral relationship for many years to come, with implications for the entire world. The people of both nations have much more to gain by maintaining a friendly and cooperative relationship with each other, rather than the other way around. It will clearly take a great degree of wisdom, an appreciation of history, and a willingness by all sides to compromise to maintain mutual peace and prosperity.

Washington is really looking for three things from Beijing: play by the same set of rules everyone else is expected to play by, level the playing field with respect to a more equal trading relationship, and act as a responsible global leader by doing its part to promote global development and maintain peace. On its face, there is nothing unreasonable about any of this, but from the Chinese perspective, China is merely doing things the Chinese way and sees no reason for any other nation to object to its actions.

Beijing, in turn, wants Washington to mind its own business and not interfere in what it considers to be Chinese domestic issues, practice what it preaches, stop being hypocritical about its own rhetoric versus its own actions around the world, and stop trying to impede China's inevitable rise. There is clearly incongruity between what both are seeking and what either may be prepared to deliver. What differentiates this challenge from that of any other two nations is that both countries need each other in order to prosper and either one can cause insurmountable problems politically, economically, and militarily for the other.

Given the inherent inequity in the two nations' trading relationship, and Beijing's ongoing insistence on continuing with its theft of IP and high level cyberattacks, it is up to Xi to demonstrate that China is willing to modify its behavior. Many in the US government will believe that when they see it – on a sustained and unwavering basis. That appears unlikely. What appears to be more likely is that Beijing will continue doing what it has been doing and getting away with whatever it can get away with. That is its business model.

With China the ascendant power and the US in gradual decline, Xi has little real incentive to change the Chinese playbook on a wholesale basis. That means that the US should reset its expectations about future Chinese behavior. The modern trading system does not and cannot prevent China's state-owned enterprises from blurring the line between commercial interests and national interest. Chinese government funds subsidize and protect Chinese companies as they purchase dual-use technology or distort international markets. To effectively counter more of the same from China in the future, the US needs a strategy, not merely tactics.

Such a strategy would ideally be executed in conjunction with other large and strong countries opposed to Chinese tactics in the West. The Trump administration's disdain for collaboration with America's historical allies, and the institutions it was central to creating in the postwar era, should be replaced with a global alliance of the willing. This is not merely America's issue or battle, for the same bones of contention Washington has with Beijing are shared, to a greater or lesser degree, by countries around the world. When America competes with China as a guardian of a rules-based order, it starts from a position of strength. That is the only way Beijing will become incentivized to change its behavior.

Although there is some degree of inevitability in the notion that Beijing and Washington will end up as rivals, that is not inevitable, nor is to inevitable that such rivalry must lead to war. Henry Kissinger has opined that the Sino-US relationship should not be considered a zero-sum game, and that a prosperous and powerful China should not, in and of itself, be considered an American strategic defeat. Both countries are compelled to interact. The question is whether they will do so as collaborators or adversaries.

China's greatest strategic fear is that an external power will establish a periphery capable of encroaching on Chinese territory (which helps, in part, at least, to explain Beijing's actions vis-à-vis the South China Sea). America's greatest strategic fear in Asia is that its interests and military capability will become overwhelmed by another power. A strategy that presumes confrontation in the future might be completely justifiable in the business, military, and cyber arenas, but that does not necessarily imply confrontation if Beijing modifies its behavior to stop stealing IP and level the playing field in the trade arena. By the same token, Washington must understand that China's rise is inevitable, just as is America's eventual decline as the world's leading power. The question is whether superpower rivalry will succumb to historical precedent.[26]

Chapter 3: Geostrategic Rivalry

<u>Careening out of control</u>

As global affairs continue to career out of control, the world's foreign-policy decision-makers may be forgiven for feeling as if they are floating around in a weightless atmosphere, wondering what they will crash into next. What distinguishes this "negative G" era from others in the past is that, when the whirlwind began, the world was not at war, nor was there a global economic crisis. Rather, it occurred while the world was at relative peace and in a comparative state of prosperity. Only rarely in the past has an era of disruption coincided with such political calm and favorable economic indicators.

This has put policymakers in a rather unenviable position. The era of disruption has taken hold, with pressure on virtually every facet of the foreign policymaking process: politics, economics, sociocultural issues, the military, cyber, technology, and the environment. It has coalesced into what amounts to mission impossible: how can foreign policy decision-makers possibly craft strategies with any hope of remaining relevant and implementable in the long-term with so many variables at play?

The world's governments would be wise to take a page from the Chinese playbook. Through its decades-long use of five-year plans, Beijing has become masterful at crafting long-term strategic vision, devoting the necessary resources and practically ensuring successful implementation. Such an approach has naturally spilled over into foreign policy, with Beijing simultaneously pursuing the BRI, a military build-up, and the pursuit of supremacy in AI as part of its foreign policymaking.

Beijing is, in effect, creating its own foreign policy reality. By having a futuristic world vision created in its own image, and by devoting incredible financial resources over many years to seeing it through, China's government is virtually ensuring that it controls much of the dialectic in global foreign policy. No other government comes close to rolling out an initiative as bold and sweeping as the BRI, and Beijing is spending more than all other governments combined in its pursuit of AI supremacy.

This orientation to the long-term, creative and original thinking, and a willingness to spend hundreds of billions of dollars in pursuit of its objectives is a big part of what distinguishes China from America at this juncture. Beijing is combining all this with an aggressive global diplomatic campaign to take up part of the slack left in the wake of the US withdrawal from much of the rest of the world, and a clear intent to not only strengthen existing partnerships in Asia, the Middle East, and Latin America but to create new partnerships in the process.

Part of China's long-term vision is to become the leading force in diplomacy, even if the US were to regain its global footing. It is ensuring that it has, and maintains, a substantial lead in that regard. At the same time, much of the rest of the world is embroiled in domestic issues which inhibits it from responding with muscularity to the emerging Chinese-driven reality. The US remains preoccupied with its perpetual divisive political squabbling, the UK is stuck in the Brexit debacle, and other countries continue to devote untold resources to resolving lingering issues.

When the only certainty appears to be continued uncertainty, and while the majority of the world's governments appear to be trying to determine how to stop careening out of control, Beijing sees the downward acceleration as an opportunity, rather than a cost. In a decade, when others are dusting themselves off and trying to figure out what comes next, China will be crafting its next set of long-term plans while sprinting further ahead in the foreign policy arena and beyond.[1]

The net beneficiary of global disruption

The merger between global nationalism and populism – having produced such presidents as Donald Trump, Narendra Modi in India, Recep Tayyip Erdogan in Turkey, and Vladimir

Putin in Russia – is no historical aberration or temporary phenomenon. It is the manifestation of a torrent of disruptive policies that have been unleashed at the national level. What is at stake is not merely the future direction of national economies but global supply chains, natural resource extraction, and trade and investment flows – all with global implications. This raises the question, will the sustained rise of nationalism and populism enable the West to continue to lead the global economy by dislocating the very postwar order it created, or will China assume that role in this decade by helping to redefine it, with a little help from new friends?

Perhaps no Western country encapsulates this dilemma better than Viktor Orban's Hungary, which has grown close to Beijing. No other member of the North Atlantic Treaty Organization (NATO) has deliberately drawn China and Russia closer than Hungary under Orban's leadership. His support for China included an unbridled embrace of the BRI and bringing Huawei Technologies (Huawei) into the country. This was all somewhat surprising, given that Orban was aligned with Trump on a range of controversial international issues, such as immigration and religion.

But Orban is one of the leaders produced by the nexus between populism and nationalism. And Hungary is certainly not the only country that produced a leader who subsequently embraced China – for example, the Philippines did the same when Rodrigo Duterte was elected president in 2016, even after it had won a major victory in The Hague against China and its expropriation of islands in the South China Sea. Many Filipinos and allies of the Philippines were totally mystified by Duterte's actions. The same was true with Orban. The Trump administration did try to get Hungary to change its tune on China, and on Russia, and on Orban's attempt to block Ukraine's overtures to cooperate with NATO, but it failed.[2]

Orban is part of a collection of countries that are, in essence, playing both sides successfully. Having alienated so many of its allies via a combination of trade restrictions and unpredictable foreign policy actions, the US has, of course, invited this type of behavior, but in the case of Orban and Duterte (and Erdogan, for that matter), it may not have mattered, because they were inclined to rattle the American cage regardless, riding a wave of nationalistic populism that lent itself to disruption in the foreign policy arena. The unpredictability of American foreign policy under Trump has not exactly been conducive to strengthening alliances, and the trade war between America and China is bifurcating the global trading system.

Orban and the others have determined, sensibly, they would argue, that choosing one side or the other is not in their long-term interests. As the damage being caused by Trump and his administration's bungling of America's hard fought relationships in Europe and around the world continued, even America's strongest and staunchest allies decided it was better to do what Saudi Arabia, Israel, Hungary, and a host of other countries have done and play both the America and China card. *There is nothing preventing any country from playing both sides indefinitely and, since it is just as likely that there will be no permanent victor in the America-China divide, or that, if there is a victor at all, that victory may not endure, it is, perhaps, in any country's interest to maintain cordial relations with both China and the US.*

It is worth remembering that Beijing has been busy creating an alternative version of world order for the better part of a decade, since Xi first came to power. It took the West a while to understand what Xi was doing by lending tens of billions of dollars to developing countries around the world and commencing the BRI, but now that it is clear that China is competing effectively with the US (and the West) on the global stage, have Western nations responded by electing leaders who will, by virtue of their nationalistic policies, ensure that Beijing will win?

In too many cases, this has translated into inward-focused, isolationist foreign policies. America's and the UK's ill-founded objective appears to be to hold on to its share of the global economic pie by essentially retreating into a nationalistic shell, relying on domestic demand and bilateral trade agreements to march forward. Although Beijing could also be accused of doing much the same, it simultaneously seeks to expand its global footprint by embracing the rest of the world (on its own terms, of course) to pick up the slack left behind by the likes of Washington and London.

So, what is likelier to yield a more favorable result in the long term? It is hard to imagine that the US and UK model will prevail in a world where developing and emerging economies seek the embrace both America and China and are willing to cede some of their sovereignty in the process. That is why Beijing's brand is gaining a lot of traction. It comes at a steep price for many of the world's poorest economies, which are, in essence, forking over natural resource and asset ownership rights in exchange for aid, knowing that they have no meaningful ability to ever repay what is in some cases tens of billions of dollars. Beijing lends them the money knowing that it will never be repaid.

The benefit for China is that, in doing so, it gets the natural resources it seeks and the right to claim ownership over the strategic national assets (such as power plants and toll roads) it is funding. When the defaults inevitably occur, as many already have, it becomes a "win-win" arrangement for Beijing, which can beat the "development" drum as it deepens its bilateral relationships around the world. In this way, Beijing is defeating the West at its own game.

No one is forcing these countries to accept China's assistance, but the truth is, many of them have very few financing options, as they tend to be bad credit risks and few if any Western countries will lend them the money they need. At the same time, there are too few dollars available from international financial institutions to meet the trillions of dollars in infrastructure development costs needed by the developing world. So, China has arrived with its development model at the just the right time and with just the right resources to meet those needs.

For these reasons, it seems clear that, as many Western nations continue to retreat from the global stage in the mistaken belief that they will "reinvent" world order in the process, they are, rather, ceding what remaining influence they have in the developing world. That is not a recipe for greater influence in the future; it is a recipe for a diminished presence and ability to shape the direction of political and economic dialogue going forward.

Beijing understands this and will continue to devote the resources necessary to maximize its global footprint as the West proceeds to destroy the postwar order it created. China is in the process of becoming the world's leading economy and most influential nation and, at this stage, there is not a damn thing the West can do about it. The Western nations which have embraced nationalism and populism only have themselves to blame.[3]

Enhancing its Soft Power Credentials

One of the ways China is becoming influential is by strengthening its soft power credentials in the green movement and other areas. Doing so is part of its geostrategic positioning, part of its calculated grand strategy to become a global power. One would not necessarily be inclined to think of soft power as being part of geostrategic power, but it has become an important part of the landscape. Would the US be thought of as the leading nation that it is today without having established its own soft power credentials?

Beijing wants to be able to say that it can, and does, compete with the US and the rest of the world in every major sphere of competition, so it is also devoting substantial resources toward being considered a leader in that area. In terms of crafting a consistent narrative to demonstrate its competitive prowess, China knows how to play the game well. What follows are two examples of how Beijing is playing that game.

The environmental, social and governance (ESG) movement that has swept the globe has been transformed from a luxury toy of the ethically engaged to a pillar of mainstream investment practice. Investors increasingly seek to align themselves with concern for the environment, the impact of their investments on society, and a desire to invest in companies run with transparency, paying heed to the interests of minority shareholders and in accordance with best accounting practices.

Some 25% of all professionally managed assets are now invested in accordance with ESG criteria, but ESG has exerted significant influence on the global investment community for only a few years. Until recently, it had barely registered as a ripple in China, despite Beijing being a major global investor. Most Chinese investors consider compliance with ESG guidelines to be an unacceptable compromise on returns, with the country's corporations viewing ESG as little more than a box-ticking compliance exercise. But China is now playing catch-up in the ESG stakes with speed, narrowing the gap between the government's global aspirations and the conventional mindset of its international investors and corporate boards.

China is in the process of transitioning from being the world's greatest polluter to one of its greatest environmental champions, reflecting Beijing's future-oriented frame of reference. From its participation in the Paris Climate Agreement to its leadership in solar technology and its move away from near-total reliance on coal-fired power plants to a pursuit of wind power, Beijing has made a noteworthy contribution to environmental consciousness.

China's heavy subsidization of clean energy is starting to bear fruit as the cost of wind and solar power dips below that generated from fossil fuels (solar power became cheaper than coal-fired energy in 11 Chinese provinces in 2019) and bolsters China's ESG mission statement, as does the burgeoning pay-off from massive investment in electric vehicle production. The change in mindset at the corporate level is being driven both by government regulation and the internationalization of China's capital markets.

The previous "box-ticking" approach, under which companies made voluntary ESG disclosures without fear of regulatory action for failing to comply, will become a more serious endeavor once regulations come into force in 2020, making ESG disclosure mandatory for 3,000 of China's listed companies and bond issuers. In 2019, China scored 21.6 in Bloomberg's average ESG disclosure score, less than half of the top rank scorer, France. That was set to change as disclosure becomes mandatory, but also as the country aims to attract international capital.

Internationalization is driving the same dynamic in China's flourishing Green finance market. From zero issuance in 2015, the country became the world's largest issuer of Green bonds a year later, accounting for 26% of sustainable bond issuance globally. Adhering to internationally agreed Green finance guidelines requires disciplined reporting if debt is to be placed with the growing global pool of ESG-focused investors.

It is also likely that China will harmonize its sustainability guidelines with the EU's Green finance taxonomy, whereby definitions of what constitutes a sustainable use of proceeds will necessarily prod the country's Green bond issuers to adopt sustainable business practices. This alignment of corporate behavior with the government's mission statement rings true, given that China is the world's largest investor in renewable energy and energy efficiency, accounting for 30% and 27% of the global total, respectively.

China's banks are also a crucial element in the ESG dynamic, with seven of the country's largest banks having signed up to the Green Investment Principles, established in cooperation with the EU, with internationalization a key underpinning, given that these banks seek to syndicate loans within a consortium of overseas peers. At the investor level, the mindset in China is also changing fast, linked to the rise of the country's asset management industry. Seven Chinese asset managers signed up to the UN-supported Principles for Responsible Investment in 2018, bringing the total number of signatories in the country to 18 – more than double the 2017 total. So, the Chinese government's aspirations in the ESG arena are becoming a reality, and China is quickly being seen as a player in the ESG space.[4]

Regarding climate change, China has for decades been hesitant to deem climate change a national security issue, because Beijing feared that crisis-oriented rhetoric about climate change would be used to legitimate interventionist actions by the West, including forcing Beijing to curtail its economic growth. While doing so, the Chinese military quietly released a 2010 white paper on national defense acknowledging that climate change contributed to security issues. China's shift from being a skeptic to a believer on the link between climate change and security was not really because its leadership had suddenly become convinced that climate change is real. The change in its public stance was a calculation that embracing the issue could enhance China's legitimacy at home and its influence abroad. At its heart were concerns about the impacts of environmental change on both domestic and international stability.

Anyone who has visited most any Chinese city will be acutely aware of its legendary poor air quality. I have visited Beijing on numerous occasions when I literally could not see across the street and have flown from Beijing to Hong Kong looking down on what appeared to be a never-ending pollutant-laden haze. China has numerous natural disasters each year from earthquakes, storms, and floods, which should by themselves have been a compelling reason to become believers in climate change. In addition, the CCP is keenly aware that as the incomes of its urban residents increase, their demands for improved environmental quality are rising, and that a leading source of provincial protests are coal-fired power plants. This convinced Beijing to pursue aggressive policies to reduce the prominence of coal as a source of power and to begin to rely more on green sources of power.

The Chinese Academy of Sciences advised in a 2017 report[5] that "water resources scarcity issues will become the core issue in the development of countries along the Belt and Road." As a result of the BRI, Chinese companies, citizens, and the state are becoming more exposed to climate-related security issues, such as extreme flooding and drought, migration, and protests over Chinese-financed infrastructure construction.

Beijing came to the realization that it was falling behind the global green movement, and that was having an impact on how it was perceived globally. It also became increasingly sensitive to allegations (especially from India) that it is attempting to control and disrupt the flow of major rivers, most of which, such as the Brahmaputra and the Mekong, originate within China. More than one billion people will be affected by Chinese decisions related to water from the Tibetan plateau. So, domestic stability, international stability, and international influence have all had a tangible impact on China's approach to climate change.

As is the case with the US, China has shown a reluctance to move too quickly or adopt any climate policies that might limit its economic growth. Although it has become a leader in renewable energy technology, China has ensured that it will be spewing fossil fuel emissions for decades to come by continuing to build coal-fired power plants at home and fund them around the world – even after signing the Paris Climate Agreement. Beijing has also been accused of flouting the Montreal Protocol on the ozone layer by releasing chemicals that deplete the ozone layer and are themselves greenhouse gases.

So, while Beijing has increasingly embraced the position that climate change poses a security risk to the nation, that has not yet translated into actual reductions in the country's emissions.[6] Its heightened sensitivity to this issue is more about appearing to be on the climate change train, and implementing some policies that are having a positive impact, but not at the cost of modifying its larger strategic objectives.

The BRI will continue apace, regardless of its economic impacts, as will the construction of coal-fired power plants. It is likely to take Beijing an extended period of time to arrive at a genuine middle ground that adequately balances its climate change concerns with its security concerns.

Rare Earth Minerals

Of course, China has established its bona fides in terms of the application of hard power, also. We will explore this throughout the rest of the book but, for now, suffice it to say that Beijing is no stranger to applying pressure where it needs to in order to achieve its objectives. In 2010, after Japan had detained a Chinese fishing trawler captain for allegedly violating Japan's fishing rights and trying to avoid inspection of his vessel, China imposed a ban on its export of rare earth minerals (REMs). Estimates vary, but China is thought to produce as much as 95% of the world's known REMs, although only about a third of the world's reserves are located there. REMs are a series of chemical elements found in the Earth's crust that are vital to many modern technologies, including consumer electronics, computers and networks, communications, clean energy, advanced transportation, health care, environmental mitigation, national defense, and many others.[7]

Despite strangely coincidental timing, Beijing said at the time that its action should not be perceived as retaliation for its dispute with Tokyo over ownership of the Senkaku Islands or Japan's detention of the Chinese fishing boat captain. Beijing argued that it had, after all, also suspended its exports of REMs to the US and Europe and had been steadily reducing its export of REMs since 2005.

It was, therefore, no surprise when, in 2019, Beijing was reportedly considering restricting the export of REMs to the US, ostensibly in reaction to the escalating bilateral trade war. Doing so would have been one of two "nuclear" options Beijing has at its disposal. The other would be to stop purchasing US treasuries (Beijing being their largest foreign purchaser, with Tokyo being a close second) or pick up the pace of selling US treasuries (which Beijing has been doing since 2013).

The Chinese government claims it possesses less than 20 years-worth of medium and heavy minerals and must reduce its export of REMs to preserve its supply. Given that a minimum of 3-to-5 years are generally required to make new mines operational, additional alternative sources of REMs remain years away. Since 2010, a number of countries have replaced Chinese-sourced REMs with that of other countries, such as Australia, Brazil, India, and Russia.

The US was, from the 1960s through to the 1980s, the world's number one producer of REMs, sourced from the Mountain Pass mine in California, which was subsequently closed due to environmental issues associated with the disposal of toxic wastewater and an inability to compete with lower cost Chinese mines, which were not required to comply with the same degree of environmental restrictions. The mine was reopened in 2017 and now produces as much as 10% of global supply, but it remains dependent on China for ore processing. The US General Accountability Office calculated, almost a decade ago, that it would take up to 15 years to re-establish a domestic REM industry sufficient to meet America's needs.

The fact that REMs are in limited supply and used to produce a wide array of products that are either in high demand, critical to green technology, or have military applications, complicates matters. The US is indeed vulnerable, but not as much as it used to be. In 2018, the US purchased less than 4% of Chinese REMs, which is not difficult to understand when one considers just how much of America's manufacturing base has been shifted outside the country over the past two decades.

A wholesale and sustained cessation of the export of REMs to the US or other countries seems unlikely. If Beijing were to implement a ban, it may prompt companies from around the world to reconsider whether they wish to continue to maintain their manufacturing base in China, or in other countries heavily reliant on China. The global supply chain is multifaceted and resilient, so while an export ban on the US would ultimately impact many of the countries US companies do business with, as was proven in the 2010 Japanese example, smugglers and black marketeers will find ways around any such ban, just as they currently do to bypass American sanctions against Iran and other countries.

The trade war with the US is serving to demonstrate that China is as vulnerable as any other country to trade sanctions and that its own actions can have a profound impact on the Chinese economy. It also serves to re-emphasize that US businesses are as guilty as those from any other country for choosing to make China a centerpiece of their global operations. They have only themselves to blame for continuing to remain in China despite the passage of numerous laws that severely restrict how they may operate and what they must give up – in terms of knowledge, production technology, and IP – for the privilege of doing business in and with China. At what point does the price become too high? The time has come for many companies to address this question.

In a world in which interconnectivity and dependency define the trade and investment landscape, the luxury of pulling high stakes triggers and expecting few enduring consequences has largely disappeared. China's rare earth bravado failed to achieve its objective in 2010 and it will fail again now if implemented. Given that Trump has proven–again and again – that he is willing to go the mat in negotiations with adversaries, there should be little doubt in Beijing's mind that should it decide to impose an export ban on REMs, the US will respond in kind.

As for Beijing's ongoing status as the top purchaser of US treasuries, if it continues to sell them, Tokyo will become their top foreign purchaser, which suits it just fine. And, as the world becomes ever more economically nationalistic, it should not come as a surprise to learn that the number one purchasers of US treasuries – by a wide margin – are, in fact, US citizens. That should serve as a reminder that China has less of a chokehold on the US economy than it might imagine.[8]

China's Neocolonialism in Africa

The same may not be said about many African countries. Some foreign policy analysts contend that China has become the new face of neocolonialism in Africa, having loaned tens of billions of dollars to the continent's governments while knowing that, in all likelihood, many of those debts will never be repaid, as previously noted. Beijing proceeded to do so on the presumption that its access to Africa's markets, enhanced influence, and ability to exploit the continent's rich deposits of natural resources would compensate it for any unpaid loans. Chinese investment in Africa has a long history, dating back to the Ming Dynasty, but it was not until the late 20th century that China pursued what is now commonly referred to as "debt trap diplomacy" in order to have its way with Africa.

In 2000, China's official loans to Africa were just in the millions of dollars. Johns Hopkins University has estimated that between 2000 and 2015, the Chinese government, banks, and contractors had loaned $94 billion to African governments and state-owned enterprises. Many countries welcomed Chinese investment because it did not come with strings attached, such as a requirement for free elections, gender equality, anti-corruption programs, or government accountability. Many African leaders' willingness to agree to Chinese funding – whether for natural resource extraction, infrastructure building, or for commercial purposes – has come at a cost.

Many people in Africa have complained that workers are not treated fairly, the environment has not been well considered, and much of the Chinese-built construction is shoddy and dangerous. Regardless of the quality of the construction, the loans must, at least in theory, be repaid to China, adding to governments' debt burden. Two HIPCs – the Democratic Republic of Congo and Zambia – have particularly high levels of Chinese government debt, raising questions about how those loans may ultimately be repaid, at what cost, and what sacrifices the governments may have to make to repay those loans. This has led some analysts to suggest that the relationship between China and Africa has become toxic.

Much of the debt of the HIPCs was written off by lenders just after the millennium. As a result of China's aggressive lending throughout the developing world, particularly in Africa, countries such as Zambia have accumulated almost as much debt as they had before the previous generation of national debt had been written off. Between 2013 and 2018, Zambia's national debt tripled as a percentage of national income. Most of it was owed to China.

Some NGOs consider the accumulation of debt unnecessary and reckless on the part of African governments, which, they maintain, certainly share the blame for the continent's predicament vis-à-vis China. After all, no one forced them to accept the loans. Some projects were considered "vanity" spending, to help get politicians elected or re-elected. In Zambia, for example, Chinese loans paid for two new airports and a variety of "roads to nowhere," while the country still lacked so many basic needs. While it takes two to tango (a lender and a borrower), development loans are often difficult to obtain, so free-spending Beijing had an obligation to ensure that the borrowers understood the implications of accepting its money, yet responsible long-term lending has often taken a back seat to near-term objectives, such as resource extraction. No one in Zambia believes that China is simply going to forgive its debt.

In 2018, Kenya's public debt first surpassed the $50 billion mark. At that time, China was Kenya's largest lender by far, accounting for 72% of bilateral debt – a 15% increase from 2016. Kenya's debt to China was also 8 times more than what it had received from its next largest lender, France. Overall, China accounted for more than 21% of Kenya's external debt that year, coinciding with Moody's downgrading of Kenya's credit rating because of its rising debt levels and what the agency saw as deteriorating debt affordability. That same year, the IMF ceased Kenya's access to a $1.5 billion standby credit facility due to non-compliance with fiscal targets, urging Nairobi to lower its deficits.

Kenya was then forced to relinquish control of its largest and most lucrative port in Mombasa to Chinese control as a result of Nairobi's inability to repay its debts to Beijing. Other assets related to the inland shipment of goods from the port, including the Inland Container Depot in Nairobi and the Standard Gauge Railway, were also threatened to be compromised in the event of a Chinese port takeover. To make matters even worse, Kenya agreed to the Railway deal with the understanding that any investment disputes would be subject to Chinese law and occur in China. Should default occur, China's Export-Import (EXIM) Bank would take possession of the assets from Kenya's Port Authority. At the same time, Zambia was slated to lose its international airport and national electricity grid to Beijing because of defaults on Chinese loans.

The Chinese know that Africa is going to become a smarter clientele continent going forward, and a more difficult and demanding negotiator in the future. The Angolans, for example, began specifying exactly the number of schools and railroad lines they would like the Chinese to build, and what they hoped to achieve as a result. The relationship was, in essence, being rebalanced out of necessity. African leaders were perhaps afraid to stand up to China, or were simply greedy, and feared that the money would not flow in the end. Many of them did not consider the consequences; nor did the Chinese.

As the world's natural resources become increasingly scarce, African countries have come to realize just how many cards they hold, and they have finally decided to stand up to China. Should African countries successfully manage the transition from nations that merely possess natural resources to manufacturing powers that can actually compete with China, the nature of their relationship with Beijing will change even further. That said, both sides know they ultimately need each other. The challenge will be to find the right balance between China's wealth, power, and money, and African countries' resources and vast potential.[9]

China's Maturing Sino-Saudi Alliance

As Washington's influence in the world and the Middle East continues to wane, Gulf countries are weaning themselves from their traditional orientation toward and dependence on the US. America's postwar political and economic supremacy in the region is now threatened as a result of its own foreign policy, but equally so by the rise in importance of the emerging powers. No country has capitalized on the shifting landscape more than China, which has, consistent with its actions globally, moved assertively to strengthen its ties with the Gulf region generally, and in particular with its most important economic and political power, Saudi Arabia.

From the Chinese perspective, energy security lies resides at the heart of the bilateral relationship with Saudi Arabia, as has been the case with many of China's most important strategic relationships over the past decade. China has adopted a multi-tiered foreign policy designed to acquire and secure long-term energy supplies by diversifying its sources of oil and gas, engaging in 'energy diplomacy,' and establishing energy reserves. With the world's largest oil reserves, Saudi Arabia was bound to play an important role in Chinese energy policy.

China and Saudi Arabia signed a Memorandum of Understanding and opened commercial offices in each other's countries in 1988, which led to the formal establishment of diplomatic bilateral ties. Their relationship has steadily grown since then. Just as China has been vociferous in its pursuit of a deeper relationship with the region, Saudi Arabia has been the most assiduous in the region in cultivating a stronger relationship with China. For this reason, Saudi Arabia has, since 9/11, been perceived with some suspicion by America – even during the Bush years. King Abdullah's first foreign visit upon assuming the throne was to China, Chinese President Hu paid two visits to Saudi Arabia in the span of three years, and President Xi has also visited the Kingdom.

A substantial boost in Chinese exports to Saudi Arabia occurred after 2000, when Chinese products became more price competitive. As a result of rising oil prices in the early part of the last decade, Saudi Arabia's appetite for Chinese products rose dramatically. As noted earlier, China has become the Kingdom's top oil export market and Saudi Arabia has reoriented its foreign and energy policy accordingly. Many Gulf states find their burgeoning relationship with China refreshing, in that China – which itself objects to perceived US interference in its domestic affairs – tends not to do the same with its trading partners.

But China's cordial relationship with Gulf States is not without sensitivities. In particular, China's repression of Muslims in Xinjiang Province has complicated its political dialogue with states in the region. Religious activists in the Gulf are bound to draw parallels between Xinjiang, Gaza, and Kashmir. Ultimately, the strength of the region's economic relations with China will dominate its political relations with Beijing, and any disagreements over state political policy will take a back seat to ensuring that regional and bilateral relations remain cordial and on the right track.

Since the acquisition of oil (and other natural resources) has remained central to China's economic and foreign policy, China has sought to transform its relationship from that of a somewhat bashful suitor toward a more formal engagement. But to do so, it must choose between working within the confines of the postwar diplomatic landscape crafted by the US or challenging that order in bold fashion. Doing so would break the century-long dominance America and its allies have had on Gulf diplomatic relations and enable China to truly begin to mold its bilateral and regional relations in its own image.

Breaking the status quo ante and undoing a century of history and influence will entail enormous effort in terms of persuasion, fiscal largesse, influence peddling, and relationship building. Africa was a comparatively easy nut to crack, since most African nations need the money and infrastructure China has provided, with many having been drawn to China simply by the fact that it has pursued a relationship with them. But the Gulf does not need China's money, or its infrastructure, and is not generally so easily accommodating to such overtures.

So what will China need to do to accomplish a similar feat in the Gulf? It would need to replace the security umbrella the US has so carefully crafted over the past 75 years. This is clearly not something that will be easily achieved – if it can be achieved at all. China is not a global naval power-although Beijing is building its capabilities in that regard in Djibouti, Pakistan, and elsewhere. But it has projected its military power in the Gulf since the 1980s through missile proliferation and arms sales. Saudi Arabia purchased intermediate range CSS-2 missiles from China as long ago as 1988, raising suspicion at the time about the Kingdom's nuclear ambitions. China met an important strategic need for the Kingdom that America would not agree to meet. The US has continued to measure its military support for the Kingdom with its strategic imperatives for Israel – something China has not done.

Chinese behavior in the Gulf is primarily driven by two potentially contradictory factors. One is China's newly found status as a "stakeholder state" favoring regime stability. However, this is somewhat inconsistent with China's tendency to elbow its way into relationships it deems important, and its history of dictating the terms on which it will address topics of critical perceived importance. China is also still finding its footing on the global stage and at times clumsily manages bilateral relations. The other is the Chinese quest for energy in light of its economic explosion, the opportunistic pursuit of which may lead China to have a destabilizing influence in the Gulf.

For now, Saudi Arabia will keep a foot in both the American and Chinese camps, judging that its own long-term interests are well served by maintaining the comparative advantages offered by both nations. That said, the pendulum has clearly shifted toward the Chinese camp. In time, as the Kingdom's economic ties grow firmer with China, their military relationship will expand. As China's military power comes to match its political and economic power globally, it will become Saudi

Arabia's strongest military ally.[10] China is quickly becoming the regional power that Riyadh recognized more than two decades ago.

<u>China's Rise in the Middle East</u>

China long ago mastered the art of casually sitting on the sidelines while regional and global economic and political forces clash, then swiftly swooping in to scoop up the spoils. That was best exemplified when Chinese oil companies won a variety of contracts from the Iraqi government following the end of the Iraq War. China did not fight in that war but that did not stop Beijing from seeking to benefit from it, nor did it stop the Iraqi government from awarding the contracts to Chinese firms at the expense of firms from the US and other coalition members. China's geostrategic positioning vis-à-vis the Middle East has been deliberately and carefully choreographed to ensure that its oil and gas purchasing power is well spent.

Beijing clearly sees the region's shifting political sands as an opportunity to enhance its economic and political role, particularly as America's power and influence continue to decline. In 2016, President Xi visited Tehran just days after global sanctions were officially lifted (Beijing literally did not waste any time attempting to establish a foothold with Iran), which resulted in some $600 billion worth of contracts for Chinese firms. China had already become Iran's number one export partner. By visiting both Iran and Saudi Arabia in the same trip, Xi attempted to leverage both countries' proxy regional conflicts for Beijing's own benefit, keeping both sides in its camp.

China has clearly established itself as the future growth market for Saudi petroleum. Saudi oil exports to China exceeded those to the US for the first time in 2009, and the kingdom exports in excess of three times more to five Asian countries (China, Japan, South Korea, India, and Singapore) than it does to Europe and North America combined. By 2030, Chinese demand for oil is expected to reach more than 16 million barrels per day. By contrast, US oil imports are expected to continue to dwindle as a result of increased domestic production due to fracking. In shifting its oil export focus, Saudi Arabia is joining the world's major Muslim powers that have also deepened their economic ties with China over the past decade.

Given the kingdom's ongoing economic crisis as a result of the chronically depressed price of oil, the Saudis need the Chinese to continue to buy as much crude as possible. The House of Saud wishes to maintain its historical relationship with Washington while giving itself the freedom to pursue alternative economic and political relationships. China's military lacks the capacity to police the Persian Gulf and safeguard shipping, and no country other than the US has the capacity to provide a security umbrella to countries in the region. The Saudis will, therefore, remain dependent on the US for security, which also suits Beijing's interests. China has been content not to be seen as actively promoting regional stability, but rather to ride the coattails of the US militarily.

China, Saudi Arabia, and the US are likely to continue to practice a rather awkward triangular balance of power in the Persian Gulf, reflective of an understanding of their interwoven dependencies, which limits their mutual capacity to deny each other a preeminent role in the region. Beijing and Riyadh realize that with US military bases in all of Saudi Arabia's fellow Gulf Cooperation Council member states, neither Beijing nor Riyadh are capable of removing Washington from its position as the predominant military actor in the Persian Gulf. Of course, neither China nor Saudi Arabia would benefit from a change in the US role, as America continues to bear both the burden and the cost of policing the region.

The path China is blazing in the Middle East is rewriting the rule book on how to become important and influential – economically, politically, and diplomatically – without using military force either to project power or as a bargaining chip. No other country in the world would dare to visit Riyadh and Tehran in the same trip and hope to maintain favorable relations with both, yet China did just that. This is more evidence at just how masterful Beijing has become at using a variety of approaches to get what it wants.

That said, only so much can be achieved by waiting in the background for the right moment to pounce. That model has worked reasonably well for China up to now, but regional and global geopolitical dynamics are shifting at an accelerated pace. Xi has an opportunity to up the ante by catapulting Beijing to the forefront of geopolitical diplomacy and crisis management. That is an objective worthy of a country which has already assumed leadership roles in so many other aspects of the global chess board.

Beijing is not afraid to enter into the swirling waters of the Middle East or to target the most historically important and trusted partners of Washington. It can do so not only because it is a valued trading partner, but also because few see China becoming less important and the US becoming more important to the region in the future. Beijing has already proven itself to be a worthy competitor in the region. Washington, Europe, and the rest of the world could learn a lot from the manner in which Beijing has acted, and continues to act, with bravado, swiftness, and resolve in pursuing its political, economic, and military ambitions.[11] The question is not whether Beijing will continue its bold push onto the global stage, but rather, what, if anything, can be done to stop it.

The South China Sea and China's misplaced national pride

Beijing has mastered the art of playing the international system against itself. Nowhere is this better exemplified, nor is China's frame of reference vis-à-vis Asia better illustrated, than by its territorial and governance claims over the South China Sea. China's government argues that its "nine-dash line" of sovereignty over the entire Sea is based on centuries of maritime history, and that China's claim is air-tight. The Chinese Foreign Ministry has even asserted that ample historical documents and literature demonstrate that China was the first country to discover, name, develop, and exercise continuous, effective jurisdiction over the South China Sea islands. The Chinese government has beaten this drum so hard and for so long that the Chinese people believe it. The nine-dash line has appeared in school room maps throughout China for decades, in conjunction with the narrative of its national humiliation by foreign powers after the fall of the Qing Dynasty.

However, the first Chinese official documented to set foot on one of the Spratly Islands was a Nationalist naval officer in 1946, the year after Japan's defeat in World War II and its own loss of control of the Sea. He did so from an American ship crewed by Chinese sailors who were trained in Miami. As for the story of the nine-dash line, it began a decade earlier via a

Chinese government naming commission. China was not even the first to name the islands; the naming commission borrowed and translated wholesale from British charts and pilots. It is unclear how the Chinese government translated all this into the bill of goods it has sold to the Chinese people, but by now, it is a source of national pride, however misplaced it may be.

The Chinese government, and its people, have essentially backed themselves into a corner. They have been drinking the nine-dash line Kool-Aid for so long that even despite the 2016 Hague ruling that there is no legal basis for China's claim over the Sea, and even though the Chinese government has failed to produce evidence of its declaration to back up its version of the facts, national pride will not allow it to admit that what the government is doing in the South China Sea is illegal under the very international maritime law (the United Nations Convention on the Law of the Sea-UNCLOS) to which it first subscribed on the very day in 1982 when the Convention became a legal instrument.

Can a state remain a party to a treaty or convention without being bound by its rules? Can contracting states adhere to an international legal regime and simultaneously opt out of any binding force required or to be required by that regime? A state can be found to be in violation of a substantive legal norm even without a coercive or compulsory judgment in a given venue, provided, of course, that there is truth to the argument supporting a violation and that it is appreciated by the alternative venue.

When Manila took Beijing to The Hague to formally contest China's various incursions into Philippine territorial waters and its exclusive economic zone, China accused the Philippines of violating the 2002 Association of Southeast Asian Nations (ASEAN) Code of Conduct, which states that unilateral initiation of arbitration is a violation because parties to the Code are supposed to resolve their differences over their overlapping territorial claims on a bilateral basis, via negotiation. Curiously, however, it was through the same ASEAN Code of Conduct that the parties reaffirmed their commitment to UNCLOS as well as to the purposes and principles of the UN Charter. UNCLOS is clearly adverse to the Chinese position. By invoking the ASEAN code (which invokes UNCLOS), China admitted to the binding force of that code. Under the law, this is the case, especially when a state's admission will be an admission against its own interests.

While China disavowed UNCLOS vis-à-vis the Philippines, it expressly invoked UNCLOS provisions in its own legal claims against Japan – so it wants to have its cake and eat it too. In 2009, China submitted a claim over the Senkaku Islands (which, like the Scarborough Shoal and the Spratlys, are believed to be natural resource rich) and turned to UNCLOS rules in defining and delineating its continental shelf beyond the 200 nautical mile exclusive economic zone, again within the meaning of UNCLOS. There is some international legal doctrine supporting the view that a state's acts in one place can be used as an admission and adversely bind that state in another set of circumstances.

The larger point is that China has not personified the Rule of Law in the Philippine case, or in others related to maritime borders, and wants to be able to cherry pick which provisions of international treaties it will willingly comply with and which it will not. That is behavior unbecoming of a rising global power and will make states which are signatories to treaties with China wonder if its signature is worth the paper it is printed on. This cannot be in China's long-term interest.

That said, given that Beijing's actions in the South China Sea occurred with little more than a strenuous objection from Washington, and that Manila has become ever closer with Beijing since The Hague ruling, there is every reason to believe that Beijing will not alter the course it has embarked on. It could even be the case that more of the Asian nations contesting ownership of the Paracel and Spratly Islands will follow Manila's lead, admit defeat, and break bread with Beijing over the issue. That would only serve to reinforce China's misplaced national pride on this issue and prompt Beijing to continue to take unilateral bold actions that are contrary to international law.[12]

China's port buying spree

One of the primary objectives of the BRI is to help transform China from a primarily continental power to a maritime power. Many of Beijing's investment activities around the world are consistent with that objective. Most countries seem to have a focus on the potential commercial benefits of the BRI, but some see what Beijing is trying to do in a different light. India has already made its concerns about Beijing's investment in Indian Ocean ports and the resulting "string of pearls" (which New Delhi believes are designed to encircle India) known to the international community. But Beijing's investment in ports and related infrastructure have stretched well beyond Asia.

Chinese interest in acquiring ownership stakes in global ports is consistent with Beijing's desire to tilt the global economic playing field in its favor while helping to ensure that the commercial processes and standards preferred by China become normalized around the world. Another purpose of the BRI is to bind consumer markets to Chinese exporters through the Initiative's physical, financial, and digital networks, which all lead back to China. This is perhaps best illustrated by China's port buying spree in recent years in Europe. In nominal terms, the EU constitutes about 22% of global GDP. Europe will remain the most important destination for finished goods throughout the BRI for the foreseeable future. The Made in China 2025 policy cannot succeed without bringing Europe into the Chinese economic orbit through the BRI.

It is estimated that the Chinese state has at least a 10% equity stake in ports throughout Europe (including in Belgium, France, Greece, Italy, the Netherlands, and Spain), and a growing investment portfolio of at least 40 ports in Africa, the Americas, Central and Eastern Europe, the Middle East, South and Southeast Asia, Australia, and the Pacific. Beijing's sometimes stealth approach to investing has resulted in its 35% stake in the Euromax terminal at Rotterdam, a 20% stake in the Port of Antwerp (Europe's two busiest ports), and 100% ownership of Zeebrugge in Belgium.

While Beijing has ensured that it extracts its pound of flesh from Europe in return for essentially making the EU the centerpiece of the BRI, it is worth adding, in fairness, that a number of European ports have benefitted directly from the Chinese investment. For example, when China's COSCO Shipping Corporation took over the Greek container and passenger port of Piraeus in 2008, fewer than 900,000 containers passed through its facilities; by 2016, it reached 3.7 million containers, and Piraeus rose in container port rankings from 93rd in 2010 to 44th in 2015 to 38th in 2017. Chinese-invested ports will eventually be connected to the *maritime* Silk Road accompanying the BRI and become part of a network of freight lines belonging to the Eurasian economic corridor. This will link European economies with the entire BRI economic ecosystem, from China through to the Mediterranean.

Those entities that are familiar with how Beijing does business will know that China Vision – how Beijing is creating an alternative world order in Beijing's image – is certainly at play with respect to Chinese infrastructure investment. According to the CSIS Reconnecting Asia database, *89% of contractors participating in strictly Chinese-funded BRI-related projects are Chinese companies, with only 7.6% being local companies and 3.4% being foreign companies.* By contrast, of the BRI projects funded by multilateral development banks, just 29% of contractors were Chinese, 41% were local firms, and 30% were non-Chinese foreign firms.

There is also growing discomfort on the part of non-Chinese entities with the close funding arrangements between Chinese firms and government-controlled financial organizations. This stands at odds with the EU's liberal notion of political economy, which depends on there being significant distance between the political and strategic objectives of the government versus the objectives of commercial enterprises.

Beijing is gradually asserting de facto control and dominance over European ports just as it did with the islands of the South China Sea but, in this case, Beijing is using a divide-and-conquer strategy to prevent the EU from taking a common stance against Beijing by offering substantial amounts of funding and investments to countries throughout the region. While Beijing's actions in the South China Sea were judged to be illegal by The Hague, its actions in Europe are legal and, as noted, create some economic benefits, even though the biggest net beneficiary will, of course, ultimately be China.

European nations should remember that Xi's goals of making China a moderately prosperous society by 2021 (when the country celebrates the 100th anniversary of the formation of the CCP), and of becoming a fully developed, rich and powerful nation by 2049 (when China celebrates its 100th anniversary as the PRC) require that Europe play along. Every European country that has already ceded ownership of critical ports to Chinese entities is doing just that. Since *the BRI cannot be completed without the active participation of Europe*, European leaders may want to consider taking a page out of Trump's playbook and find a way to establish a more equal footing with

Beijing. They, too, will have a stake in the success of the BRI. Cross-border investment is *supposed* to be a two-way street.

The EU should consider putting pressure on countries such as Greece and Hungary to agree to a common set of guidelines with respect to screening how Chinese investments are made and how Chinese-owned assets are run and operated. The sale or lease of any asset – but especially strategically important assets – should follow a set of guidelines adhered to by all EU states. Foreign entities should abide by the same set of rules. More broadly, all EU member states should take collective responsibility for protecting European interests, the adherence to international law, and the preservation of a regional and economic system which does not prioritize a China-centric view of the world while ensuring that special advantages are baked in for China.[13]

Europe is, of course, not the only place where China has embarked on a port buying spree; China will soon operate the Israeli port of Haifa. When this was first announced in 2018, the Americans thought the Israelis had lost their senses, if not their priorities. Security is always foremost in Israelis' minds, Haifa is the country's primary port, and American military ships dock there, so what exactly was the Israeli government thinking? Well, it appears to have been thinking about business and its long-term economic future. China is by far Israel's largest and most significant Asian business partner, and its third largest exporting country overall. Chinese investments and construction in Israel reached $12.2 billion between 2005 and 2019, and in 2018, exports of electronic components from Israel to China increased by 80%.[14]

Israel wouldn't have been the first country to put business ahead of other concerns when considering whether to give China the keys to its most prized port, but it would probably have been the last country that anyone would have thought would actually do it. The appeal for China is quite clear – Haifa is an important strategic vantage point, with easy access to the Europe and the Suez Canal. But for Israel, apart from earning good will from Beijing, its own advantages are less clear, and in doing so, it rattled its most important strategic partner in the world – the US.

Part of the mystery can be resolved by considering what else Israel might have had to offer China. Afterall, countries all over the region and all over the world fell all over themselves to become part of the BRI, and China has superior relations with a number of Middle Eastern countries – Saudi Arabia being at the top of the list (as we have seen). While China certainly also has an interest in Israel's high-tech industry, the Israeli government is presumably not quite so eager to hand off the keys to that kingdom to Beijing. The port at Haifa undoubtedly offered a viable alternative. Israel needed to offer Beijing something meaningful without putting the country's most important security interests at risk.

The state-owned Chinese company Shanghai International Port Group (SIPG) won the bid to expand Haifa's port in 2015 and its work is to be completed in 2021. SIPG is owned by the State-owned Assets Supervision and Administration Commission of the State Council (responsible for managing the country's state-owned enterprises), which reports directly to the State Council of the PRC (the country's chief administrative authority). So, SIPG is a rather important entity in the Chinese government. Its terms of reference called for it to run the Haifa Port for 25 years; another Chinese firm also won the bid to build a new port at Ashdod. Surprisingly, those decisions were made by the Israeli Transportation Ministry and the Ports Authority without the involvement of the country's National Security Council or Navy.

The civilian port at Haifa is also the exit route of the adjacent navy base, where Israel's submarine fleet is stationed (and which, according to foreign media reports, maintains a second-strike capability to launch nuclear missiles). China's involvement in other large Israeli infrastructure projects – such as the Mount Carmel tunnels and the light-rail train in Tel Aviv – also did not involve the government authorities that one would think would ordinarily be associated with such decision-making.[15] They all appear to be business and/or political decisions.

Israel is also wanting to expand its range of options. For decades, the US/Israel relationship has been paramount. And it will remain so. But at the time, Israeli Prime Minister Netanyahu was open about his courting of support from China, India, and Russia, among other countries. Israel is a small country that packs a big punch that gets noticed by these large powers. They, too, see advantages to having strategic partnerships with Israel – one of the world's leading nations in technology and military hardware. Multiple alignments are a smart play for Israel, and any country in its position would likely do exactly the same thing.

That said, Israel may ultimately pay a price for proceeding with the arrangement. The Trump administration has made it clear that, if SIPG does indeed manage the Port, certain aspects of intelligence sharing would be impacted – fervent Israel supporter and close ally or not. America and Israel clearly have a difference of opinion about the nature of any threat posed by China. Then again, America has the luxury of turning away from China by virtue of its size and strength. Israel does not have the same luxury.

For its part, China knows a good thing when it sees it. Israel is one of the high technology start-up capitals of the world and leads the world in areas of cybersecurity, medical, and automatic driving car technology (among others). China knows that it still has some things to learn and has determined that Israel is a useful way to achieve part of that. Managing the Port is the icing on the cake.

China's great rejuvenation

Xi's primary foreign policy objective is to achieve the "great rejuvenation of the Chinese nation"[16] by the middle of this century. He has demonstrated a willingness to assume greater levels of risk in pursuit of China's interests but, as the case of Israel clearly demonstrates, Xi has also shown a propensity to create and seize strategic opportunities as he attempts to once again make China a leading great power. In part, he is doing so by adopting a "Neo-Tributary" approach to regional affairs in which the economic and political destiny of every Asian country runs (from Xi's perspective) through China. Beijing's interests and preferences are therefore the key factors guiding any decision of geopolitical consequence, especially in the Asia-Pacific. It is quite willing to directly challenge the interests and prerogatives of China's neighbors and assume the leadership role that the US has played in the region in the postwar period.

We should expect that China will continue to look for ways to enhance its growing power, further establish itself at the center of Asia's regional political and economic architecture, and to advance its interests, even if (or, more correctly, *especially* if) it generates greater friction in the geostrategic arena. Xi will continue to present China as the champion of globalization and open markets, even though China's domestic reality is tightly controlled. This is part of its carefully choreographed narrative – maintaining a dual personality on the global stage.

China's previous geopolitical weakness meant that any question about whether China's views and actions were aligned with those of the liberal international order were largely academic. As China's rise achieved greater consequence, beginning in the 1990s, American leaders started to call for China to act as a responsible stakeholder in accordance with the liberal international order. But China's actions – particularly under Xi – have made it increasingly clear that Beijing's approach to international relations has grown increasingly ambivalent.[17]

China's orientation toward international relations is being defined by a set of core objectives – among them is protecting the territorial sovereignty of the nation, maintaining its growth at a level that will enable the government to ensure ongoing domestic stability, similarly ensuring the enduring supremacy of the CCP, and creating sufficient influence among nations around the world so that its political and diplomatic power will remain unquestionable in the future.

In short, the CCP wants to make sure that China remains strong, prosperous, influential, and respected. In doing so, it wishes to avoid the middle-income trap (wherein it would become stuck at a middle-income level and unable to push through to that of a wealthy nation) through a combination of technological innovation, a strong military, and an ability to have an impact on global norms.

In a general sense, China has pursued a risk-averse strategy and seeks to avoid direct conflict with the US, although it has not hesitated, as previously noted, to push up against established norms and boundaries in the process. And it has done so with remarkable success. As Beijing becomes increasingly brazen in its actions, it is experiencing greater resistance from Washington. The question is just how far China can continue to push and how much resistance America will exhibit before a confrontation ensues – politically, technologically, or militarily.

Xi appears to be banking on the belief that the continuation of disruption in global politics will be a net positive for China, which will enable it to be able to increase its global influence around the world while quietly building up its military and steering his country through an economic transition that accommodates and takes advantage of the world's largest middle class. The great rejuvenation coincides well with the great transformation of China from an exporting nation to a consuming nation that further integrates itself with the global economy by achieving an equilibrium between what it sells and what is buys from the rest of the world.

Xi is also betting that America is only willing to go so far, spend so much, and devote so many resources toward challenging China without fundamentally altering the manner in which it functions. With a $700+ billion defense budget, how much *more* can the US be expected to spend on defense before upsetting its own fiscal balancing act? China already has the world's largest navy; in the coming decades it will challenge US military supremacy in ways that will present an even more difficult dilemma to Washington: will it outspend China or can it find a way to outsmart it, as China is attempting to do (this is explored further in Chapter 6).

In 2019, The Worldwide Threat Assessment of the US Intelligence Community stated that China's leaders will increasingly seek to assert its model of authoritarian capitalism as an alternative – and implicitly superior – development path abroad, exacerbating great power competition that could threaten international support for democracy, human rights, and the rule of law.[18] In the absence of some type of reform to China's political model – which seems highly unlikely at this juncture – one should presume that there will be irreconcilable ideological tension between the Chinese and US governments that will become a permanent element of their bilateral relationship.[19]

As China and the US become more competitive, they risk locking themselves in an increasingly intensifying security dilemma, wherein one of their actions makes the other feel less secure. Can cooperation endure on such a basis? As the stakes continue to rise, the US may feel the need to essentially put China in its place while it still can. This could take the form of a limited engagement in the South China Sea or perhaps the attempt to do the thing China's leaders fear the most – encircling China with a larger string of military bases in the Pacific and surrounding oceans.

This, of course, already exists, but what if, for example, the Philippines were to change its now long-held position and invite the US Navy back, or New Delhi were to seek a more robust naval relationship with Washington, or Japan's ability to project its naval power were to be dramatically increased? One look at the Asian map is a constant reminder to China that the US has a lot of allies in the region, while China has very few. As for the Sino-Russian alliance, it is a marriage of convenience that may last for some time but it is questionable just how much of substance may be achieved as a result of that collaboration. The two countries are more akin to adversaries than allies as they jostle for favorable positioning on the global stage.

To remain strong, the US will need to reassure its allies by redoubling its commitments, expanding and accelerating its engagement, and reaffirming its determination to sustain a sphere of influence. But Washington should not approach this global competition with China on the basis of outdated assumptions, a fundamental misunderstanding of China's ambitions or capabilities, or a miscalculation of its own power and leverage. Washington should accept that strategic competition with China is inevitable and that, with such a worthy adversary, absolute security is not possible. That so many US allies are already operating within overlapping American and Chinese spheres of influence[20] should be all the evidence that Washington needs that the ground is shifting beneath its feet. US primacy cannot be perpetually sustained. Eventually, China *will* match or exceed US capabilities and positioning in a host of areas, including political, economic, and diplomatic influence, technological prowess, and global leadership.

Chapter 4: Economic Considerations

<u>The contest for systemic leadership</u>

From America's perspective, Beijing and Washington's trade war is, at its most fundamental level, about the pursuit of trade parity, transparency, and equality. It is also, of course, about which country will lead the global economic system into the rest of this century. Despite the trade war and a gradual slowing of the global economy, there has been no generalized decline of the US economy in absolute terms. Since Trump assumed power in 2017, the US economy has grown faster than any other leading industrialized economy since the end of the Cold War. Any deterioration in America's *potential* for global economic leadership stems from a decline in its will rather than in its capability – at least, for now. The main reason for any US economic decline in relative terms is the dramatic rise in China's capabilities. America and China are now broadly equal in several key metrics, including GDP in purchasing power parity terms and levels of trade. China is likely to continue grow approximately 4-6% annually – double or triple the anticipated US rate of 2 to 3% for at least another decade.

That said, there are at least three potential scenarios for the evolution of global economic leadership over the next decade. The first and most likely outcome is a systemic stalemate that emerges without effective leadership from either America, China, or any other country. The continuation of this "G-Zero" world could have deleterious consequences. The danger is that the world falls into the "Kindleberger trap" of the 1930s, which deepened the impact of the Great Depression when the declining UK no longer had the capability to lead and the rising US did not yet have the will to do so. No country provided the open markets, lending, and liquidity needed to avoid international economic conflict or a downward spiral.

Parallel issues exist today. Will China be able (and willing) to translate its growing capability into an effective and acceptable leadership role? If not, will the US regain its will to do so? If neither can or will step up to the plate, could the G-Zero model proliferate and endure? Is this our new normal? And, even if China or the US had the will to step up, would it necessarily make a difference in a world that has become accustomed to the idea of seeing America eventually fall off its perch? The norms of the postwar international economic order are strongly embedded in the global economy and could prevail even without the most prominent countries' leadership. The institutions that were created at Bretton Woods 75 years ago have proven resilient and could even further evolve to maintain their legitimacy and authority.

The second scenario envisages the continued rise of China to eventually lead a new economic system. Many believe that a gradual assumption of global leadership by China is inevitable. China has been in the habit of confounding predictions regarding when it will hit conservative time benchmarks (for example, not long ago, the prevailing view was that China may become the world's largest economy by 2030. Some economists now see that occurring early in this decade[1]). Every indication from the past decade of US administrations has led to the conclusion that, whatever the timing, the US will not walk away quietly.

Could this clash of the titans lead to a "Thucydides Trap" for the global economic order – when a rising power generates fear and tension with the established power, which can escalate toward war? When incumbent Great Britain resisted rising Germany in the late 19th century, the first era of globalization ended and war resulted. The US resisted assuming leadership in the 1930s, the Great Depression ensued, the US economically confronted a rising Japan, and war was again the result. Although the stakes are equally high, the nature of warfare has changed the calculus implied in actually engaging in war. If America were inclined to spar militarily with China, it would presumably have done so when Beijing was constructing its military bases in the South China Sea. That is as good an indication as any of Washington's predilection for military battle with Beijing. Economic battle is an entirely different matter.

The third, and likeliest, scenario may be that the US regains its footing, restores its alliances, and reinvigorates its economic dynamism – implying a lengthier transition period, but with China snapping at its heels all the way. While this may seem to some an unlikely prospect, multipolar leadership has proven to be successful several times in recent modern history. Examples include the late 19th century and the early interwar period, during much of which either the UK, France, the US, or a combination of them provided the foundation for global economic stability and prosperity. In the postwar era, the EU and US effectively functioned as a "G-2", managing the global and monetary trading system for prolonged periods, but that arrangement is coming to an end.

In the current decade, an American and Chinese-led world would function within the existing multipolar and institutional frameworks but be more fully influenced by China. The AIIB and New Development Bank are good examples of how this is already working in practice; Beijing would naturally like to see more Chinese-driven institutions created in due course. As we have already seen, China is in the process of shifting the Western-created institutions (such as the UN) in its own direction. As Chinese influence in these institutions rises, America's must inevitably fall, as it is in the process of doing.

That said, some examples of leadership by both countries over the past decade reveal which scenario may be most likely. Consider that China resisted devaluation during the Asian financial crisis, which could have greatly exacerbated the calamity. It joined the WTO, which helped spur it to promote domestic reforms. It moved more swiftly and forcefully than many expected in response to the Great Recession. It has provided generous loans to the IMF in recent years, created the AIIB, and launched the BRI. And China has generated nearly a third of total global growth since the Great Recession. On the other hand, it has contravened international rules and norms on numerous occasions, its massive currency manipulation resulted in the loss of huge amounts of output and jobs from other countries, and its forced technology transfers and IP piracy have similarly taken a massive economic toll.

Beijing clearly values the existing system enough to take steps to preserve it when systemic stability is threatened, as occurred during the Asian crisis and Great Recession. It appears to have concluded that it can get away with substantial cheating within the system to promote its national objectives, since its economic and political power have deterred other countries from launching effective steps to counter it. China will therefore likely be content for some time to continue to enjoy the best of both worlds under the current regime – have its cake and eat it, too. The risk, of course, is that it could at some point miscalculate and trigger a backlash, presumably led by the US, against its free-riding, which could threaten the sustainability of the system and risk plunging the world into the "G-Zero" leaderless context. Such a result could be approaching, given the aggressive moves against China taken by the Trump administration.

The US has a similar story to tell. Since 2008, it nearly caused a global economic collapse, engaged in at least two wars, failed to respond well to the negative domestic impacts of globalization, withdrew from the Paris Climate Accord, NAFTA, and the TPP, failed to conclude the Transatlantic Trade and Investment Partnership, has been unwilling to lend additional funds to the IMF, and its fiscal stimulus of an already fully employed US economy is irresponsible in macroeconomic terms. America's behavior indicates that it has lost interest in providing leadership to the global economy and has embarked on a path of domestic and international economic destruction though its brazen rejection of multilateralism, while embracing isolationism, nationalism, and populism.

The paradox is that, if America were to continue on the path it is on (which seems highly *unlikely* in the long-term) China may *have* to assume global leadership, by default, in order to preserve the global economic and political architecture. Ironically, the most logical way for China to proceed down such a path would be to stimulate the launch of a new round of liberalization negotiations at the WTO. It could also choose to join the TPP and convert it into the Free Trade Agreement of the Asia-Pacific among the 21 Asia-Pacific Economic Cooperation (APEC) nations, generating pressure on the Europeans and other nonregional countries to support a new global initiative.[2] Both are certainly possible – with or without the US maintaining its de facto role as global economic and political leader of the world. China is perfectly capable of acting independently with any initiative at any time.

Both governments have an inherent interest in resolving their differences, and that will occur in due course, because they must. A perpetual state of heightened economic conflict between them is simply inconceivable. Once Trump is gone, and assuming America has come to its senses, it should not take too long for Washington to get its act together. Part of the reason is that many Americans, and a multitude of people and nations from around the world, have become desperate for a sensible, practical, and manageable world order. China will continue down the path it has embarked on until and unless it is forced to change direction. The world can only hope that the CCP is smart enough to recognize what is in its, and China's, own interest in the longer term.

<u>Gaming the system</u>

Following China's accession to the WTO in 2001, and up until 2016, trade friction between America and China took place within the frameworks that had been established by China's accession protocols and the WTO rules. Such issues were previously generally managed via bilateral dialogue, the WTO dispute settlement system, domestic trade remedies, and quiet diplomacy. But China's economic system is a unique and complex blend of private and public institutions, government participation and oversight, and private sector participation, which makes it difficult to distinguish between the actions of the state versus that of private sector actors. The distinction between the public and private sectors is a conceptual fault line under WTO law.

The WTO regulates a range of public activities that impact the ability of private actors to engage freely in markets. Challenges arise where the nature of the bodies that WTO law seeks to regulate is opaque or unclear.[3] This has especially been the case with China's emphasis on developing indigenous technology, which began with its 11th Five-Year Plan beginning in 2006. These challenges presented by the Chinese economic system since that time were "finessed" by the treatment of China as a nonmarket economy in antidumping and countervailing duty cases, but whether China can continue to be treated as a nonmarket economy is a matter of considerable controversy.

Friction between China and other advanced economies has increased as Beijing has sought to use state-centered industrial policies and state-owned enterprises to adopt more advanced industrial activities, which foreign firms were not allowed to participate in fully. The Obama administration sought to use regional trade agreements such as the TPP and the Transatlantic Trade and Investment Partnership to write trading rules to, in principle, deal with the problems presented by China that could not be addressed through WTO rules. The idea was that, if a critical mass of Asian and other major trading countries would sign on to the rules, China could be pressured either to follow them or at least negotiate with the US and other agreement signatories.

Trump abruptly shifted gears, however, preferring instead to use access to the US market as leverage to renegotiate the terms of US engagement bilaterally, even when this approach itself involved blatantly disregarding WTO rules. While Trump was trying to retreat from the rules-based system, many other countries continued to see being part of the system as clearly in their interest. Ironically, Trump's actions may have made other countries work even harder to build an even stronger rules-based system, not only to strengthen their position, but to incentivize America to return to the rules-based trading system.

So both Beijing and Washington are contributing in different ways to eroding the existing global economic regime: China's economic model does not really fit into the Western-designed rules-based trading system, and America under Trump is working against the system it helped create by prioritizing bilateral trade agreements over multilateral trade regimes. In combination, both countries are contributing toward undermining the postwar trading system by weakening adherence to the rules and norms that have contributed to the system's success. If nothing fundamentally changes, trade wars and increased protectionism could become the rule, rather than the exception.

The economic costs to the global economy could be considerable if countries and businesses lose confidence in the enforcement of trade rules, resulting in a loss of perceived legitimacy. Although China's economic system in some ways undermines the rules-based trade order, Beijing is additionally incentivized to promote it because China gets to continue to be a member of various trade agreements while remaining outside the scope of their intended method of operation, which suits Beijing just fine. When Trump withdrew from the TPP, Beijing wasted no time doubling down on becoming its leading advocate, picking up where America left off, and adding it to the list of agreements it gets to continue to be part of without fully complying with it in the process. That is Beijing's way of subtly benefitting from gaps and inconsistencies in the system.

A more brazen example is how the Chinese government continues to claim that its Made in China 2025 program (in place since 2015 and intended to move the country away from being the world's "factory", producing low value products, toward producing higher value products and services) does not discriminate against foreign firms or force technology transfer. That is clearly not the case. The program explicitly uses subsidies that favor domestic over foreign production, a clear violation of the WTO Agreement on Subsidies and Countervailing Measures, which expressly prohibits such subsidies.[4]

As we have already seen, China is masterful at using the systems designed by the West to help make it the economic goliath that it is today. That of course includes the WTO, where it has been pursued by other countries with vigor through the Organization's dispute resolution procedures. China has been a third party participant in more cases brought to the WTO since its inception than any other single country except Japan.[5] What follows is a small sampling of bilateral and multilateral commitments made by China by virtue of becoming a member of the WTO that remain unfulfilled:

- Despite repeated commitments to refrain from forcible technology transfer from US companies, China continues to do so through market access restrictions, the abuse of administrative processes, licensing regulations, asset purchases, and cyber and physical theft;

- China committed to open the electronic payment services market in 2006. This commitment was confirmed in a 2012 ruling by the WTO's dispute settlement body resulting from a US legal challenge. Today, no foreign electronic payment services companies conduct business in China's domestic market;

- China's use of export and import substitution subsidies has been ubiquitous throughout the past two decades in sectors as diverse as automobiles, textiles, advanced materials, medical products, and agriculture, despite explicit prohibitions in the WTO Agreement; and

- China has repeatedly committed to review applications of agricultural biotechnology products in a timely, ongoing, and science-based manner. However, Chinese regulatory authorities continue to review applications slowly and without scientific rationale, while Chinese companies continue to build up their own capabilities in the area of agricultural biotechnology. [6]

China has repeatedly deployed illegal export restraints, such as export quotas, export licensing, minimum export prices, export duties and other restrictions, and on scores of raw material inputs as determined in multiple WTO cases brought against it by the US and other WTO members. Beijing has used these illegal export restraints to provide substantial cost advantages to a wide range of downstream producers at the expense of foreign producers, while creating pressure on foreign producers to move their operations, technologies, and jobs to China.

Any review of China's trade regime will also show that China's regulatory system is so opaque that it is often difficult for US companies – or even the US government – to fully comprehend China's legal requirements in a particular area of the economy. This problem is exacerbated by China's extremely poor record of adhering to its transparency obligations as a WTO member. Such shortcomings create their own trade barriers and undermine the competitiveness of China's trading partners.

WTO membership comes with expectations that an acceding member not only will strictly adhere to WTO rules but also will support and pursue open, market-oriented policies. Not only has China failed to comply with these expectations, it has moved further away from open, market-oriented policies and has more fully embraced a state-led, mercantilist approach to its economy and international trade. China's market distorting policies and practices harm and disadvantage its fellow WTO members even as it reaps enormous benefits from its WTO membership.[7]

Some WTO members have pursued China on these, and other issues, while others have remained silent. But the fact that a country that actively abuses gaps and inconsistencies in the WTO's operational guidelines, as China continues to do with regularity, and is being allowed to continue to not only do so but retain its membership in the Organization, points to a broader issue that plagues not only the WTO but many other multilateral organizations. This must also be addressed in due course, though it is difficult to muster the political will to do so in such organizations. China knows that and is betting on its continuation.

<u>China's perspective on the trade war</u>

Beijing and Washington naturally have a different take on how and why their trade war started, who is to blame, and how it will be resolved. As an American, I naturally gravitate toward the US position, which is, in short, that China has been raking the US over the coals on trade and getting away with whatever it can for decades. The record is demonstrable, clear, and undeniable. However, I am thoughtful enough to recognize that it takes two to tango and that, in large part, America has itself to blame for ensuring that China has become the epicenter of global manufacturing by joining the rest of the world in rushing to set up manufacturing operations there, agreeing to legal, regulatory, and judicial conditions that no foreign investor in its right mind would ever agree to, and that American companies' pursuit of profit appears to have blinded them to the many risks associated with doing what they were doing in China the way they were doing it for as long as they have been doing it.

China's perspective is that no one forced any of these companies to make China the global epicenter of manufacturing, no one forced any country, business, or consumer to purchase their products, and no one forced any of the companies operating there to stay. So, it should be no surprise to anyone that, in June 2019, the Chinese government released a 5,000-word government white paper[8] on the state of trade talks with the US, which offered a uniquely Chinese view of the matter. What follows is a brief summary of some of the key points raised (based on an English translation of the paper). Some of these points readers may find ridiculous; other points they may view as absolutely true:

- The economic and trade friction provoked by the US damages the interests of both countries and of the world;

- China's technological innovation is based entirely on self-reliance. Accusing China of IP theft and forced technology transfer is utterly unfounded;

- China is fully committed to IP protection. It has established a legal system for the protection of IP that is consistent with prevailing international rules and adapted to China's domestic conditions;

- China has always pursued international technical cooperation with mutual benefit and a "win -win" philosophy as the basic value orientation;

- The tariff measures the US has imposed harm others and are of no benefit to itself;

- The US has backtracked on its commitments in the trade talks;

- In response to the economic and trade friction started by the US, China has been forced to take countermeasures, as bilateral trade and investment relations have suffered;

- The US has insisted on including mandatory requirements concerning China's sovereign issues in the deal, which only serve to delay the resolution of remaining differences; and

- The US government bears sole responsibility for the severe setback to the China-US economic and trade consultations.[9]

A couple of these points are hard to argue with, such as that the trade war *is* against the interests of the both countries and the world, and that China *has* established a legal system for the protection of IP that has been adapted to China's domestic conditions. Other points, such as that China's technological innovation is based entirely on self-reliance and that China has always pursued international technical cooperation with mutual benefit make non-Chinese policy analysts want to burst out laughing.

On the other hand, accusing China of cheating is hypocritical when almost all trade policy actions taken by the Trump administration are themselves in breach of WTO rules, a fact implicitly conceded by Washington's determination to destroy the dispute settlement system. The US negotiating position vis-à-vis China is that "might makes right". It doesn't help that the US side of the debate is increasingly about whether integration with China's state-led economy is even desirable. Liberal commerce is increasingly seen as "trading with the enemy" and relations with China viewed as a zero-sum conflict. Yet, an effort to attempt to halt China's economic and technological rise is almost certain to fail, and will almost certainly result in deep hostility among the Chinese people.[10] Since China's rise is inevitable and irreversible, wouldn't it be better to find a way to collaborate and cooperate, with some achievable and verifiable boundaries in place, instead?

America's take

Trump led America into the trade war for a simple reason: he believed that China had been gaming the system and taking advantage of America for decades. He didn't blame China for doing it; he blamed successive America leaders for allowing it to happen. And he was right. Nation-states can sometimes be like people; they will attempt to get away with whatever they can. That is their nature. If monitoring and enforcement mechanisms are not robust enough to catch malfeasance and punish it, then who is to blame? As discussed earlier, the US government had failed to reign in China's excesses and take it to task for a litany of grievances-among them, IP theft of a grand scale, currency manipulation, a failure to abide by previous agreements, and an outlandishly unbalanced current account surplus on the Chinese side. The problem just got worse over time.

Americans are naturally divided about whether a trade war is a good thing or a bad thing, but the majority don't like China too much (never mind that probably 90+% of them have never visited the country, nor do they necessarily know much about China). That previously referenced Pew poll on the subject in August 2019 confirmed that 60% of Americans had an unfavorable view of China (up from 47% the prior year) and that 24% regarded China as America's top threat in the future.[11] Yet, that same month, an NBC/Wall Street Journal Poll[12] noted that 64% of Americans believe in free trade.

This is an example of cognitive dissonance: citizens of the world's largest economy (the US, soon to be its second largest) do not like the world's second largest economy (China, soon to be the largest), although they were instrumental in making it the second largest economy, and even though they believe in free trade. Many Americans may not make the connection. Be that as it may, they know when they're getting screwed (even if they are partly to blame). To put it in simple black and white terms, the US *goods and services* trade with China totaled an estimated $737 billion in 2018. Exports were $179 billion, and imports were $558 billion, resulting in a trade deficit with China of $379 billion in 2018. China is America's largest *goods* trading partner, with $660 billion in total two-way goods trade in 2018. Total goods exports totaled $120 billion, while goods imports totaled $540 billion. The US goods trade deficit with China was $419 billion in 2018, an 11.6% increase over 2017. China accounted for 21% of US imports in 2018.[13]

When the trade war first began, the Trump administration propagated several myths to the American people in its battle against China. One myth was that China pays for the tariffs. At the beginning of the imposition of tariffs, this was actually a frequent talking point from the White House, but it simply is not, and was never, true. Americans pay for those tariffs via higher-priced imports from China. There is no way that tariffs on goods that account for that much of the US economy will have no impact on US businesses and consumers. How did Trump expect to perpetuate such a fiction? Despite the economic pain associated with the imposition of the tariffs across a broad swathe of the American economy, even the most severely affected farmers tend to agree that something needed to be done, and that short-term economic pain would eventually be replaced by economic gain in the longer-term.

Another myth is that it can coerce China and sever that relationship with minimal cost to the US domestically. Those on the receiving end of the tariffs in America, such as farmers and importers, know that is simply not true. That is also why the US government has had to give tens of billions of dollars in subsidies to the farmers to keep them from going bankrupt as the trade war continues, and why more US businesses are being forced to alter their manufacturing base away from China and modify their purchasing and sales sources. The trade war will result in many changes in the way American businesses manufacture and in how American consumers purchase.

Consumer behavior does not necessarily change easily or quickly, but it does eventually adjust to new circumstances. Consider the price of gasoline. During the Great Recession, American consumers did not change their driving patterns all that much as the price of gasoline rose to $3 or $4 per gallon, but they did when it rose above that. Where I lived at that time, in Connecticut, drivers would routinely drive 10 or 15 miles per hour over the speed limit on the highway before gas got expensive. At $5 per gallon, most were inclined to drive at 55 miles per hour, where gas mileage could be optimized. Put another way, if a gas price increase is temporary or reasonable – or, at least, perceived to be so – consumers may be less inclined to change their driving habits. If it is judged to be significant or permanent, consumers will purchase smaller cars and tend to drive only when necessary. On this basis, it would appear that American and Chinese consumers appear to think that the impact of the tariffs is both significant and permanent.

Consider that Shopkick, the operator of a US-based shopping rewards app, surveyed more than 30,000 of its users in June 2019 and learned that 44% of respondents planned to shop and purchase less as a result of rising prices on consumer goods resulting from the tariffs on Chinese goods. In the survey, 38% of respondents said they expected a household cost increase of up to $500, and 30% said they anticipated that the cost increase will be more than $1,000 per year. 60% of shoppers in the survey said they planned to modify their shopping habits, and 25% said they will switch to purchasing more American-made goods. Shopkick concluded that if the tariffs announced at that time were actually implemented, annualized consumer cost was likely to double.[14]

A Marketplace survey[15] in China in 2019 confirmed similar sentiment. Marketplace interviewed ordinary Chinese about their spending and purchasing habits, found that their places of employment had generally experienced a decline in activity and revenue, and confirmed that they, too, were spending (and saving) less. This was well before all the tariffs had taken effect, or before the ones that had taken effect had necessarily been fully implemented. Since most Chinese belong to the ranks of the growing middle class and since most have *some* discretionary income, but certainly not an unlimited amount, this type of "street" sentiment was indicative of the true impact such economic actions have on individuals, businesses, and the economy more generally.

Additional surveys on both sides of the Pacific confirmed something similar. So, American and Chinese consumers determined as of 2019 – less than 2 years after the trade war had started – that the tariffs were noteworthy and likely to be permanent. After all the flag waving and nationalistic rhetoric that both Trump and Xi had encouraged since this imbroglio began in 2017, and following all the false starts and absence of progress in the negotiation process in the 2 years that followed, should it have been any wonder that they had arrived at that conclusion?

If these alterations in purchasing power do in fact become permanent, the change in consumer sentiment does indeed stand to have a real impact on manufacturing, processing, distribution, and purchasing habits in America, China, and throughout the world. Whether either China or the US stand to gain economically as a result will take years to be determined, but in the end, consumers on both sides of the Pacific could end up being the winner because of their predilection to modify their purchasing habits early and en masse.

Impacts far and wide

The Sino-US trade relationship is far more nuanced than many headlines suggest – in the US and around the world. In America, the bilateral trading relationship supports approximately 2.6 million jobs across a range of industries, including jobs that Chinese companies have created in

America. As the Chinese middle class continues its rapid expansion (the number of Chinese middle-class consumers is expected to exceed the entire population of the US by 2026), US companies face significant opportunities to tap into a new and lucrative customer base that can further enhance employment and economic growth – if the two sides can sort out their issues over trade. According to one estimate, by 2030, US exports to China could rise to more than $520 billion.[16] Great potential growth and prosperity stand to be gained, from both sides, based on the reestablishment of a strong relationship.

That depends, however, on whether meaningful progress can be made that goes to the heart of core issues – particularly from the American side. The American government's concerns about the bilateral trade relationship stem from specific practices endemic to China's economic model that systematically tilt the playing field in favor of Chinese companies in the global arena. Progress on specific trade issues will require China to comply with its WTO commitments, which implies reforms that touch on areas of state control over the economy. That is not something the CCP is much inclined to do. In addition, new trade rules will be required in order to address China's economic practices not covered via its WTO commitments, including state-owned enterprises (SOEs), digital trade, and subsidies.[17]

While the many benefits of the relationship are tangible, so are the economic costs. The short-term effects of higher US tariffs are manageable for China because of the size and diversity of its economy, the longer-term ramifications for growth are likely to be more serious – certainly more serious than the Chinese government would ever admit, and largely underestimated. For China, the trade war is a demand shock, and the sector where that has the most implied impact is the technology sector, where the combined effects of investment restrictions, export controls, and tariffs will be felt the most. Technology is also where China's ability to raise its dwindling productivity growth resides. Beijing may put a brave face on it, but the Chinese economy is clearly under pressure.

The European economy has more to fear from Chinese retaliation against American exports than from US tariffs on Chinese goods and services because the share of European content in US production is twice as high as it is for Chinese production. For the EU as a whole, involvement in US and Chinese production represents a bit more than $400 billion (or 2.4% of GDP). The European sectors that are most exposed – that is, those whose involvement in US and Chinese production far exceed the EU average – are transport equipment, motor vehicles, rubber and plastics, chemical products, and pharmaceuticals. All of these sectors have medium to high technological content. So, countries such as Germany, France, the UK, and some Nordic nations are at greatest risk. The indirect effects could be more detrimental, not least because the European economy is increasingly dependent on trade, and much more dependent on trade than the US. The world's two biggest national economies are also the two biggest trading partners for the EU, with the sum of EU two-way trade with both countries representing about 8% of EU GDP.

For Canada, the dispute could end up helping some manufacturers and suppliers, as US buyers look for domestic substitutes or suppliers in a third country. Since the US buys machinery and plastics from both Canadian and Chinese exporters, the new tariffs could divert trade in favor of Canadian suppliers. A UN study suggested that countries not directly hit with bilateral tariffs benefit most from trade diversion and see Canada's exports to the US jumping by as much as $20 billion in the near-term. However, Canada will likely suffer collateral damage as the tariffs sour business sentiment and put planned investment at risk – though there may end up being little effect on Canadian GDP growth. Other countries, which have a high share of exports to China – such as Chile and Peru – are particularly exposed as the yuan weakens and Chinese demand slows.[18]

The impact the trade war has had on the service industry is one of its hidden sides. Tariffs on goods disrupt value chains but also impact the service providers who form an integral part of them. Consider that up to 30% of the value of a car is derived from service providers. Think of it this way: service providers connect the dispersed production stages of global value chains (such as transport, logistics, communications, financial, and business services). As of 2015, 69% of global GDP was in the service sector, as was 79% of US GDP.[19]

A natural byproduct of the imposition of the tariffs was also tighter investment screening procedures, which disrupted investment flows to services sectors across the world. Several countries became increasingly selective about which investments to allow into their markets. The US targeted the Chinese acquisition of service companies in the US, particularly with respect to technology companies and firms that possess a great amount of data about US nationals. It was, ironically, restrictions on *data flows* that had the potential to cause the most amount of disruption to all services sectors. This had a real impact on "tradability" of services, which was boosted by the Internet revolution and has even more potential to do so with the introduction of 5G technologies. The stakes are high regarding policy choices impacting data governance. So, while service industries are often invisible, they are far from mere bystanders in this trade war.[20]

In short, there are no bystanders. The American and Chinese economies have extended their tendrils into virtually every country on earth, impacting billions of consumers. All countries and all consumers will feel some sort of impact from this trade war as a result. The trade war has prompted countries to shift alliances, businesses to change manufacturing processes and locations, the modification of sourcing patterns, and what may end up being a permanent change in the products consumers will buy, and from whom. Neither Beijing nor Washington anticipated the potential long-term impacts of the trade war, but the fact that it was so long in coming may have guaranteed the depth and breadth of its lingering impact.

Intended and unintended impacts

While the imposition of the tariffs is the best known manifestation of Trump's assault on all things Chinese, less recognized are the many changes that have occurred vis-à-vis how Chinese businesses are granted access to US markets, how they may acquire companies in the US, transfer IP from the US to China, or conduct research in the US. A long-term structural trend had already been under way to shift some manufacturing activities out of China, and not just by American companies. For example, Samsung moved many tens of thousands of jobs to Vietnam from China years ago, and Li & Fung, a Hong Kong-based supply chain manager of retail stores that was founded in China, for the first time has a base of operations in Bangladesh.

Foreign businesses across China have put in place contingency plans should tariff rates rise above 25% on the goods they produce. How disruptive such change in their production processes may be will depend on the exporter's global footprint. For a globalized consumer goods company, the US may represent less than 20% of its output from China, and the company may already have a network of manufacturing plants around the world. Adding spare capacity to such plants by swapping production between plants in Brazil and China – so that the Brazilian plant can produce for the US – would incur additional operating costs, but not capital investment. Eastern Europe, India, Turkey, and the Philippines are countries that have the capacity to provide workers and supply chain infrastructure.(Vietnam is seen by many to be at capacity, and producing in Mexico is seen as less desirable by some manufacturers because of high local value-added requirements contained in the US–Mexico–Canada Agreement).

Chinese FDI in the US dropped 83% in 2018 to $5 billion, from $29 billion in 2017 and a record $46 billion in 2016. The amount fell partly because Beijing sought to rein in deeply indebted investors and partly because of the enhanced scrutiny of Chinese investments. China ended up not pursuing transactions worth $2.5 billion in 2018 because it knew they would not be accepted by the Committee on Foreign Investment in the United States (CFIUS), which reviews foreign investments that have national security implications. Chinese investment in the US information and communications technology industry plunged to $200 million in 2018 from $2.5 billion in 2017 (a whopping 99% decrease). US FDI in China dipped only slightly, by comparison, to $13 billion in 2018 from $14 billion in 2017. US investment in the Chinese information and technology industry dropped to $2.1 billion in 2018 from $4.1 billion in 2017 (a 51% decrease).[21]

No Chinese company wants to be caught up for months in a review process with the CFIUS, with the high risk of the transaction being turned down. US sellers do not want such uncertainty, either. As a result, many Chinese strategic investors have self-censored and decided not to make acquisitions in the US, or to make smaller amounts of investment in areas that are not considered sensitive or strategic. This is having significant impact in the US start-up space, where Chinese investment has been integral to the marketplace.

Chinese entities are estimated to have poured approximately $14 billion into US startups since 2000, with 80% of the deals having occurred since 2014. Investments from Chinese state-owned investors had all but disappeared by 2019. As recently as mid-2018, there were about 5 such deals each month. These investors, which were controlled by the Chinese government, would now find it impossible to get approval for an investment in a US company building sensitive technology. Chinese venture capitalists have tried to steer clear of the technology CFIUS is closely probing, such as AI, data analytics, and cyber security. Some 40% of the Chinese venture capital deals in 2018 went to biotechnology and pharmaceutical companies.[22] Uncertainty about the future of Chinese investment in technology start-ups will undoubtedly linger well into the current decade.

In 2018, Trump signed into law the National Defense Authorization Act for Fiscal Year 2019, which contained the Foreign Investment Risk Review Modernization Act (FIRRMA), the first significant reform of CFIUS in more than a decade. The most important changes brought by FIRRMA were the significant expansion of the scope of transactions subject to review by the CFIUS, which may now request that the President prohibit or unwind specific transactions. CFIUS has jurisdiction to review "covered transactions". Under the previous standard, a "covered transaction" was any transaction that would result in control of a US business by a foreign person. Under FIRRMA, the definition of "covered transaction" was expanded to include:

- Non-passive investment in a business that (a) owns, operates, manufactures, supplies or services critical infrastructure; (b) produces, designs, tests, manufactures, fabricates or develops critical technologies; or (c) maintains or collects sensitive personal data of US citizens that may be exploited in a manner that threatens national security;

- Any real estate transaction (both developed and undeveloped) that is proximate to (a) an air or maritime port, or (b) a US military facility or other sensitive government locations;

- Changes in the existing rights that a foreign person has with respect to an investment in a US business if that change could result in control; or

- Any transaction or agreement designed to evade or circumvent CFIUS review.

Previously (and unbelievably, given what the CFIUS is and is intended to do), submission of transactions to CFIUS was a *voluntary* process, in that no laws or regulations required companies to file a notice (although companies that did not file risked CFIUS initiating its own investigation and potentially blocking a deal). Under FIRRMA, however, parties to a transaction must submit to *mandatory* reporting, if the involved foreign investor is one in which a foreign government has a substantial interest and such foreign person would acquire a substantial interest in a US business that involves critical infrastructure, critical technologies, or that maintains or collects sensitive personal data.[23] (Of course, "substantial interest" remains to be defined in future regulations).

So, since the US has become "inhospitable" to Chinese investment in sensitive sectors, where might the Chinese money flow instead? As noted earlier, Israel is certainly one place to try to make up the difference. One wonders how long it will take the Israeli government to tighten its regulatory environment further to prevent the Chinese from doing more of the same there. UK start-ups continue to receive Chinese investment in fintech and health tech, alongside investment in more mature industrial sectors. Italy's government has proactively reached out to China seeking further investment in a variety of areas. And Chinese companies continue to explore acquisition targets, from luxury goods to technology, quietly, in Japan.

Opportunities for Chinese researchers to work at leading facilities in the US are also being restricted. Where visas *are* issued to researchers, they tend to be for shorter periods, making researchers uncertain whether they will be able to complete their projects. As a result, fewer researchers and students are likely to want to go the US. Johns Hopkins University briefly halted its visiting-scientist program in 2018 to revise its application requirements. Apart from the reduced tuition income that will result, fewer large Chinese donors will provide funding to build new world-class research facilities on US campuses in the future. And Chinese green card holders in the business arena have noted that their green-card-to-passport application process has ground to a complete halt.

Xi's continuing exhortations for China to increase its "self-reliance" (independence from foreign technology and other foreign influences) have added to the centrifugal forces contributing to the America-China divide. Companies on both sides of the Pacific are exploring options for creating separate corporate structures for their China- and US-focused operations,[24] expecting the divide to become permanent. American companies have expanded rapidly overseas for decades and have bandwidth to adapt their operations to new market realities with relative ease, but the majority of China's companies are relatively new to the game. That has not stopped them from proceeding apace to catch up.

China's overseas investments

Consistent with so much about China's thrust onto the global stage over the past decade, its outward foreign direct investment (OFDI) has grown far faster than OFDI from most other transitional economies. Chinese OFDI is largely politically driven, aimed at achieving specific nationalistic objectives, such as securing natural resources, acquiring strategic assets in key technologies and service industries, and creating national champion companies. China's approach to OFDI is often aggressive and increasingly colors its relationship with recipient nations at all levels of development and income.

Until 2000, OFDI from China was negligible. That year, Premier Zhu Rongji officially announced that overseas investment would be one of the main objectives of the government's 10th Five-Year Plan (2001-05), giving birth to its "go global" strategy. Premier Wen Jiabao reinforced the importance of overseas investment in the 11th Five-Year Plan (2006-10). The government-led strategy proved to be effective. By 2006, yearly OFDI flow was 19 times that of the amount in 2000, growing at an average rate of 116% per year, dwarfing average world OFDI growth of 6% over the same period. By 2016, China's OFDI had reached $196 billion, but in 2017, it dropped for the first time since 2001, by 19%, to $158 billion. Chinese investment in the US in 2017 was a little more than $6 billion, a decline of 62% from 2016. By contrast, Chinese OFDI in Europe exceeded $18 billion that year, up 73%.[25]

China has tailored its approach to OFDI based on the relative economic and political strength of the recipient country, in exchange for specific benefits. So, in HIPCs, China tends to offer to build infrastructure in exchange for the right to access raw materials. In developing countries, China may offer to help develop an indigenous industry; in emerging markets, grant greater access to the Chinese market; and in developed countries, expand reciprocal agreements related to cross-border investment. In each case, *China weighs the relative costs and benefits associated with expanding its relationship with a given county vis-à-vis what it will receive in return.*

Beijing's overall strategy for SOEs is to "grasp the large and let go of the small", aiming to create national champions from large SOEs through extensive government support, while giving small and medium-sized SOEs greater exposure to the market. SOE's receive direct financial support from the government in the form of below market rate loans, direct payments, and other subsidies associated with official aid programs. The China Development Bank (CDB), China EXIM, and Sinosure (the national political risk insurer) are the primary government organs that provide such support, although other state-owned banks and specially created funds also provide backing.

Chinese SOEs pursue OFDI in the primary sector, where investments are dominated by a few giant firms. A second strategic objective is to spur investment that acquires sophisticated, proprietary technology, technical skills, industry best practices, and established brand names and distribution networks. OFDI also serves as a strategic objective at the macroeconomic level, relieving some of the imbalances that have been built up by economic policy that distorts the marketplace. In the process, OFDI reduces the massive capital stock the government has accumulated while allowing for investment diversification, particularly away from US and other government bonds. Such investment often takes the form of merger and acquisition activity. Lenovo's purchase of IBM's computer unit and Huaneng Group's acquisition of InterGen are good examples of this. These were accomplished before the US more closely scrutinized Chinese OFDI from a national security perspective.

Some governments remain wary that such investment will lead to the "development trap": a flood of cash that results in heightened corruption and largesse without building indigenous capacity, knowledge, management skills, or that allows movement up the global economic value chain. The blowback China has received from some African countries objecting to its one-size-fits-all approach to OFDI has prompted China to reconsider its approach. An increasing number of countries are no longer simply rolling out the red carpet. Natural resource export earnings must now be deposited into offshore escrow accounts, with the value of the exports determined at the time of export, rather than in advance, for example.

This is a far cry from how Chinese OFDI started in some of these countries, with the Chinese simply dictating the rules of engagement. Developing countries accounted for 95% of Chinese OFDI stock by the end of 2006, with a significant percentage in countries with weak governance and rule of law. Many of these countries subsequently experienced the classic "resource curse" in which valuable reserves of minerals or fossil fuels enhanced corruption and conflict rather than promoting economic development. Chinese SOEs have typically stepped into this environment with the advantages of political backing and government subsidized and insured investment. China has typically used significant sweeteners to win contracts.

To secure investment deals, the Chinese government typically offers infrastructure projects, soft loans, and grant programs as a package deal with a proposed natural resource investment. With government financing and political support, Chinese SOEs avoid risks that often plague investments in resource-rich, economically poor countries. Political and reputational risks are therefore usually minimized, and financing uncertainty is eliminated. Such risks hinder Western multinational enterprises (MNEs) that must respect the bottom line but tend to be of little concern to Chinese SOEs.

China's relationship with other emerging markets can be more complex. Subsidized Chinese OFDI may crowd out less substantial or unsubsidized OFDI, or investment from other emerging market countries. At the same time, many emerging markets view Chinese investment into their countries – particularly in infrastructure and industrial projects – as a valuable resource for economic development, especially since it comes with few strings attached. China's strategy has been to negotiate such investment through diplomatic channels, with investments taking the form of partnerships and quid pro quo loans, as opposed to being exclusively under Chinese control. Emerging markets have more negotiating power than HIPCs, and China knows it.

Using such sweeteners as diplomacy, ideology, and camaraderie tend not to work in developed countries, where China finds it is playing on a more even field. When placed in a competitive environment with a formidable opposite number, *China tends to use a sledgehammer to get what it wants – crossing a line, retreating, then doing so again, until a new line of been established and Beijing gets what it wants* (as previously noted). Points of conflict with developed countries tend to occur in three areas:

- OFDI by Chinese SOEs is seen as unfairly competitive vis-a-vis private sector companies. By virtue of government ownership and backing, Chinese SOEs often operate investments in risky environments where Western multinationals may prefer not to operate, and at reduced cost, thereby outmaneuvering Western firms. As Western MNEs generally operate based on market conditions, albeit with advantages from established reputations, technology, and industry best practices, they and their home countries believe the playing field is no longer level. China's growing non-commercially motivated OFDI has the potential to distort global markets, leading to long-term loss of productivity and efficiency.

- Chinese official aid to unsavory governments in order to lubricate OFDI contracts raises governance and humanitarian concerns and, therefore, hackles among developed country governments. China's general willingness to befriend rogue or unsavory governments – funding projects in countries such as Sudan, Iran, and Venezuela – creates tension with the developed world. Some of this tension may actually stem from the fact that the exercise of realpolitik by China puts it on top and outwits Western firms that have had their activities circumscribed in such countries due to sanctions, reputational risk, or political risk.

- As already noted, Chinese SOEs' attempts to acquire ownership interest in, or assets of, large developed country MNEs operating under market conditions have unnerved some developed country governments, which fear losing market access to strategic resources, as well as their technological and advanced practices edge.

If it were not for the West's preoccupation with achieving a higher moral standard and adherence to international standards of acceptable behavior, China would not have been as successful as it has been in fostering OFDI in the developing world. China is in the process of beating the West at its own game – identifying what it sees as the West's 'weakness' on the grand chess board and filling in the gaps. If the West played the game the same way, China's investment ambitions would be more restricted, or at least more expensive.[26] But the West is not going to change its stripes any more than China will be changing its own.

In some ways, China is better at achieving capitalist nirvana than the countries that invented it. China has quickly learned the benefits of establishing more equitable and mutually beneficial bilateral economic relationships. Soon enough it will master that game, too. Once that occurs, China will be able to truly demonstrate why this is the Chinese century. Until then, the developing world will have to figure out a way to encourage China to leave something other than a football stadium behind.[27] Developing countries are becoming smarter about establishing boundaries to attempt to rein in some of Beijing's most egregious offenses, but they still lack the ability, and sometimes, the will, to take China to task when it crosses the line.

Credit where credit is due

China will remain an easy target for criticism on a whole host of issues, but it should not be forgotten that, as a nation, it is doing what many other nations do to project its power and enhance its influence. Beijing just goes about doing so somewhat differently than most other countries do. Should it only be criticized for that, particularly if some good comes of it? China is in a unique position to influence the global economy and the future course of globalization. The question is whether it will do so responsibly, and at what cost for other countries?

Although the BRI is seen by some as a blatant attempt to exert Hard Power among 65 participating nations that require new or upgraded infrastructure, the program will enhance Beijing's economic and political influence. It will also greatly enhance transportation systems, power projects, and other essential construction in a lot of countries that badly need it. No other country is willing to lead such an effort, or devote such financial, engineering, and construction resources to that task, so China should be given credit where credit is due. If another country were to undertake such an endeavor, it would also undoubtedly seek to garner some form of influence in the recipient nations. It would be disingenuous to suggest otherwise. More good is likely to come from the BRI than harm, but expectations and impacts should be managed by host countries. After all, they are not being forced to accept Beijing's offer of assistance, nor to grant Beijing carte blanche to simply do as it pleases once it arrives.

Although China has for decades been addicted to coal-fired power plants and was for years building a new plant every week, it is on its way to becoming a green powerhouse. Beijing declared its intention to take the lead on climate change reduction after signing the 2015 Paris Climate Agreement. By 2025, most new cars in China will be fully electric vehicles, putting it well ahead of the targets set by a variety of developed nations to do the same. China already accounts for more than 60% of the world's high-speed rail and has committed to achieving blue skies in all of its major cities by 2021. The Western press does not spend much time reporting on such facts.

China has also become a leader in the digital economy, including cashless payments. In major cities, as many as 90% of all commercial and retail transactions occur through digital payment systems such as Alipay and WeChat. Through Alibaba, e-commerce delivery in large Chinese cities is the fastest in the world. The company consistently breaks records for single day sales. A number of Chinese universities have become among the top ranked in the world,[28] with dozens more expected to join their ranks in the coming years. While Western universities continue to dominate the rankings, students from around the world already attend Chinese universities.

These are examples of some things that China is doing right, and very well. *China is projecting its power and influence in a uniquely Chinese way while having foresight and a willingness to act on what it sees as its, and the world's, future, in a decisive way.* One great benefit of being an authoritarian government is that there is no need for a lot of debate about what to do and how to do it. Of course, that has pluses and minuses attached, but the Chinese can build a convention center or complete a toll road in the time it can take some municipal authorities in the US to repair an escalator at a metro stop. In fairness, much of what goes on in China gets little press outside its borders, including on many of the initiatives it is undertaking to try to correct past mistakes.

There is no question that China will play a major role in the globalization process going forward. The question is how it will choose to do so. Will it become a leader in providing foreign assistance and alter the manner in which it distributes foreign aid? Will it continue to demand repayment of loans that cannot be repaid by HIPCs? Will it continue to demonstrate leadership in some of the world's most pressing ongoing environmental challenges? These are among the issues that Beijing must consider if it wishes to be perceived as a net positive force in the global economy.

The Chinese perception of its own impact on the world can be very different from that of the rest of the world. To date, China has a mixed record of net pluses and minuses from the perspective of the global community. Beijing is uniquely positioned to act as an interlocutor of the world's emerging and advanced economies. Since the turn of the century, it has notably ramped up its engagement in regional and multilateral agreements and pursued deep engagement with developing countries in trade, investment, and security. It now has the ability to enhance such efforts with greater credibility.

The AIIB and New Development Bank are poised to become leaders among the international financial institutions, and China is well positioned to flex its economic muscle through these institutions, the BRI, and its growing influence among the MDBs and other global organizations. The Chinese government should take a more enlightened approach toward shaping the direction the future course of globalization will ultimately take. However, as its economy continues to be buffeted by the trade war, and the government finds it increasingly difficult to generate sustained levels of GDP growth above 5 or 6%, it appears less and less likely to place a priority on revamping its image in the international arena.

Some uncomfortable truths

The stakes of the outcome of America and China's trade war are obviously high, particularly when considering that the result may determine which country comes out on top of the battle for supremacy on the global economy. In that regard, most observers rightly tend to focus on the economic impacts. Bloomberg Economics believes that uncertainty over the future of global trade could reduce world GDP by 0.6% in 2021, relative to a scenario with no trade war. That is roughly double the direct impact of the tariffs themselves and the equivalent of $585 billion, based on the IMF's estimate of world GDP of $97 trillion in 2021. China would be hit hardest, with its GDP down by 1% compared with 0.6% for the US.[29] Most people would probably have expected the numbers to be more robust, given all the airtime, rhetoric, and bluster involved.

But there are clearly other issues at hand. Consider that, in taking the actions he has, Trump risks making America's economy resemble the state-dominated economy run by the CCP. To rescue the American agricultural sector in the wake of the trade war, by mid-2019, Trump had already released $28 billion in government subsidies. He had tried to force American companies to move their production bases outside of China, and he pressured the US Federal Reserve, whose independence was previously considered sacrosanct, to lower interest rates in an attempt to boost the US economy and drive down the value of the dollar. Those are all actions much more akin to a state-controlled economy rather than one dominated by the free market.[30]

Globalism has been slowly deconstructing the same American economy that helped transform it into the behemoth it has become. The offshoring of US jobs has reduced US manufacturing and industrial capability, as well as the associated innovation, research, development, supply chains, consumer purchasing power, and tax base of state and local governments. Many American corporations have increased short-term profits at the expense of such long-term costs. China is not to blame for that but, rather, a failure to adopt a similar orientation to the future, as Beijing has.

The US has depleted its manufacturing, industrial, and engineering capabilities by transferring much of it abroad (a lot of it to China) for the past two decades. That self-imposed sectoral recession has been very good to Asia. Indeed, Beijing owes much of its rapid rise as a world power to the transfer of American jobs, capital, technology, and business knowledge to China so that American shareholders could receive capital gains and corporate executives could receive bonuses for producing them by lowering labor and production costs. For some reason, neoliberal economists cannot seem to comprehend that if US corporations produce the goods and services that they sell to Americans offshore, the offshore locations are also going to be the beneficiaries.[31]

And herein lies an uncomfortable truth. America tends to be quick to point the finger of blame for the trade war solely in China's direction – just as China has done in reverse. Everyone outside of China knows what part Beijing has had to play in this drama, but how many Americans are reflecting on what role the US has played in it? American business's pursuit of the almighty dollar – at seemingly any cost – has blinded many of them from engaging in meaningful strategic planning, in thoughtfully considering the long-term consequences of their actions action, and from having an orientation that extends beyond the next quarter.

Both China and America stand to learn a *lot* from each other as this slugfest continues. The Chinese government is already in the process of pivoting, but the same can be said for the US government, which continues to wait for China to change its behavior rather than casting an eye toward the future and what demands will be required to embrace it and benefit from it. It is easy to criticize China's Five-Year Plans as little more than an exercise in centralized state planning, but to achieve and implement such Plans, a great amount of effort and ability to execute must be demonstrated. That kind of discipline is going to be required for America to remain an effective competitor going forward.

Chapter 5: Science and Technology

Science and technology will become the life blood of the Chinese economy in this decade and will be its life blood in the future. That is, in part, because the country has become sufficiently advanced to be able to effectively compete with America and other technological leaders in the West. It is also the key to China's ability to innovate and compete in the future, as it is for other advanced economies. Innovation-driven growth is also required for Beijing to smoothly deleverage away from its manufacturing base model of growth, which is slowly running out of steam.

Improving productivity drove ballistic growth in the two decades following Deng Xiaoping's opening up of the Chinese economy in 1978. Its productivity boom carried on through the 2000s as China became a member of the WTO, which enabled the country to reform its SOEs. In the decade that has just passed, its productivity gains have faltered; credit-driven investment in low return capital has propped up its growth. China must address its slowing productivity gains to produce a smooth rebalancing of the economy. Productivity growth will not come from textiles, steel, or the property market, and the flourishing services sector will require cutting edge technology to remain competitive. To pull it off, China will need to acquire and deploy advanced technology quickly and efficiently throughout its economy.

China's ability to do that will be determined by its ability to close two productivity gaps. The first is between its advanced industries and the rest of the world, which requires importing foreign technology via trade and investment. As we will see, that is where America's restrictions on China's investment in US technologies could make a real difference. The prospect of higher marginal returns by investing in the interior of the country should be attractive to domestic and foreign investors alike. The CCP's challenge is to find a way to reform the economy so that it will simultaneously address both sets of needs. Xi's "self-reliance" theme will take it only so far. If China cannot find a way to either create or acquire the same technologies that America, Israel, and South Korea have, the game will be over before it begins in earnest.[1] The chances that that will happen are slim to none, however.

Supremacy in the cyber arena

From the time he assumed power in 2012, Xi made it clear how important a role he believed the Internet would play in China's future. To his credit, he recognized even then that the future will be digital, and that those countries that can get ahead and stay ahead in the race for digital supremacy will hold a natural technological advantage. He set China on a path that would help ensure its future economic competitiveness by harnessing the power of the Internet. Based on the manner in which he has unleashed China's participation in that race, the Xi era will be remembered for putting an end to the West's naive optimism about the potential of the Internet to liberalize global polities.

Chinese military doctrine has long articulated the use of a wide spectrum of warfare against its adversaries. Much of what is known outside of China about its approach to asymmetric warfare is contained in a book first published in 1999 and translated with the title *Unrestricted Warfare*. The first rule of unrestricted warfare is that there are no rules, and nothing is forbidden. The book advocates tactics known as shashou-jian (Assassin's Mace), the concept of taking advantage of an adversary's seemingly superior conventional capabilities by "fighting the fight that fits one's own weapons" and "making the weapons to fit the fight". It proposes ignoring traditional rules of conflict and advocates such tactics as manipulating foreign media, flooding enemy countries with drugs, controlling the markets for natural resources, joining international bodies so as to be in a position to bend them to one's will, and engaging in cyberwarfare.

Having had nearly two decades to develop this philosophy, Chinese military strategists are, of course, prepared to use conventional weapons to fight their enemies but, especially where it lacks a competitive advantage, one of its tactics is to use cyberwarfare to make up the difference. Since the turn of the century, China has set in place an impressive cyberwarfare infrastructure that includes citizen hacker groups, military units. and an extensive cyberespionage network around the world. Some of that cyberwarfare infrastructure has been used to obtain the technology that has powered China's meteoric rise over the past two decades.

Noteworthy in that regard was China's threat in 2003 to ban government procurement of Microsoft software, hardware, and technology unless Bill Gates agreed to provide China with a copy of its proprietary operating code,[2] which he had refused to reveal to Microsoft's largest US commercial clients at the time. After Gates agreed to provide it, China then copied the Cisco network router found on almost all US networks and most Internet service providers. It then sold counterfeit routers at cut-rate discounts around the world. The buyers apparently included the Pentagon and a host of other US federal agencies. A subsequent report by the FBI concluded that the routers could be used by foreign intelligence agencies to take down networks and weaken cryptographic systems.

Armed with intimate knowledge of the flaws in Microsoft's and Cisco's software and hardware, China's hackers had the ability to stop most of the world's networks from operating. Chinese networks would also have been vulnerable but, as part of its deal with Microsoft, the Chinese modified the version of Microsoft software sold in China to include a secure component using their own encryption. They also developed their own operating system (Kylin) and secure microprocessors for use on servers and Huawei routers.

By 2003, the Chinese government had created cyberwarfare units with defensive and offensive capabilities, complete with weapons that had never been seen before, including the ability to plant information mines, conduct information reconnaissance, change network data, release information bombs, dump information garbage, disseminate propaganda, apply information deception, release clone information, and establish network spy stations. By 2007, China was penetrating US and European networks, successfully copying and exporting huge volumes of data. China has since developed its cyberwarfare capabilities into a finely tuned and largely unrivaled machine.

By 2007, Chinese hackers were able to carry out the Byzantine Hades cyberattacks with little more than a peep of condemnation from the US government. The attacks, which were traced to the Chinese military, ended up getting broad media attention years later, in part because part of the theft of designs of Americas F-35 fighter jet (which enabled China to produce its own stealth fighter, the Chengdu J-20). It was only beginning with the Obama administration that the US devoted substantially more resources to the problem and began to respond more robustly.

In 2014, the US Justice Department indicted five Chinese military hackers from Unit 61398 for their alleged role in economic theft, but by that time, Chinese cyberespionage had grown to become a goliath. The whole system runs through a corrupt nexus of government officials, military officers, business executives, and academics throughout China. It makes money back by developing products based on the stolen information. The system even extends to transfer centers that process stolen information and transforms them into usable designs.

When, in 2015, both countries signed the US-China Cyber Agreement, Washington sent a list to Xi of Chinese hackers identified as having stolen commercial secrets from US businesses, requesting their arrests. Chinese authorities made some arrests but, by passing the evidence against Chinese hackers to Chinese authorities, the US unintentionally helped the Chinese government close gaps in its system of economic theft. The Chinese authorities presumably took this information as a road map for how US investigators detect attacks and used the information to adjust their methods and make cyberattacks progressively more difficult to identify.

The Agreement stated that neither country would "conduct or knowingly support cyber-enabled theft of IP, including trade secrets or other confidential business information, for commercial advantage." The Agreement also established a system for high-level dialogue between the US and the CCP. However, it only prohibited "cyber-enabled theft of IP", which did nothing to address intellectual theft through other means, rendering it relatively toothless. And it failed to forbid economic theft more generally – only one method of economic theft – while leaving unmentioned that the CCP itself is behind so many of the attacks against the US.

Recognizing how inadequate the agreement with China was, and remains, and how Beijing has trampled all over it, Trump has taken America's "objections" to China's cyber capabilities to a whole new level. However, Beijing is already well on its way to creating cyber neocolonialism, which relies on its Information Industrial Complex to project its cyber power on to the US and the world. China may eventually reign supreme in this area, and there is little the US or any other country can do about it. The most the US can hope for is to at least match the Chinese modus operandi, on its own terms. That implies ramping up the silent, behind-the-scenes cyberwarfare that is already in the process of reshaping how the wars of the future will be fought.[3]

Why the US government's concerns about Huawei are justified

From all that you have read so far in this book, it should be clear now that a pattern is developing. China is preparing to assume a seemingly preordained role as the world leader in a plethora of areas. It is diligently preparing to assume that role. It is driven. It is focused. And it will stop at nothing to ensure that it has all the advantages it can glean from the existing world order to create a world order in its own image. Technology is absolutely critical to achieving that objective, and there is little that is more important in that regard than cutting edge telecommunications – specifically 5G technology.

The Huawei saga has served to illustrate this point. America's issues with Huawei are as much about who has access to, and thus controls, the data of the future, as it is about superpower politics and the rule of law. Huawei is the world's largest supplier of telecommunications network equipment and the second-biggest maker of smartphones.[4] Unlike other big Chinese technology firms, it does much of its business overseas and is a market leader in many countries across Europe, Asia, and Africa.

5G is the next generation of wireless networks that promises to be 100 times faster and more reliable than current technology. It is a market that will be worth hundreds of billions of dollars, as 5G will require compatible new phones and communications equipment. Huawei has already built up such a strong lead in 5G technology that it is already practically irreplaceable for many wireless carriers. And that presents a challenge for the US and many other countries around the world. Some Western intelligence sources believe the company is state-owned and has deep connections to China's intelligence services. Its founder was an engineer with the People's Liberation Army (PLA), and it is worth adding that no large Chinese company is fully independent of the government.

China's 2015 National Security Law requires any domestic firm to assist the government for national security purposes. Every company operating in China is required to give Chinese authorities their source code, encryption keys, and backdoor access to their computer networks in China. In other words, businesses must now hand Chinese agents the lifeblood of their companies and products, while also giving the CCP a free pass to spy on their networks. In 2017, China's Cybersecurity Law went even further, giving the government unrestricted access to almost all data held by Chinese companies. The companies that hold data routinely obey government demands to provide access to it. So, doing the math, whatever data Huawei has access to belongs to the CCP.

Back in 2012, the US House Intelligence Committee designated Huawei a state-controlled enterprise that provided an opportunity for the Chinese government to tamper with the US telecommunications supply chain. It was then that the CFIUS decided to block acquisitions, takeovers, or mergers involving Huawei and ZTE (one of China's leading telecommunication manufacturers), given the perceived threat to US national security interests. The US government then decided that sensitive US government systems should not include Huawei or ZTE equipment, including component parts. Government contractors – particularly those working on contracts for sensitive US programs – were also ordered to exclude ZTE and Huawei equipment from their systems.

In 2017, ZTE pleaded guilty to conspiring to evade embargoes by selling US equipment to Iran. The US Commerce Department said ZTE subsequently violated the settlement and barred it from buying any US components – which severely restricted many ZTE operations. The ban was then lifted, at the behest of President Trump, in a concession to Xi, which surprised and angered many in the US government. The 2019 National Defense Authorization Act finally banned US federal agencies from buying Huawei products.

Given its concerns about potential national security implications of utilizing Huawei products, the US has pushed for a ban on Huawei technology with the Australia, the EU, the Philippines, Poland, and a number of other countries. Security concerns have led Australia, Japan, New Zealand, and Taiwan to completely ban the company's technology.[5] The UK said it could work around the issue and Germany has refused to take the US position on the subject.

Knowing what is known about Huawei and how the Chinese government acquires data from Chinese companies, it is truly surprising that *any* Western government would willingly agree to utilize Huawei and other Chinese telecommunications products. Washington is wanting to position itself in a superior competitive position just as Beijing is, but this is ultimately about who controls the future. Only one country can reign supreme. China and Huawei have made it clear this is a race they intend to win.[6] Will the rest of the world allow that to happen?

<u>Innovation nation</u>

The rest of the world may not have much of a choice if the 2019 rankings of the Global Innovation Index (GII) are any indication. In that Index, Switzerland, Sweden, and the US were the top three ranked countries (respectively) in terms of innovation, which is a little surprising since most people are not accustomed to thinking of Switzerland and Sweden in those terms. The Index covers 128 countries based on 80 indicators, ranging from traditional measurements such as investment in research and development and international patent and trademark applications, and some newer variables such as mobile-phone app creation and high-tech exports. The GII also considers innovation in an economic context. Despite signs of slowing global economic growth, innovation continues to blossom, particularly in Asia. Given the mounting economic pressures being exerted by the trade war, sound government planning will be critical to the success of future innovation.

Here, China has a distinct edge; it was ranked 17th in the Index, sandwiched between Hong Kong and Japan (which, one would have thought, would actually have ranked higher). If that is not an impressive enough statistic, consider that in 2010, China was ranked 43rd,[7] and in 2015, it was ranked 29th,[8] so China is rapidly moving up the ranks and will surely hit the top 10 before 2025. The GII serves to illustrate that those countries that prioritize innovation through their policies have seen significant increases in their rankings. By contrast, in some high-income countries, research and development expenditures are growing slowly or not at all.[9] That is a clear challenge to the US government, for China has already demonstrated that it fully understands what is at stake.

China has a strong innovation culture, but the interplay between innovation and politics is complex. China's nationalist approach to technology runs counter to the dominant global trend for investment and innovation. The country's impressive display of innovation occurred during a period of relative political openness. A widely held assumption in the West is that there is a causal relationship between personal freedom and innovation, but that does not appear to be the case in China, where the country seems more driven than ever to keep innovating. China is testing long-standing assumptions about the relationship between politics, society, and technological innovation.[10]

The trade war is not really all about trade; it is also about whether America or China will lead global innovation in the future. Some would argue that China already has a huge lead. The country has installed more high-speed rail lines than the rest of the world combined, and mobile payments are 50 times as large in China than in the US. In 2018, more electric vehicles were sold in China than in the rest of the world, and more than twice as many industrial robots were in use in China than in the US. If the definition of innovation is turning ideas into outcomes, China is already an innovation economy. That is just what the Trump administration is worried about.[11]

Although China spends more than $200 billion on research (second only to the US), generates close to 30,000 PhDs in science and engineering, and leads the world in patent applications each year, its record is mixed in terms of the actual impact of innovation, as measured by the success of companies in commercializing new ideas and competing in the global market. China has some unique strengths in innovation, which includes the rapid commercialization of new ideas by virtue of the size of its consumer base. It also has the world's most extensive manufacturing ecosystem, enabling continuous innovation in production processes that reduce costs and improve quality, and has created capacity for research with a growing number of universities and research institutions, as well as an expanding pool of talent. On the minus side of the ledger, China's slow regulatory processes and weak IP protections prevent foreign investors from wanting to bring their best and brightest researchers and innovations to the country.

China has the potential to build on its strengths in innovation and become a global leader – creating a "China effect" on innovation around the world. This is based on China's momentum in consumer-facing industries and manufacturing, and its growing capacity for innovation in industries where it is not yet globally competitive. Not only can the country serve as the locus of innovation for a growing number of companies that want to penetrate China and other fast-growing emerging markets, but the Chinese approach to innovation can spread, helping companies everywhere turn ideas into products and services more quickly and for less cost. Completing the journey from innovation sponge (absorbing and adapting existing technology and knowledge from around the world) to global innovation leader is not just a way to signal China's progress as an economy and society. The boost to productivity that innovation provides is critically important for sustaining China's growth, as previously noted.

China has reached a point where innovation is no longer a conceptual idea – an aspiration that would reflect the rising power and sophistication of the Chinese economy. In the coming decade, innovation will be a vital tool for China to raise productivity and sustain growth. Innovation will be key to retaining and extending China's competitiveness in global markets. At the same time, China can become a global center of innovation, and its rapid, nimble approaches could be adopted around the world.[12] Don't be surprised if, a decade from now, China's effect on innovation will be widely acknowledged and even deliberately emulated by other leading nations.

An emerging CRISPR superpower

One area of technology where China has clearly excelled is clustered regularly interspaced short palindromic repeats (CRISPR), which uses DNA sequencing to accomplish gene editing. CRISPR is highly controversial in large part because gene editing offers both promise and peril; it can potentially offer a cure for some of humankind's most persistent and intractable diseases, and it could cross previously unrealizable scientific boundaries into the unknown, with uncertain consequences. China made headlines in 2019 because one of its scientists had genetically modified a human embryo. That China was the first to cross that threshold raised questions about just how far it would go using CRISPR to achieve its aims.

As of 2019, the US still held more CRISPR-related patent applications than China, but not by much (872 versus 858)[13]. In some areas, such as agriculture and industrial applications, China holds more patents and has published more papers than any other country. US universities have a long history of drawing top scientists from around the world to drive their scientific ambitions. Chinese universities routinely entice Chinese gene-editing scientists to return from the US; international scientists are also migrating to China to conduct their research.[14] The Chinese government has even highlighted gene editing as a focal point in its current Five-Year plan,[15] and has committed to streamlining the regulatory environment that restricts it.

The primary sectors in which it is directing its efforts are agriculture, human medicine, and basic research. Across China, there are at least four groups of CRISPR researchers gene editing monkeys, dogs, mice, rats, pigs, and rabbits. Some projects, such as the collaboration between the Salk Institute in California and researchers in China, are splicing human cells to animal embryos.[16] The goal is to create organs, like kidneys or a liver, that can be harvested for transplantation into humans. The embryo study was carried out in China specifically to avoid getting caught up in ethical, moral, or legal entanglements. Such considerations are less prevalent in China more generally than in many Western countries.

Beyond animal research, at least 20 research groups[17] across China are using CRISPR to modify crop genes as part of a wider technology-based effort to enhance agricultural production.[18] Feeding China's 1.4 billion people and ensuring that the country has a reliable food source into the future is naturally a primary concern for the government. Food is, in that regard, a national security issue, and the CCP has spent tens of billions of dollars on agricultural research over the past two decades.[19]

It is difficult to say whether, in this race, the tortoise or the hare will win. While China is clearly advancing rapidly in the field of CRISPR research, it is worth remembering that the first use of gene editing without the use of CRISPR help, intended to increase human resistance to HIV, was accomplished in the US, as was the first attempt to edit cells inside a human body. The first initiative to edit a gene to cure cancer was in the UK. There are currently two competing CRISPR trials – in China and the US – attempting to enhance the human immune system's anti-tumor capabilities, targeting the same gene in T cells. In that sort of race, it matters less who gets there first, but that they get there.[20] China is certainly driven, and has the bravado, necessary to get on top and stay on top in this race.

Has the US surrendered to China on scientific research?

As the CRISPR race illustrates, China is a worthy competitor against the US in the scientific arena. As in other domains, the CCP has not hesitated to devote tens of billions of dollars to areas that are important to China's future. That is part of the beauty of being a one-party authoritarian government: the CCP does not need to ask permission from anyone to do anything. The same is, of course, *not* true vis-à-vis the US, where any outlay of large amounts of government funds must be approved by any number of congressional committees. The difference between the two approaches is already having an impact on China's ability to race ahead in AI and 5G; the same may soon be said about other areas of scientific endeavor.

The US intelligence community's 2019 Worldwide Threat Assessment[21] report identified a number of research areas that will determine global military and economic superiority in the coming decades; AI, gene editing, synthetic biology, 5G, and quantum computing were among the areas specifically referenced in the report. It noted that America's lead in the science and technology fields has been significantly eroded in recent years.

The decline is the result of steadily declining US budgets for basic scientific research and a lopsided emphasis on the life sciences, to the detriment of emerging technologies. According to the National Science Foundation (NSF), the US government spent $67 billion on basic and applied science and technology research in 2017 – less than 2% of all federal spending and just 0.3% of US GDP. Trump's budget for 2020 included a 10% cut in the Centers for Disease Control, which he came to regret after the outbreak of the COVID19 virus early in 2020.

In 1956, US investment in scientific research represented about 1.1% of the federal budget and a mere 0.2% of GDP. But following the successful Soviet launch of Sputnik in 1957, investment in basic and applied scientific research surged, peaking at 3.6% in 1965. As the Cold War ended, such funding declined to where it is today, and the funds that are available are distributed in a lopsided manner. Though a range of US federal departments and agencies conduct and fund scientific research – from the departments of Agriculture, Energy and Defense to the National Aeronautics and Space Administration - some 46% of all federal civilian science money goes to just one agency: the National Institutes of Health (NIH). That is why the intelligence community can say that the US remains dominant in biomedical science.

Current federal investment in all other areas of critical scientific research is minuscule. The Energy Department invests more than $18 billion a year in research and development – almost a third of American spending on non-biomedical science. About half of that is devoted to nuclear security and energy – important issues, to be sure, but not cutting-edge fields critical to creating a thriving, competitive economy in the future. Much of the federally funded research in the areas highlighted by the US intelligence community – such as AI, computing, and physics – passes through the NSF.

The NSF provides about a quarter of all federal research grants and covers fields such as engineering, mathematics, computer science, and the social sciences. It also funds the purchase of large-scale scientific equipment. NSF-funded researchers have won 236 Nobel Prizes. In 2017, the Foundation's total research budget was a mere $5.6 billion (or 0.1% of the federal budget and less than 20% of the budget of the National Institutes of Health). Its budget had been declining for years as a percentage of the federal budget and had been cut by 10% from 2017 to 2018.[22] Rather than *raising* funding for the NSF, the Trump administration proposed to make additional cuts to total funding for the NSF, from $8.1 billion to $7.1 billion in 2020 – an additional 12% *decrease*.[23] By contrast, in 2019, China's funding for scientific research had reached 2.5% of its GDP[24] and was slated to continue to increase. Historians will no doubt look back at such statistics and wonder what on earth the US government was thinking.

It is hard to maintain leadership in any field with shrinking budgets. The same is true when falling behind on the education front. China opened more than 1,800 new universities[25] from 2001 to 2014 (that's more than 2 per *week*) and produced nearly five million science, technology, engineering, and medicine (STEM) graduates – nearly 10 times the equivalent American figure. (The US graduates around 1.8 million students per year in all subjects, from about 2,600 four-year colleges and universities.[26]) One of the biggest cross-national tests of student performance is the Program for International Student Assessment (PISA), which measures reading ability, math, and science literacy skills every 3 years among 15-year-olds in dozens of developed and developing countries. The most recent PISA results, from 2017, placed the US at an unimpressive 31st out of 70 countries (just ahead of Latvia). China came in at 10th place, just behind South Korea.[27]

In short, the US is being outmatched. Government funding of basic and applied scientific research is not only lagging, but falling dangerously behind China, and too little corporate funding is being spent on the basic research that leads to transformative discoveries. US companies spend about $24 billion per year on basic research – about a third of the annual federal investment – but more than 10 times that, in excess of $300 billion, on development. That is not enough for the US to maintain its lead over China, and Beijing knows it.

The US has the world's best research universities and a strong culture of innovation. All that it really needs to do is devote more funds to scientific research to give China a run for its money. At a minimum, the federal government should restore funding to 1965 levels and commit to doubling non-biomedical research funding in the key areas identified by the Worldwide Threat Assessment report. Doing so would require about $12 billion per year over three years, or just 0.25% of the federal budget. To beat the Soviets to the moon, NASA received more than 4% of the federal budget in 1965 and 1966. If it really wants to have a hope of maintaining its scientific edge, that type of commitment is once again required.[28]

But will it be enough in the face of what is, in essence, a state-sponsored foreign technology transfer apparatus? Beijing has enacted some two dozen laws that have created a technology-siphoning machine. That apparatus maintains databases of foreign co-optees and distributes stipends, sinecures, and cash to foreign donors of high-tech innovations. China has targeted all sources of American innovation, including universities, corporations, and government labs, exploiting both their openness and naïveté, with methods and tradecraft custom-tailored to each target.

At American universities, China takes advantage of the commitment to intellectual freedom on campuses. In US corporations, the lure of access to the Chinese market gives Beijing tremendous leverage in eliciting technology transfer from American firms, combined with financial incentives for employees to purloin IP for personal gain. US government labs have an historic commitment to international scientific cooperation but an uneven record of monitoring that cooperation for unsanctioned transfers of information. That is now slowly changing, but it will take time to ween the institutions of their trusting ways.

While Chinese intelligence has a strong track record of attempting to recruit ethnic Chinese, primarily because of cultural and language affinity, recent cases of espionage and technology transfer suggest that the Chinese government has broadened its tradecraft to recruit nonethnic Chinese assets and collectors as well, perhaps as a way of complicating US counterintelligence efforts. China's most systematic channel for identifying foreign-based nontraditional collectors is its Recruitment Program of Global Experts, commonly known as the Thousand Talents Plan (or the Thousand Talents Program (TTP)). The TTP is a massive and sustained talent recruitment campaign designed to recruit leading experts from overseas to assist in the country's modernization drive. Initiated in 2008, the Program recruits leading overseas scientists and experts who work in areas that are deemed a high priority for achieving China's modernization goals.[29]

Unbridled access to technology

The Chinese government's current system for processing and reverse engineering stolen designs has grown significantly larger than it was during the Cold War and has developed from a strictly military operation into a system permeating the entire Chinese government. *It is an elaborate, comprehensive system for identifying foreign technologies, acquiring them by every means imaginable, and converting them into weapons and competitive goods.* The departments in charge of reverse engineering are officially called China's National Technology Transfer Centers (or National Demonstration Organizations) and became established by policy in 2007. Among their names are the State Administration of Foreign Experts Affairs (under the State Council), the Science and Technology Office (under the Overseas Chinese Affairs Office), and the National Technology Transfer Center (under the East China University of Science and Technology).

These organizations do not attempt to hide their purpose; their charters explicitly name "domestic and foreign technology" as targets for "commercialization". The transfer centers play several roles, which include processing stolen technology, developing cooperative research projects between Chinese and foreign scientists, and running programs designed to 'encourage' Chinese nationals who have studied abroad to become part of the organizations. *China's meteoric economic rise can, at least in part, be attributed to this system of minimal investment in basic science through a technology transfer apparatus that worked to suck in foreign proprietary achievements while most of the countries which they were stealing from had no idea what they were doing. China could not have experienced the dramatic economic transformation it has experienced in the 21st century, nor have sustained its progress as it has, without inexpensive and unrestricted access to other countries' technology.*

State theft as a business

China's military, the PLA, is required to cover a portion of its own costs. Its decades-long focus on building external sources of cash has made its military leaders some of the most powerful people in China. With only 70% of its operating expenses covered by the state budget, the PLA must make up the difference and generate supplemental funds for its modernization. Just as is the case regarding the nexus between government and private business, the lines between the military and the state, versus the military and the private sector, are thin. *The PLA maintains thousands of front companies in the US, whose sole reason for existing is to steal and exploit US technology.* According to the US Defense Threat Reduction Agency, the Chinese regime operates more than 3,200 military front companies[30] in the US dedicated to theft.

Project 863 (also called the 863 Program) was started by former CCP leader Deng Xiaoping in 1986. According to a report from the US Office of the National Counterintelligence Executive, it provides funding and guidance for efforts to clandestinely acquire US technology and sensitive economic information. Project 863 originally targeted seven industries: biotechnology, space, IT, automation, laser technology, new materials, and energy. It was later updated to include telecommunications and marine technology.

The Chinese government also runs the Torch Program to build high-tech commercial industries, the 973 Program for research, the 211 program for "reforming" universities, and countless programs designed to attract Western-trained scholars back to China. Each of these programs relies on foreign collaboration and technologies to cover key gaps, encouraging Western-trained experts to help China's technological development by returning to China or "serving in place" by providing needed information gained while working for their Western employers. Project 863 maintains a library of tens of millions of open source articles in scores of databases that contain more than four terabytes of information gleaned from American, Japanese, Russian, and British publications, military reports, and standard specifications.

One of the most powerful organizations behind economic theft is the 61 Research Institute, under the Third Department of the PLA's General Staff Department (GSD). The man in charge of it, Major General Wang Jianxin, has some powerful connections at the most senior level of the Chinese government. The names of many known military hacker units in China begin with the number '61', and there are at least 11 units under the GSD's Third Department with that designation, including Unit 61398, under which five military hackers operated, who were indicted by the US Department of Justice in 2014.[31]

China's quest for AI supremacy

In the race to achieve AI supremacy, only a handful of countries and companies have any real hope of winning. Among them, China, Germany, Japan, Russia, South Korea, and the US are the leading national contenders. Chinese and American companies lead the pack of commercial contenders, including Alibaba, Baidu, Tencent, Amazon, Facebook, and Google. What distinguishes all of them is the resources they have already devoted and the achievements they have already made in the AI arena. They are so far ahead of other countries and companies that those which are not already in the race have little hope of catching up.

While Germany, Japan, and South Korea are focused primarily on commercial applications, Russia excels in military applications, and the US maintains its general lead (for the time being) in the space. China is particularly well placed to assume the global AI lead because it has capital, people, data, and computing power in abundance, and is deploying all of them in a targeted manner at the same time in pursuit of AI supremacy. While most countries that are either in the race or intend to get in the race may spend tens or hundreds of *millions* of dollars in pursuit of AI supremacy, China plans to spend at least US$150 *billion* to achieve that goal by 2030, when it intends to the world's leading AI power. It would not be surprising if Beijing took the lead well before then.

China has two other resources that make it a promised land for AI. The country already has approximately 40% of the world's trained AI scientists and most large universities have launched AI programs, meaning that percentage will only increase. Also, China's enormous population generates more data than any other nation, given its 750+ million daily Internet users. Almost all of them go online from smartphones, which generate far more valuable data than desktop computers, primarily because they contain sensors and are mobile. Moreover, unlike in the West, where citizens are preoccupied with civil liberty protections, the Chinese are not necessarily so concerned about privacy, which makes openly collecting data easier.

While the quantity of Chinese AI research has grown dramatically, researchers in the US remain responsible for a lot of the most fundamental groundbreaking work. However, the White House Office of Science and Technology Policy, which was instrumental in leading AI policy work during the Obama administration, was depleted of 70% of its staff at the outset of the Trump administration, depriving the US government of critical expertise and insights on AI at a time when China is planning its own AI revolution.

What Chinese researchers have been very good at doing is focusing on an idea and expanding on its different applications. In fact, the Chinese have become prominent in adding value to existing research, with researchers in China wasting no time to produce papers on various applications, which can then be further developed. Chinese researchers usually speak English, so they have the benefit of access to all the work disseminated in English. By contrast, the English-speaking AI research community is much less likely to have access to work written in Chinese, and the velocity of work is much faster in China than in most of Silicon Valley.

China's government is proceeding at warp speed to rapidly make up for any lag it has with Western firms and governments. Chinese companies believe that by rotating Chinese staff to Silicon Valley and American staff to Chinese campuses, they can accelerate the timeline for reaching parity with the US. For the time being, however, the size and experience of China's AI workforce is a fraction of that of the US. Half of the top 10 employers of AI talent in China are US firms – including IBM, Intel, and Microsoft – which are integral to the development of China's human capital in AI.

For some types of high-value semiconductors, China has had to rely on imports for virtually all of its needs. To address this, the Chinese government implemented the previously referenced Made in China 2025 policy, designed to comprehensively upgrade Chinese industry and become the global leader in manufacturing, while at the same time achieving self-sufficiency and reducing reliance on other countries. The policy outlines a wide-ranging strategy for harnessing and promoting the acquisition of foreign technology through outbound investment, including the use of industrial funds, state-owned capital dividends, and other channels to support the creation of advantageous manufacturing capacity to implement overseas investment acquisitions and counteract China's comparative manufacturing disadvantages.

That said, many countries have become concerned that Made in China 2025 is not simply an effort to become more competitive by a country that lags behind in some areas. Governments around the world are increasingly concerned that such investments by Beijing inside and outside of China are not simply a product of market forces but are guided by the CCP rather than the private sector, particularly where high-tech is concerned.

Led by the US, there is now a growing backlash among Western governments against permitting future sensitive technology-oriented investments in their countries by Chinese investors. Many in the West may find China's way of doing business distasteful, but there are no real rules dictating how to achieve AI supremacy. Like it or not, China is well on its way to getting there. It will do the West no good to simply complain about how China gets to the AI finish line. Perhaps it should play the game in a similar fashion, for, in the end, it will not matter so much how a country achieves AI supremacy, but that it does so. China deserves credit for recognizing early on the importance AI fluency implies for national competitiveness in the coming decades. Other countries should either find a way to maintain their position or get out of the way, because nothing will stop Beijing in its quest to achieve AI supremacy.[32]

AI with Chinese characteristics

In some respects, the real race in AI between China and the US will be between the two countries' big cloud companies, which will compete to be the provider of choice for companies and cities that want to dive deeply into AI. China's tech giants are ready to compete with Google, Amazon, IBM, and Microsoft to serve up AI. While Alibaba's core business remains selling goods and providing a platform for business-to-business trade, it has spawned other lucrative operations, including a platform for logistics and shipments, an advertising network, and cloud computing and financial services. The company's ubiquitous mobile payments app, Alipay, is run by a sister company, Ant Financial, which also offers loans, insurance, and investing via a smartphone.

Alibaba announced in 2017 that it would spend $15 billion over the following three years on a research institute called the DAMO Academy (Discovery, Adventure, Momentum, and Outlook), dedicated to exploring fundamental technologies. This is evidence, as if it were needed, that China long ago dispensed with a reputation for simply copying Western innovations. According to the Organization for Economic Cooperation and Development, R&D spending in China grew tenfold between 2000 and 2016, rising to $412 billion.[33] As of 2018, the US still spent more ($477 billion versus China's $371 billion[34]), but very soon, China will be the leader in that category, as well.

DAMO will effectively triple Alibaba's research budget, to more than $7 billion. This most likely means that Alibaba will overtake IBM, Facebook, and Ford, and will narrow the gap with the world's leaders – Alphabet and Amazon – which spent $16 billion and $14 billion on R&D in 2017, respectively. DAMO will include a portfolio of research groups working on fundamental and emerging technologies including blockchain, computer security, fintech, and quantum computing, with AI being the biggest focus with the greatest commercial potential.

Alibaba appears to be inspired by the way the DARPA funds different teams competing on the same project, and it is clearly learning from Alphabet and Amazon, as well. It has released a cloud machine learning platform (the first from a Chinese company), which was launched in 2015 and has been upgraded significantly since then. The tools it offers are similar to those on Google Cloud and Amazon Web Services, including off-the-shelf solutions for such services as voice recognition and image classification. Developing these tools was a major technical undertaking for Alibaba and signals both how ambitious the company is to shape the future of AI and how big a role cloud computing will play.

Alibaba's cloud already supports several other companies' Deep Learning (DL) frameworks, including Google's TensorFlow and Amazon's MXNet. By supporting its competitors' frameworks, Alibaba gives developers a reason to use its platform instead, but Alibaba is creating its own DL framework. In 2017, the company released an AI program capable of reading a piece of text and answering simple questions about that text more accurately than anything ever built before. Alibaba has already used the program to improve its automated customer support on its online marketplace and it plans to deploy language understanding across all of its platforms and technologies.

Alibaba's AI researchers are working on other cutting-edge projects, such as generative adversarial networks, a machine learning approach developed by a Google researcher wherein two neural networks compete against one another, with one trying to generate data that seems as if it comes from a real data set, while the other tries to distinguish between real versus fake examples. Most Westerners may not realize it, but Alibaba is already exporting AI technology as the world's fifth-largest cloud computing provider (after Amazon, Google, IBM, and Microsoft[35]). Alibaba is arguably already ahead of the competition in some areas. In 2017, it announced a collaboration with the Malaysian government to provide smart city services, including a video platform that can automatically detect accidents and help optimize traffic flow. Alibaba may have already done more to change the way business is done in China than any other organization.[36] It is ambitious on every front.

While the quantity of Chinese AI research has grown dramatically, researchers in the US remain responsible for a lot of the most fundamental groundbreaking work. *What Chinese researchers have been very good at doing is focusing on an idea and expanding on its different applications.* In fact, the Chinese have become prominent in adding value to existing research, with researchers in China wasting no time producing papers on various applications, which can then be further developed. Chinese researchers usually speak English, so they have the benefit of access to all the work disseminated in English. By contrast, the English-speaking AI research community is much less likely to have access to work within the Chinese AI community, and the velocity of work is much faster in China than in most of Silicon Valley[37]– among the many distinct advantages China possesses.

A plethora of concerns

There are a number of additional concerns about how China will manage its rise to become a great AI power. Among them is the potential that the benefits of Chinese technological breakthroughs will be muted by data protectionism. The 2017 cyber security law requires foreign firms to store the data they collect on Chinese customers within the country's borders; foreigners cannot use Chinese data to offer services to third parties. If data cannot be pooled, the algorithms that run autonomous cars and other products may not be the most efficient. There is also, of course, the risk of reprisals from foreign firms on Chinese firms and citizens outside of China.

Ethics and safety are linked where AI is concerned. In the US, the technology giants of Silicon Valley have pledged to work together to ensure that any AI tools they develop will be safe. All the leading AI researchers in the West are signatories to an open letter from 2015 calling for a ban on the creation of autonomous weapons. Equivalent Chinese discussions about the limits of ethical AI research are more opaque, however. Chinese AI companies have incentive to think about some of these issues, since rogue AI would be a problem for the planet wherever it may emerge. There is a self-interest case to be made for the formulation of global safety standards, but it is hard to imagine that Beijing will lead the charge on that.

China's AI plan is clearly about maximizing AI's value to the state. AI techniques are ideally suited to identifying patterns in the massive amounts of data that Chinese censors sift through on a daily basis in order to maintain the government's grip on its citizenry. It is easy to imagine how the same data may be used to enhance the government's plans to create a Social Credit system that scores individuals based on their behavior and its perceived desirability. Once perfected, such algorithms would likely be of interest to autocratic regimes around the world. China's tech firms are in no position to prevent the government from taking advantage of such tools.

One of the world's largest Internet and AI firms, China's Baidu, preached data transparency in public even as it had been appointed by the Chinese government to lead a national laboratory for DL. That ought to have caused a severe case of cognitive dissonance to AI ethicists in China and beyond. Western firms and governments are no angels in the areas of data collection and espionage, but at least they are engaged in an open debate about the ethical implications of AI, and intelligence agencies in many other countries are constrained by democratic institutions.[38] Neither is true of China.

When, in 2014, the US Air Force wanted to make military robots more perceptive, it awarded Boston-based AI start-up Neurala the contract, but when Neurala needed money to finance the project, it got no help from the American military. The company ended up turning to China's Haiyin Capital,[39] backed by state-run Everbright Group, for an undisclosed sum to support the Air Force contract. Everbright was initially owned by China's State Administration for Foreign Exchange,[40] the wholly government-owned entity that manages the country's foreign exchange reserves. In 2008, it was sold to the China Investment Corporation,[41] the country's wholly government-owned sovereign wealth fund. So, *the Chinese government ended up partially funding the US Air Force's contract to make military robots more perceptive.*

In fact, *Chinese firms have routinely become investors in American start-ups, particularly those working on cutting-edge technologies with potential military applications.* These are companies that make rocket engines for spacecraft, sensors for autonomous navy ships, and printers that make flexible screens that can be used in fighter-plane cockpits. Many of the Chinese firms are owned by state-owned companies or have direct connections to Chinese leaders. According to the US Department of Defense (DOD), Beijing actively encourages Chinese companies with close government ties to invest in American start-ups specializing in critical technologies such as AI and robots to advance China's military capacity, as well as its economy.

US government controls intended to protect potentially critical technologies against countries like China have fallen short. It took a while, but such transactions eventually started ringing alarm bells in Washington. US lawmakers raised broad questions about the nature of China's economic relationship with the US well before the Trump administration started applying tariffs on Chinese products, in an effort to reduce the inherent inequity in bilateral trade between the two nations.

Neither the high-tech start-ups nor their Chinese investors had been formally accused of malfeasance, and some experts admit that much of the activity could indeed be perfectly innocent. Chinese businesses have money and are, after all, looking for returns, but the fund flows fit China's pattern of using state-guided investment to support its industrial policy, enhance its technology holdings, and acquire military-related technology. Yet, some start-ups – especially those making hardware rather than revenue producing mobile apps – have said that Chinese money has at times been the only available funding. If one is inclined to give them the benefit of the doubt, some Chinese investors appear to have a bigger appetite for risk and a willingness to get things done quickly, which is exactly what most start-ups need.

Although Neurala apparently made efforts to ensure that Haiyin Capital had no access to its source code or other important technological information, Haiyin's participation raised enough concern inside the Pentagon that some in the DOD argued that the US government should steer clear of the contract that it awarded to the company. To address concerns that it was not tapping a sufficient amount of innovation from start-ups, in 2015 the Pentagon set up Defense Innovation Unit Experimental, to enable investments into promising new companies. That same year, Haiyin Capital also invested in XCOR Aerospace, a US commercial space-travel company that makes spacecraft and engines and has worked with NASA. Haiyin Capital's founder later admitted that part of his firm's goal is to build Chinese industrial capabilities, noting the difficulty with which Chinese firms are able to obtain space technology from abroad because of American export controls.[42]

The race for faster neural network processors

Part of China's race with the US for AI supremacy includes 5G technology and Beijing's drive to achieve mass-production of neural network processors by 2020, with the intention of applying the chips to improve manufacturing, while putting into hyperdrive its move into smart cities. America's NVIDIA is the leader in neural processor chips, which are used by the world's largest tech companies to power everything from AI data centers to semi-autonomous cars. The company estimates that its total AI-related revenue will reach nearly $40 billion by 2025. China has taken notice of NVIDIA's AI chip dominance and has specifically named the company as one that it would like its domestic companies to challenge. China's Ministry of Science and Technology (MST) wants a chip that delivers performance and energy efficiency 20 times better than that of NVIDIA's M40 chip, branded as an "accelerator" for neural networks. Although it was first produced in 2015, the M40 is still used in a plethora of AI projects.

Chinese officials and tech companies each have good reason to target NVIDIA, which has provided chips for robots, drones, and autonomous vehicles, and has partnered with such auto makers as Toyota and Volvo. In response, in 2017, an investment fund owned by China's State Development and Investment Corporation led a $100 million funding round in Cambricon, a Beijing AI chip startup. Cambricon subsequently announced the creation of two server chips that could substitute for NVIDIA chips in some AI projects, while Huawei began collaborating with Cambricon to produce AI chips for phones and other devices. Plenty of other Chinese companies jumped into the fray, with Horizon Robotics having raised $100 million and Deephi raising $40 million in 2017.

Although it wants to rely far less on foreign chip makers for commercial and military applications, China has struggled for years to make its chip industry more competitive. The US and other governments closely scrutinize proposed acquisitions of domestic semiconductor technology by Chinese companies. The US government has canceled multiple proposed purchases of US chip makers on national security grounds.[43] The concern is that cutting-edge technologies developed in the US could be used by China to bolster its military capabilities and gain a competitive advantage in strategic industries.

An unpublished 2017 Pentagon report warned that China was skirting US oversight and gaining access to sensitive technology through transactions that did not trigger CFIUS review, including joint ventures, minority ownership stakes, and early-stage investments in start-ups. AI and similar technologies are so new that existing regulatory mechanisms related to export control and national security have not found a way to account for them. Further revision of the CFIUS guidelines would require the Committee to heighten scrutiny of buyers from nations identified as potential threats to national security. The legislation would provide a mechanism for the Pentagon to lead that identification effort, with input from the US technology sector and the Commerce and Energy Departments.

As the legislation was making its way through Congress in 2018, a contentious issue was a provision that would give the CFIUS increased jurisdiction over a wide variety of transactions between US companies with "critical" technology (innovations that will sustain a US competitive edge in the future) and any foreign company. US technology company lobbyists tried to water down provisions that the industry deemed to be too restrictive on non-sensitive transactions, such as computer hardware sales and software licensing. Other industry lobbyists were concerned that stronger US regulations may not succeed in halting technology transfer and could trigger retaliation by China in the process.[44] The truth is that, in the absence of a lobbying effort by US technology firms, modifications to the CFIUS would have swiftly passed in Congress in 2018, lending credence to the argument that the Chinese have a distinct advantage when it comes to passing legislation and getting things done. They do not engage in a long drawn out debate about it – they just do it.

As previously noted, in 2018, President Trump signed FIRRMA into law, which established more vigilant reviews of foreign investments into American companies on national security grounds. Now that start-ups and minority investors are specifically included in the vetting process, countries such as China will no longer be given a free pass to slip under the radar undetected when making investments into sensitive areas of industry. According to the US Defense Innovation Unit Experimental, in 2015 alone, Chinese investors invested between $3 and $4 billion in early-stage venture transactions. Between 2015 and 2017, the Unit estimated that China contributed 13% of its total investment funds into US-backed companies, ranking second only to Europe as the largest foreign source of capital for start-ups.

Part of the reason this becomes so important is that China's sovereign, provincial, and local governments, along with state-owned enterprises, firms, and individual investors, often form their own funds and pool their capital into each other's investment vehicles. Some have also adopted Western-sounding names, making it even more difficult to distinguish between Chinese and non-Chinese sources of investment. The US government believes that, in many cases, Chinese investments into US start-ups are not simply innocent investors seeking high returns on their capital but, increasingly, seeking information and insight into the inner workings of these start-ups.

Some analysts also believe that *investing in start-ups may help prevent the ideas and technology they represent from becoming part of the US military*. The DOD does not use technologies supplied by early stage companies with foreign investors, for fear that they could either share or steal information or clandestinely offer a back door into sensitive government computer systems. The implementation of FIRRMA gives the CFIUS enhanced discretion to review a host of new types of cross-border transactions in sensitive sectors and/or businesses. However, to fall within the purview of FIRRMA, investment must either include seats on a board of directors or access to sensitive material. And, just what constitutes "critical technology" will remain somewhat ambiguous. Some Chinese and other foreign investment that should fall within the purview of FIRRMA will remain outside its scope.[45]

There is certainly an argument to be made that *the US and other countries should focus at least as much on accelerating their own AI development as on restricting access to it*. Much of the work that is done on AI, machine learning, and DL takes place out in the open and is highly transparent. Companies such as Google and Facebook not only publish numerous papers detailing their latest ideas, but also the open source software and hardware that they use to do so. *America's best hope of staying ahead in AI is to keep alive the type of vibrant, open research and development culture that has made Silicon Valley the global hub for the blossoming of ideas and investment in the field*.[46] That may prove increasingly difficult with the tightening of protective legislation, in combination with a more competitive and combative tone having been set by Washington toward Beijing specifically with respect to trade, and more generally.

Warp speed

While the Obama administration sought to *increase* support for AI research and development in its final years, and planned a range of initiatives to embrace AI in the future, in its first year in office, the Trump administration actually proposed *cutting* AI research to a variety of institutions supporting it. At the same time, China is spending enormous sums on technology. Already by 2014, the Chinese government had created a 1 trillion renminbi (US$150 billion) investment fund to turn the Chinese semiconductor industry into a global powerhouse. That was just an initial foray into the space.

While the US civilian sector races ahead of the US government in money spent and innovation achieved, and the government remains indecisive about how best to embrace the private sector to achieve AI supremacy, China has not been shy about pursuing AI in a manner deliberately designed to fuse together the most AI-capable aspects of its civilian and military sectors in AI. Beijing is proceeding full steam ahead, having created a Military-Civilian Fusion lab at its equivalent of America's MIT (Tsinghua University), to provide a formal platform for dual-use AI. In 2017, China also established its first national DL laboratory, through Baidu and in partnership with three universities. Baidu has enthusiastically embraced AI technology, in essence reinventing itself around AI. As of 2017, the company had a 1,300-person strong AI team working on a range of cutting-edge initiatives.

As the US government slowly ramps things up in the AI space, China's government is proceeding at warp speed, rapidly making up for any lag it has with Western firms and governments. It would not be surprising if it took the lead well before 2030. Chinese companies believe that, by rotating Chinese staff to Silicon Valley and American staff to Chinese campuses, they can accelerate the timeline for reaching parity with the US. For the time being, however, the size and experience of China's AI workforce is a fraction of that of the US. *Half of the top 10 employers of AI talent in China are US firms – including IBM, Intel, and Microsoft – who are integral to the development of China's human capital in AI.*

Governments around the world are beginning to grapple with the potential implications of AI on a range of societal sectors. As was the case under the Obama administration in the US, the Chinese plan also calls for government action to mitigate the economic pain and social instability of worker displacement. Given China's government-led transition of hundreds of millions of laborers from the agriculture to manufacturing sectors, it clearly has meaningful experience in this area, but its AI-related efforts have only just begun.

Unfortunately, under the Trump administration, the US is no longer attempting to plan for these challenges. The White House Office of Science and Technology Policy, which was instrumental in leading AI policy work during the Obama administration, was depleted of 70% of its staff when Trump first took office in 2017, depriving the administration of critical expertise and insights on AI, while China is using the Obama playbook to plan its own AI revolution.[47]

<u>China's game plan</u>

China lags behind the US and the UK in terms of fundamental research capability, which is a big reason why there is a shortage of talent. Despite its recent push to devote serious resources toward achieving AI supremacy, fewer than 30 university research labs in China are focused on AI, and they are unable to develop enough talent to meet the recruiting needs of China's AI industry. Chinese AI scientists have also disproportionately specialized in areas such as computer vision and voice recognition, creating gaps in some other areas. Beijing knows that, in order to turn the tide, one of the things it must do is increase the number of universities focused on AI, in order to produce more graduates prepared to contribute to the nation's AI effort.[48]

Another area where China has fallen behind, as previously noted, is its dependence on foreign suppliers for microchips. For some types of high-value semiconductors, China has had to rely on imports for virtually all of its needs. The "Made in China 2025" policy is meant to address that. The policy outlines a wide-ranging strategy for harnessing and promoting the acquisition of foreign technology through outbound investment, including the use of industrial funds, state-owned capital dividends, and other channels to support the creation of advantageous manufacturing capacity to implement overseas investment acquisitions[49] and counteract China's comparative high-tech manufacturing disadvantages.

That said, many countries have become concerned that Made in China 2025 is not simply an effort by a country that lags behind to become more competitive. Governments around the world are increasingly concerned that such investments by Beijing, inside and outside of China, are not simply a product of market forces but are guided by the CCP (rather than the private sector), particularly where high-tech is concerned. Circumstantial evidence confirms this suspicion. For example, Chinese investment in the US and elsewhere has skyrocketed since 2015. *Between 1990 and 2015, Chinese investment in the US totaled $64 billion. In 2016 alone, Chinese investment in the US totaled $45 billion – triple the amount in 2015 – with another $21 billion awaiting either regulatory of financing approval.*[50] The investment rush has ended for the time being.

Such investments reveal a broader coordinated strategy by Beijing – to appear to have transparent and straightforward ambitions, and be playing by the rules, when not necessarily doing so. For example, Fujian Grand Chips is an ostensibly "private" Chinese company that attempted to acquire German machine maker Aixtron in 2016. Shortly before it attempted the public takeover, another Fujian-based company – San'an Optoelectronics – unexpectedly canceled a critical order from Aixtron on dubious grounds, sending its stock tumbling and presenting Fujian Grand Chips with an opportunity to purchase Aixtron for substantially less.

It turned out that both Fujian Grand Chip and San'an Optoelectronics shared a common investor: a national semiconductor fund controlled by Beijing. Aixtron makes devices which produce crystalline layers based on gallium nitride that are used as semiconductors in weapons systems. The acquisition was stopped by the US and German governments at the last hour but is illustrative of how Beijing can drive Chinese FDI in a highly coordinated manner. As the stakes associated with acquiring cutting edge AI technology become higher, such concerns can only become even more sensitive with time.[51]

As this chapter has illustrated, China is extremely capable and driven. When it aims to be a leader in a particular sector or acquire a certain technology, it does so with precision. There is no question that Beijing aims to be a leader in AI, semiconductors, and any number of other sub-sectors of the technology-driven 21st century economy. It has the advantage of having a lot of money to spend, and plenty of people and resources to devote to the issue. Since it certainly appears that the US government will not be devoting similar resources to the tech sector, it is merely a question of time until China captures that title, too. In the battle for the future, the CCP understands very well what is at stake. It took the US and the West too long to realize what China was doing, and by the time they did, Beijing was already approaching strongly from behind. Soon enough, the West will be looking at China in the tech space from the front window, rather than from the rear-view mirror.

133

134

Chapter 6: Military Power

The defining character of the Sino-US relationship has, for decades now, been based on a gradual transition of power. Beijing recognized this early on, but a lot of powerful people in Washington didn't realize what was happening until relatively recently – a bit late in the process. They had believed that the bilateral relationship was primarily about commerce. Now that it is apparent what the relationship really is about – the slow devolution of power away from Washington and toward Beijing – it is having a profound impact on how the two nations interact and compete. As China continues to grow stronger, it will become increasingly less inclined to compromise on issues it views as important to Chinese national interests. In response, Washington may find it increasingly challenging not to overreact.

If the power transition were to ever flare up militarily, there are two likely flash points: Taiwan and the Spratly Islands. Since Taiwan separated from China in 1949, the island has been a persistent source of irritation to China. Since 1950, when Taipei first became formally allied with Washington, Beijing has drawn a line on the subject of Taiwanese independence and, in an odd way, Taiwan has served as a sort of stabilizing influence between China and the US. The US opposes any unilateral attempt to change Taiwan's status by Beijing but has also acted as a buffer against Beijing's predilection toward a forceful reunification with Taipei and the island's various political moves for and against independence.

That said, as China continues to modernize and strengthen its military power, the balance of power over the Taiwan Strait will change. The threat of the use of force is in the interest of both China and the US, on the assumption that a military confrontation will never happen. Although one could certainly argue that no such confrontation has occurred in the 70 years since Taiwan became the Republic of China, and now that economic relations between Beijing and Taipei are the strongest ever (with China purchasing 28% of Taiwan's exports[1] and accounting for 19% of Taiwan's imports[2] in 2018), the risk of military conflict must be considered extremely low.

Beijing has never wavered in terms of the importance it attributes to eventual reunification with Taiwan. Since China's military is now in the position to give the US a proper challenge, it is difficult to say if or when Beijing may judge that the cost-benefit analysis has shifted in its favor. The US policy of measured arms sales to Taiwan is a point of ongoing contention between Beijing and Washington. Several times over the past two decades the arms sales have led to a deterioration in bilateral relations, but the two nations have maintained high-level military contacts,[3] and avoided conflict. To be clear, none of the three governments in question seek or desire armed conflict. Taiwan may well remain one of the world's most intractable political and military dilemmas of the 21st century, but China is more inclined to "resolve" the issue by force than it ever has been in the past. That does not mean that it will necessarily do so.

Given the de facto expropriation of the Spratly and Paracel Islands by Beijing, they, too, may remain both a potential flash point and stalemate in terms of great power confrontation going forward. Once China had militarized the islands, with little more than a glance from Washington, Beijing's ability to exert some aspect of military control over the South China Sea was a fact. It is now hard to imagine that the US would attempt to take over the islands in any scenario short of war. But in the event of war, the Spratlys would perhaps be America's first target, to deny Beijing the ability to project its air and naval power from the South China Sea. With the price of military conflict between the two nations being so high, it is presumed that the status quo that exists in 2020 will remain the status quo for many years – perhaps decades, to come.

<u>Beating America at its own game</u>

As American foreign policy was adrift over the first two decades of this century, the CCP realized that it had a strategic opportunity to fill in the gaps the US left behind by virtue of its isolationism and proceeded to build its own set of alliances to make up for lost time. China's leadership seeks to secure the CCP's objectives without jeopardizing regional stability or the Party's monopoly grip on power – both of which remain critical to the country's economic development. China's leaders have deployed a multitude of tactics – short of armed conflict – to pursue China's strategic objectives through activities deliberately designed not to provoke armed conflict with the US, its allies, or other actors in the Indo-Pacific region.

Such tactics are particularly evident in China's actions in the South China Sea, where Beijing went as far as it could possibly go with its military buildup of the Spratly and Paracel Islands without prompting a counter-military move by the US. Beijing probably felt that Washington's Pivot to Asia during the Obama administration justified its move, but no impartial observer would equate the two actions. China is clearly willing to employ coercive measures to advance its interests and mitigate opposition from other countries.[4] The question is, just how far is it willing to be pushed before military engagement becomes the result.

Having spent the past two decades observing US actions in Afghanistan, Iraq, and Syria, China has been able to observe American military fighting capabilities.[5] The PLA has transformed itself from an antiquated fighting force to a highly capable, modern military. Its modernization has largely optimized the PLA's air and naval forces, conventionally armed ballistic missiles, and counterspace and cyber capabilities. Given its global military responsibilities, the US is less able to optimize its own armed forces solely as they apply to Asian scenarios. Since the end of the Cold War, America's military has largely been focused on low-intensity conflict. Much of the significant increase in the US military budget since 2000 (from $430 billion in 2000[6] to $686 billion in 2019[7] – a 60% increase) was devoted to funding combat operations in the Middle East or to developing capabilities most relevant to those operations. The Pivot to Asia had more to do with the re-allocation of 60% of America's existing sea power to the region.

As China prepares for conflicts close to its periphery, its mainland provides ample secure staging areas for operations. This enables the PLA to focus primarily on "tooth" (combat forces) elements of potential combat as opposed to "tail" (support assets). But the growing number and variety of

Chinese missiles will almost certainly challenge America's ability to operate from forward bases. A larger proportion of US aircraft would be forced to fly from bases that are either susceptible to attack or farther from the theater of conflict, complicating US efforts to gain air superiority over an Asian battlefield.

China has replaced many of its obsolete second-generation aircraft, which made up an overwhelming proportion of its force in 1996, with modern fourth-generation designs. These aircraft now constitute approximately half of the PLA Air Force fighter inventory. The net effect of such changes has been to narrow, but not close, the qualitative gap between the US and Chinese air forces. US commanders are equally concerned by the development of Chinese air defenses, which would make it more difficult to operate in or near Chinese airspace in the event of a conflict. In 1996, the vast majority of China's 500+ long-range surface-to-air missile systems were Chinese duplicates of the obsolete Russian SA-2 missile (with a range of roughly 35 kilometers). By 2010, China's newer missiles had ranges of up to several hundred kilometers. Combined with more capable fighter aircraft and the addition of new airborne warning and control system–equipped aircraft, the Chinese integrated air defense system has become formidable.

While US air forces have made improvements to their penetration capabilities, with the addition of stealth and suppression of enemy air defenses aircraft, Chinese defense systems have steadily improved, even against the latest American weaponry. America's ability to penetrate and strike targets opposite Taiwan with minimal risk to US aircraft declined significantly between 1996 and 2017, although its ability to penetrate targets in the Spratly Islands has improved. This is because the same number of critical but scarce US assets (such as standoff weapons and stealth aircraft) can be allocated to attack much smaller targets, and because those targets are closer to "friendly" coast lines.

China has also developed an increasingly robust over-the-horizon (OTH) intelligence, surveillance, and reconnaissance (ISR) capability, having launched its first operational military imaging satellites in 2000 and having deployed its first OTH skywave radar system in 2007. That system can detect targets and provide a general, though not precise, location as far away as 2,000 kilometers from China's coastline. The development of China's space and electronics sectors has enabled Beijing to increase the pace of satellite launches and deploy a wider range of sophisticated ISR satellites. China's development of anti-ship ballistic missiles – the first of their kind – present a new threat dimension for US naval commanders. The US military is in the process of developing effective countermeasures. Anti-ship ballistic missiles therefore may not, in the end, pose the kind of one-shot, one-kill threat sometimes portrayed in the media.

However, the ongoing modernization of Chinese air and submarine capabilities represents a more severe potential threat to the American military. Between 1996 and 2015, the number of modern diesel submarines in China's inventory rose from 2 to 37, and all but 4 were are armed with cruise missiles (as well as torpedoes). Chinese submarines would present a credible threat to US surface ships in a conflict over Taiwan or the South China Sea. The US military has refocused on developing missiles better suited to the high-threat environment.

The PLA is not yet close to catching up to the US military in terms of aggregate capabilities, but it does not need to catch up to the US to dominate its immediate periphery. The advantages conferred by proximity severely complicate US military options, while providing major advantages to the PLA. Over the next 5 to 15 years, if US and PLA forces remain on roughly current trajectories, Asia will witness a progressively receding frontier of US dominance. PLA forces will become more capable of establishing temporary local air and naval superiority at the outset of a conflict, though the US would probably still prevail in a protracted war. If a conflict were to erupt between them, US and Chinese forces would likely face losses on a scale neither has suffered in recent decades.

Although the US will probably not have the resources to prevent further erosion of the balance of military power over the next decade, it can adjust its force structure, operating concepts, and diplomacy in ways that will slow the process down and limit the impact on deterrence and US strategic interests. In the longer term, technological and economic variables will determine whether and when the larger trend can be reversed, or the balance stabilized.[8] Of course, stabilization implies that bilateral relations get back on track, which is unlikely for the foreseeable future. When bilateral relations do finally start to improve, an assessment of the damage done in the interim will need to be made, and a path forward carefully crafted.

<u>Room for collaboration</u>

Since Nixon's famous visit to Beijing in 1972, America has been engaged in collaboration with China, never imagining that the developing country Nixon first visited would turn into such a worthy adversary in such a short period of time. For anyone who understands China – its motivations, objectives, and capabilities – there could be no doubt that it would eventually reassume its place as a leading nation on the global stage. The America-China divide, and their mutual battle for global supremacy, will remain *the* central theme for the world's nations from multiple perspectives – including, of course, the military arena – for the foreseeable future.

While China has one of the world's largest armies and its largest navy, it is worth noting that the US still spends far more on its military than does China (3.2%[9] of GDP based on an economic size of approximately $21 trillion[10] in 2018, or about $670 billion for the US versus 1.9%[11] of GDP based on an economic size of approximately $14 trillion[12], or about $266 billion for China). China has some distinct advantages by virtue of the size of its armed forces, its ongoing investment in advanced technology and, of course, its proximity to the region.

Despite America's Pivot to Asia, America will continue to need to commit additional funds to the region in order to remain militarily competitive there. The US military requires more in terms of conventional forces, including larger stockpiles of munitions, stronger passive and active defenses, sea and airlift power to project and disperse troops, advanced air battle management systems, and ships ready to fight in the Asia Pacific. It also needs more investment in advanced technologies – including AI, cyber, hypersonic technology, and electronic warfare – to ensure that the US military can access and operate effectively in the region.

How future US presidents decide to utilize the US military will also be crucial. An America that is gearing up for future potential conflict with China can ill afford to become embroiled in yet another Afghanistan or Iraq. And while remaining focused, Washington can also ill afford to allow the Islamic

State or any other such terrorist group to gain or regain strength.[13] This ensures that future American presidents will almost certainly be required to close in on a trillion dollar annual Pentagon budget – *even if* its budget allocation process were to become more streamlined and cost-sensitive.

America's principal military objectives are to maintain security, avoid conflict, reduce risk, and manage existing and emerging security challenges to minimize outcomes that undermine US interests or limit its potential future opportunities. The US government perceives that China has similar interest in avoiding conflict, reducing risk, and managing tension but it expresses these goals in somewhat different terms. The Chinese government believes that the proper framework for managing such bilateral issues is to build a new type of relationship to address the issues as much as the outcomes themselves. And it wants to be treated as an equal partner.

The US fully understands that China firmly opposes US military operations outside its territorial waters, and that China asserts that such acts are constituent elements of a strategy to contain China, but it also strongly believes that this Chinese perception is disproven by four decades of policy and practice. The US sees its postwar security commitments as having created a security environment in which unprecedented economic prosperity has occurred in Asia, as well as in China. The American government believes that China is pursuing changes to the status quo in incremental ways that could preclude direct military responses. The US worries that such moves serve to undermine its credibility in the region, particularly among its allies and partners.

Over the longer term, the bilateral relationship will become more durable and effective when it serves to strengthen regional and global security, especially if it were to address common challenges that both countries face. An example of a common challenge with implications for regional and global security is North Korea, where both Beijing and Washington share a roughly common objective. The countries have common policy interests in the denuclearization of the Korean Peninsula, but there has been little discussion between them regarding crisis scenarios addressing regime viability. It is not hard to imagine a situation in which special operations forces from both China and the US operate in North Korea during a crisis. If this were to be in an uncoordinated manner, the safety and security of each force, and the achievement of their broader security goals, could be put at risk.[14]

When needed, Beijing and Washington have found a way to align their military interests. A great example occurred in 2018, when a team of American, British, Norwegian, and Chinese experts assembled to remove highly enriched uranium from a research reactor in Kaduna, Nigeria, that nonproliferation experts had long warned could be a target for the Boko Haram terrorist organization, which had for years been active in the area. China played a central role in transporting and storing the plutonium, the operation occurring only hours after President Trump had made an explicit threat to China about enhancing America's nuclear arsenal.

In the mid-1990s, China helped Nigeria commence work on what would become Nigerian Research Reactor 1 (NIRR-1), located at Ahmadu Bello University in Kaduna. Opened in 2004, NIRR-1 was classified as a miniature neutron source reactor, designed for scientific research, neutron activation analysis, education, and training. The reactor powers scientific experiments, not the local power grid, but the design used highly enriched uranium (HEU), otherwise known as weapons-grade uranium, which forms the core of any nuclear weapons material. The Nigerian material had been more than 90% enriched, making it an attractive target for terrorists to create a dirty bomb.

While virtually all of the cost of the $5.5 million operation was borne by the US, the final destination for the HEU was China, making its role critical. The Antonov plane carrying the HEU (and American inspectors and security) arrived at Shijiazhuang airport just as the arrest of Huawei's Meng Wanzhou had inflamed fears of a formal bilateral trade conflict between Beijing and Washington. Beijing carried right on with the operation, with the Chinese National Nuclear Corporation noting at the time that China's role was evidence of its commitment to the peaceful use of nuclear energy. It remains a mystery what happened to the HEU after that, but it is presumed that China put it to good (civilian) use.[15]

The episode was an excellent example of how China can, and does, at times step up to the plate and make meaningful contributions to international operations, from peacekeeping to anti-terrorist operations. China's role is becoming increasingly important and the US government recognizes this fact. It is reasonable to expect that Beijing will most definitely wish to contribute to future such efforts, not only as a responsible global leader, but also to raise its global profile and footprint. It is similarly reasonable to presume that the state of bilateral relationships could also prove to be an obstacle to such actions, going forward.

How America is aiding Chinese weapons research

As part of its effort to lure Chinese scientists back to China, Beijing has placed particular emphasis on recruiting scientists working at research laboratories in the US that are linked to America's nuclear and hypersonic weapons programs, other sensitive military research, those working for NASA, and leading US defense contractors. Many of the scientists returning to China have, for example, worked at the Los Alamos National Laboratory in New Mexico, the Lawrence Livermore National Laboratory in California, and the US Air Force Research Laboratory at Wright-Patterson Air Force Base in Dayton, Ohio – which are among the most sensitive military research laboratories in the US and the world. While the number of those scientists and engineers who have worked at such laboratories and returned to China is unknown, so many scientists who worked at Los Alamos have returned to Chinese universities and research institutes that they are referred to as "the Los Alamos Club".[16]

Research at Los Alamos spans a wide range of sensitive domains, such as super and quantum computing, particle accelerator weapons research, cyber security, and a host of other leading defense technology initiatives. The Los Alamos website states that 4% of its nearly 10,000 employees are of Asian origin. China's recruitment of scientists and engineers from America's leading national laboratories dates to 1949, when the PRC was founded. One of the earliest of China's successes was with Qian Xuesen, who returned to China from the Massachusetts Institute of Technology in 1955 and subsequently led the country's space and military rocket research. But Beijing has intensified its efforts in recent years by using the lure of money in addition to patriotism, and the promise of career advancement, to attract scientists with overseas experience in defense research.

Another important scientist who returned from Los Alamos to China was Professor Chen Shiyi, who, as Director of the State Key Laboratory for Turbulence and Complex Systems at Peking University, played a key role in the development of China's hypersonic glide vehicle. In 2016, China tested its new hypersonic vehicle – capable of traveling at speeds of up to 11,000 kilometers per hour (about 10 times the speed of sound). At such speed, China could send a nuclear warhead anywhere on the planet in just over an hour, *too fast for any known anti-ballistic-missile system to respond*. To conduct such complex and sophisticated research requires sophisticated testing facilities, including high-speed wind tunnels. Shiyi is an expert on turbulence, one of the most challenging problems in physics, and his laboratory built the first wind tunnels in China. He was also the driving force behind China's decision to build the sophisticated wind tunnel needed for this very sensitive and strategic research.

One of the first things Shiyi did when he returned to China was to found the Los Alamos Club. Its members included former US researchers at other top Chinese defense research institutes, such as Peking University, Tsinghua University, CAS, the University of Science and Technology of China, the Harbin Institute of Technology, and Fudan University. Another member of the Club is Dr. He Guowei, a researcher with CAS's Institute of Mechanics, who left Los Alamos shortly after Shiyi. Also a turbulence scientist, his team is now developing computer models for submarine development. His team's research allowed the technology that is enabling China to build quieter submarines and more easily detect foreign submarines.

There can be little doubt that the US national security establishment has known about and wrestled with this issue for decades, which begs the question, what are the net benefits to America to continue to allow *any* foreigner to work on such sensitive projects? Would there be any price to be paid by America if it simply stopped doing so?[17] In 2018, the Trump administration decided to find out by considering imposing strict measures to block Chinese citizens from performing sensitive research at American universities and research institutes. The exact types of projects that would be subject to restrictions were unclear at the time, but what was being considered were measures to stop collaboration on advanced materials, software, and other technologies that were central to

Beijing's efforts to dominate cutting edge technologies such as AI, advanced microchips, and electric cars.

The restrictions were never formally adopted by the US Commerce Department, which is itself surprising and hard to understand in the current political climate, except when one considers that large US technology companies opposed the crackdown because they have staked so much of their own future growth on the Chinese market. The US universities that rely on Chinese students for so much of their income also opposed the proposal. If the restrictions had been adopted, no doubt the Chinese government would have imposed similar restrictions (even though it would clearly not have been in its own long-term interest).

The US already restricts who can work on sensitive technology. Researchers on classified projects are carefully vetted and must obtain security clearances. The next level down are research projects that are subject to export controls, including many with potential military applications, such as computer programs and hardware that might be used to model nuclear explosions. Companies and universities working on this material need to obtain a special license from the government to employ foreign researchers.[18] Despite all this, it is clear that the Chinese government knows how to work within the system of constraints to ensure that its needs are met. The only way the US government can hope to more effectively restrict Chinese access is to expel all Chinese scientists from sensitive US projects and facilities and forbid future access. It would take a war between China and the US for that to happen, however.

Cutting edge weaponry

Should great power conflict arrive between Beijing and Washington, there will be an impressive array of weaponry at the disposal of military commanders on both sides. America has, of course, been a pioneer in developing cutting edge weapon systems, and remains the leader in that regard, with the latest fighter jet having been added to its inventory (the F-35 Lightning II fighter, billed by Lockheed Martin as the most lethal, survivable, and connected fighter aircraft ever built) and with futuristic weapons, such as the Tactical High Power Microwave Operational Responder microwave system designed to protect military bases against swarms of drones,[19] also now in its formidable arsenal.

Such weaponry has certainly not escaped Beijing's notice, and it has also produced some highly sophisticated weapons of its own. During its 2019 celebration of the 70th anniversary of the birth of the PRC, China's display of firepower was evidence (as if any were needed) of the emergence of a new "strategic triad" of weaponry. The existing nuclear triad of land-based bombers, intercontinental cruise missiles, and submerged ballistic missile submarines is in the process of being replaced by stealthy drones, hypersonic cruise missiles, and special forces using advanced helicopters and small high-speed boats.

China's hypersonic cruise missiles can fly at speeds up to 10 times faster than conventional cruise missiles.[20] The Dong Feng (DF)-41 intercontinental ballistic missile is believed to be the most powerful missile in the world, with a range of up to 9,300 miles[21] (longer than any other missile) and capable of carrying 10 independently targeted nuclear weapons. Each warhead has yields of about 150 kilotons (equivalent to 150,000 tons of TNT).[22] At 25 times the speed of sound,[23] it would take only 30 minutes from launch to reach the US. China has been testing hypersonic glide vehicles since 2014 and is expected to deploy its first model in 2020.[24] The DR-8 supersonic drone can fly up to five times the speed of sound[25] and get close enough to aircraft carriers to send targeting information back to missile launchers.

The "carrier killer" DF-21 anti-ship missile, developed over the past decade, has a range of more than 1,000 miles and far surpasses the range of any warplane on US flight decks today. The DF-17 hypersonic glider can fly beyond Mach 5, is maneuverable (designed to evade anti-missile defenses), and can carry a nuclear warhead. The HSU-001 robot underwater vehicle (i.e. drone) is used for reconnaissance against submarines and ships by diving into the water from the air. It would also be useful for secretly mining an enemy harbor.[26] And the Sharp Sword drone is bat wing-shaped, designed for use from aircraft carriers, and possesses two internal bomb bays.[27] China has clearly demonstrated that it is a leader in military technological innovation.

Beijing's massive advanced weaponry buildup was a major reason why the Trump Administration withdrew from the 1987

INF Treaty. China was never a party to that Treaty, so withdrawing enabled the US to produce countermeasures to some of Beijing's new weaponry. During the INF's 32-year lifespan, while Russia and the US were abiding by its terms, China was busy developing its formidable missile arsenal – within launch ranges that the INF prohibited (ground-launched nuclear and conventional cruise and ballistic missiles of 500-5,500 kilometers). As of 2017, approximately 95% of China's missiles would have violated the INF, if China *had* been a signatory.[28] Beijing certainly has no intention of joining a new INF Treaty now, which means a new arms race is sure to be the result.

Aside from increasingly disruptive cyber technologies, China's missile-centric military buildup may be the single biggest factor eroding American power and influence in Asia. Beijing is, in essence, producing such powerful and technologically advanced weaponry that the US should have no incentive to engage in a conflict. Multiple range ballistic missiles that travel at many times the speed of sound provide little opportunity to be intercepted – at least, based on current counter-measure technology. So, the US has little option but to take a page out of China's own playbook and produce a similar set of weapons with similar capabilities. If Beijing were to ever become incentivized to join Moscow and Washington at the arms control negotiating table, it would only be because Russia, and especially the US, created a countervailing array of weaponry that eroded Beijing's growing advantage on the Asian battlefield.[29]

This impressive display of weaponry is unlikely to have been developed solely via indigenous sources of technology and design. China has a well-documented history of espionage and IP theft in the military sphere, which continues unabated. As has already been noted, it uses a variety of methods to acquire foreign military and dual-use technologies, including targeted FDI, cyber theft, exploitation of private Chinese nationals' access to proprietary technologies, deployment of its intelligence services, computer intrusions, and other illicit approaches. China has obtained the foreign technology it needed to achieve its breakthroughs in military technology through a combination of imports, the establishment of foreign research and development centers, joint ventures, research and academic partnerships, talent recruitment, and various forms of espionage.[30]

Some of the US companies that do business in China indirectly benefit the Chinese military. Although Google has a well-documented distaste for working in lockstep with the US military, some of its collaboration with Chinese companies in the civilian sector in China ends up transferring technology to the Chinese military.[31] Plenty of other US companies in the high-tech arena are guilty of the same thing, enabling China to acquire sensitive, dual-use, or military-grade technology or equipment from the US, including aviation and antisubmarine warfare technologies.[32]

A good example occurred in 2014, when IBM sold its x86 server division to Chinese computer company Lenovo. The $2.1 billion sale included the x86 BladeCenter HT servers used in some critical US Navy systems, including its Aegis Combat System, which controlled the Navy's ballistic missile and air defense systems. When a business with products used in critical government and military networks reveals its code to another government, it becomes a national security issue. The US Navy was subsequently forced to identify and purchase new servers, concerned that Chinese government agents could remotely access the systems by compromising routine maintenance. A vulnerability on Lenovo computers was subsequently discovered, which took advantage of the Lenovo System Update, leaving the door open for hackers. The servers were used by Navy assets, including its guided missile cruiser and destroyer fleets, and ballistic missile and anti-air defenses.[33] With or without America's help, China is proceeding to modernize its military at a blistering pace.

The DOD is busy considering future war scenarios. US military planners presume that any conflict with China would probably first occur in the waters off its eastern coastline and would involve an intense US drive to destroy China's anti-access/area denial (A2/AD) capabilities, attempting to render China's vast interior relatively defenseless. Beijing is busy strengthening its A2/AD systems with advanced aircraft, ships, space, and cyber capabilities. To pose a credible challenge, the US must develop and deploy an array of attack systems intended for long-range strikes and advanced missile defense systems capable of detecting, tracking, and engaging advanced air, cruise, ballistic, and hypersonic threats.

In order to prepare for multi-domain engagements, America's 2020 military budget includes $58 billion for advanced aircraft, $35 billion for new warships (the biggest shipbuilding request in more than 20 years), $14 billion for space systems, $10 billion for cyberwar, $4.6 billion for AI and autonomous systems, and $2.6 billion for hypersonic weapons.[34] The US military is focused on a future war-scape that presumes that American forces are no longer focused on Afghanistan, the Middle East, or terrorism, but rather on being able to utilize its most sophisticated weaponry to overpower China (or Russia) in a conflict that lasted days or weeks, rather than months or years. In these wars, the mastery of technology, not counterinsurgency or nation building, would likely prove to be decisive.[35] The very nature of warfare is in the process of being reinvented before our eyes.

The outer space weapons race

China, Russia, and the US are all in the process of being in a position to utilize space to fight the wars of the future. In 2019, the Pentagon formally launched the Space Development Agency, intended to form a central part of Trump's Space Force, with the understanding that this century's wars will, at least in part, be fought either in or by utilizing space. The agency's priority will be to develop a network of low earth orbit satellites to more effectively track hypersonic missiles, which can travel at 5 or 10 times the speed of sound. The agency will be focused on experimentation, prototyping, accelerated fielding, and leveraging commercial technologies and services.[36] The new Agency will also help defend satellites from attack by ensuring that all US military and intelligence satellites are visible and controllable. If an adversary tries to deny the US government access to its satellites, it wants to be able to respond in an integrated and coordinated manner.

Space and cyberspace had already been named as the primary focus for fighting future wars by the PLA in its guiding military strategy announced in 2016. China's real goal is apparently to gain control of the Earth–Moon system, a concept that has also been around since the Cold War between the US and Soviet Union. While the US decided in the 1960s and 1970s that long-term survival on the Moon was technologically impossible, the Chinese have committed themselves to that goal, which made its 2019 landing of a spacecraft on the dark side of the moon seem less like a benign bit of space exploration and more like a deliberate enhancement of its potential military capabilities in outer space. To be clear, *Beijing's ambitions for space missions are not just about science; China is actively developing assets for its space programs that will enable it to militarily control parts of space.*

China sees space warfare as its best chance to directly compete with the US militarily, since it has nowhere near the assets and firepower capability that the US military has. Rather than trying to match the US Navy and Air Force, China believes it could gain an advantage through production of specialized missiles, spacecraft, and platforms to be based on the moon. *Many Chinese military analysts see space warfare as inevitable and argue that, since it will become the center of gravity in future wars, it must be seized and controlled so as to achieve space supremacy.*

As part of a push to develop weapons meant to cripple the core strengths of the US military, in 2007, China destroyed one of its own weather satellites using a SC-19 anti-satellite (ASAT) missile. In 2013, the country claimed it had launched a "sounding" (research) rocket, but it was later revealed to have been China's Dong Ning-2 ASAT missile, and in 2014, Beijing did the same, portraying it at the time as an "anti-intercept test". *China's subsequent ASAT tests have used targets at lower altitudes. The US is particularly vulnerable to such weapons because of its reliance on systems that use low-earth orbit, which is a primary reason why NASA is forbidden from cooperating with China in space. China is developing a larger missile defense system that some analysts expect to be deployed by the early 2020s.*[37]

Chinese scientists have also achieved success in their development of a high-power microwave (HPM) weapon, a type of weapon that possesses unique advantages in speed, range, accuracy, flexibility, and reusability. HPM is a directed energy weapon that combines "soft kill" (electronic countermeasures that alter the electromagnetic, acoustic or other signature of a target, thereby changing the tracking and sensing behavior of an incoming threat) and "hard kill" (measures that physically counterattack an incoming threat, thereby altering or destroying its payload in such a way that the intended effect on the target is severely impeded[38]) capabilities through the disruption or even destruction of enemy electronics systems. The PLA's future HPM weapons could have multiple defensive and offensive functions that would enhance its combat capabilities. HPM systems are able to destroy electronic equipment, and in an age when most combat systems rely on electronics, such weapons could change the way wars are fought.

The PLA's breakthrough in HPM weapons reflects a track record of consistent progress over the course of decades. Until the past several years, the decades-long research on HPM weapons had, apparently, reached a dead end, until the US Air Force Research Laboratory successfully developed its Counter-electronics High-Powered Microwave Advanced Missile Project, which could target an enemy's electronics from an aircraft or missile. While the full extent of current US program is, of course, classified, the PLA's reported advance in the development of HPM weapons appears to indicate that Chinese capabilities have the potential to keep pace with those of the US in disruptive military and space technology.

The eventual fielding of the PLA's HPM weapons will serve as a critical force multiplier for its war-fighting capabilities. In the near term, deployment of this weapon could be as a ship-borne anti-missile system (or a way to reinforce China's air defense systems). Such a weapon system has the potential to undermine the efficacy of even the most advanced US missiles, such as the Long-Range Anti-Ship Missile under development. Used on its own, and especially if it were used in conjunction with Chinese ASAT weapons (or incorporated with missiles to overcome enemy air defenses), HPM weapons can likely degrade and/or damage the electronics of an incoming missile by interfering with data links, global positioning system (GPS) receivers, and other guidance mechanisms.[39]

This shift toward the areas of cyberwarfare, electronic warfare, and space warfare using autonomous weapons was formally introduced through the Chinese military's Strategic Support Force (SSF) branch in 2015. The SSF brought the military's new weapons under one roof and demonstrates a bold move toward the weaponization of outer space and broad information capabilities. During the Cold War, the US, UK, and Soviet Union signed the Outer Space Treaty (in 1967), which was either ratified by or acceded to by 105 countries (including China). It set in place laws regarding the use of outer space and banned any nation from stationing nuclear warheads, chemical, or biological weapons in space. However, *the Treaty does not prohibit the placement of conventional weapons in orbit, so such weapons as kinetic bombardment (i.e. attacking Earth with a projectile) are not strictly prohibited.*[40]

In addition to HPW, China's military is developing powerful lasers and electromagnetic railguns for use in a future war involving space-based attacks on satellites. Laser attack systems have significant advantages over more conventional weapons – including those with fast response speed, robust counter-interference performance and high target destruction rates –especially for space-based ASAT systems. An ASAT attack in space would employ ground-based radar to identify a target satellite, a special camera to provide precision targeting, and a deployable membrane telescope that would focus the laser beam on the target satellite. Chinese researchers have proposed building a 5-ton chemical laser that will be stationed in low-earth orbit as a combat platform capable of destroying satellites in orbit. Given the amount of funding devoted to that objective by the Chinese military, the satellite-killing laser could be deployed as soon as *2023*, if not sooner.

Beijing clearly wants the world to believe that it can rapidly militarize space. Developing dedicated space combat systems is in line with China's long-term goal of achieving global strategic ascendency. China's space program is dual use, supporting both civilian and military needs. For example, China's Shenzhou and Tiangong manned spacecraft were used to perform military missions; its coming space station and plans for a future base on the moon also will have military applications. The combat space station could attack key US satellites, preventing the American military from communicating with its forces and interfering with its ability to conduct surveillance, blinding it in the event of war.

In 2015, the PLA published the book *Light War*, which assigned a central role to fighting future wars using lasers. The book argues that *future warfare will be dominated by combining Big Data analytics using cyber warriors armed with AI, robot lasers, and directed energy weapons.* The Chinese effort could neutralize decades of investment by the US in its own directed-energy weapons, which are also expected to be deployed in the early 2020s (high-powered compact laser guns are slated for deployment in the 2030s). China's disclosures about the coming weaponization of space should greatly concern US and allied defense planners. *The US really had no choice but to change its long-held policy of not deploying arms in space.*[41]

Russia appears to be making a similar move with the creation, in 2015, of a new branch of the Russian armed forces – the Aerospace Forces – which brought its air force and Aerospace Defense Forces under a unified command. The focus of the Russian joint command center is somewhat different from the US, however. In addition to space forces, it will also oversee the Russian air force and its anti-missile defenses so as to defend Russian airspace from airborne and space-borne attacks. The Russian government said at the time that a key reason for proceeding with the Aerospace Forces was that Russia, the US, and China were all working on ASAT weaponry that could bring war into space, prompting the imperative of new defensive strategies.[42]

Could space be a new frontier for Sino-American competition *and* cooperation?

Part of Trump's grand plan for launching his space initiative was to reactivate America's space program, sending astronauts to the moon and even targeting landing humans on Mars by 2033. The construction of a permanent space station and rocket launch platform on the moon will be critical to human exploration of wider space, and both the Chinese and American governments (and a host of private companies) are already working toward that objective. Since achieving such an ambitious goal is a monumental task, the door is actually open for Sino-American collaboration, since neither country has unlimited resources, and both are entering uncharted territory.

When China's Chang'e-4 spacecraft landed on the dark side of the moon in 2019, NASA's Administrator sent his congratulations via Twitter, describing the mission as "a first for humanity and an impressive accomplishment."[43] China then revealed that scientists of the two countries had been in close communication throughout the process. The Americans had revealed the location of its satellites in orbit around the moon and China shared the longitude, latitude, and timing of Chang'e-4's landing. That was a sharp contrast to their otherwise tense relationship and implies opportunities for further cooperation.

Sino-American space cooperation would presumably encourage other countries (such as India, Israel, and Russia) to join the effort to develop space instead of choosing sides. Since the end of the Cold War, international space cooperation has notably increased. Apart from the International Space Station (launched in 1998, and operated jointly by the US, Japan, Europe, Russia, Canada, and Brazil), four major satellite positioning systems now operate in space (GPS (US), BeiDou (China), GLONASS (Russia) and Galileo (Europe)). They complement each other to provide the most accurate positioning services.

Sino-American space cooperation and exploration would serve to stimulate development of a host of related services and industries, such as manufacturing, agriculture, natural resources, energy, and tourism. These would almost certainly contribute positively to growth for the global economy, promote new industrial technologies, and help address some global challenges, such as climate change and energy depletion.[44] If Beijing and Washington can indeed find a way to work together in a substantive and long-term-oriented manner in space, it could provide a framework for future cooperation on earth. Perhaps the kind of bilateral cooperation portrayed in the fictional 2015 film The Martian may not be so far-fetched, after all.

The quantum race

While potential collaboration in space sounds great, virtually everywhere else in the military (and political, economic, technological, and other) arenas, America and China are competing head on. This is certainly true in the race for supremacy in quantum technology, which seeks to harness the distinct properties of atoms, photons, and electrons to build more powerful tools for processing information and clearly has potential military applications. Both countries are pouring billions of dollars into research and development to lead the race in quantum computing, attempting to attract (and keep) the best scientists, and file as many patents as possible. In 2018, China successfully filed nearly twice as many patent applications as the US for quantum technology, which included communications and cryptology devices. The US still leads the world in patent-related quantum computing, as a result of heavy investment by Google, IBM, Microsoft, and some other tech giants.

China wants to lead in this field and is positioning itself as a powerhouse in quantum science. Chinese researchers have achieved a track record of consistent advances in basic research, and in the development of quantum technologies in recent years, including quantum cryptography, communications, computing, and progress in quantum radar, sensing, imaging, metrology, and navigation. China's leaders recognize the strategic potential of quantum science and technology to enhance the economic and military dimensions of national power.

Rather than rely primarily on the integration of foreign technologies in its pursuit of indigenous innovation, China intends to achieve disruptive, radical innovation in strategic emerging technologies. As Beijing advances a national strategy for civil-military integration, these technologies will be leveraged for a range of defense applications. The same will of course be true for the US. The sensitivity and strategic objectives associated with these technologies are certainly not conducive to scientific collaboration with any other country, much less the US.

China's widespread deployment of secure quantum cryptography and quantum communications is intended to create new networks that will be, at least in theory, unhackable. Eventually, quantum computing will create unparalleled computing capabilities, with impactful applications that include cracking prevalent types of encryption. Such an objective will take many years – perhaps decades – to achieve. But advances in quantum science could have a real impact on the future military and strategic balance between America and China. The winner in this race stands to leapfrog ahead of its rival in terms of technological advantages in solving previously unsolvable computations, making incredible advances in medicine, and, of course, waging war.

In 2019, Google said it had attained a milestone in computing-achieving quantum supremacy via an experimental demonstration of the superiority of a quantum computer over a conventional computer. The researchers at Google said that quantum "speedup" was achievable in a real-world system and was not precluded by any hidden physical laws. They predicted that quantum computing power will grow at a double exponential rate, surpassing even the exponential rate that defined Moore's Law, which saw traditional computing power double roughly every two years. The experiment sampled randomly generated numbers produced through a specialized scenario involving quantum phenomena. The researchers determined that their quantum computer beat regular computers at the task, which involved calculating the output of specialized circuits.

While Google's processor took about 200 seconds to sample one instance of the quantum circuit one million times, a state-of-the-art supercomputer would require approximately 10,000 years to perform the equivalent task. Performing the same experiment on a Google Cloud server would take 50 trillion hours; using the quantum processor, it took only 30 seconds. Quantum processors based on superconducting qubits (the basic unit of information in a quantum computer, analogous to a bit in a standard computer) can now perform computations beyond the reach of the fastest classical supercomputers available today. The experiment was the first computation that could only be performed on a quantum processor.[45]

This has potentially profound impacts on information security and the ability to conduct cyberespionage. A transition to quantum cryptography could ensure that China or the US will be more secure against each the cyber threats posed by the other. The US has yet to progress toward quantum cryptography at scale. Quantum navigation may allow greater independence from space-based systems, and the realization of quantum radar, imaging, and sensing would enhance domain awareness and targeting, potentially undermining US investments in stealth technologies. Taken together, such advances could enable the Chinese military to make up in computing for what it may lack in conventional military power.[46] Washington needs to devote substantially more money and resources to the quantum race if it wants to stay ahead of the curve.

The Chinese government seeks to build an entirely new kind of Internet that is completely secure and impervious to hackers. In 2017, Chinese scientists set a new distance record for beaming a pair of entangled particles-photons of light that behave like twins and experience the exact same things simultaneously, even though they are separated by great distances. The principle is called quantum entanglement, which is one of the subatomic world's strangest phenomena. China smashed quantum entanglement's previous distance record. In a groundbreaking experiment, a laser on a satellite orbiting 480 kilometers above the earth produced entangled photons that were transmitted to two different ground-based stations 1,200 kilometers apart, without breaking the link between the photons. That distance was 10 times greater than the previous record for entanglement and was the first time that entangled photons had been generated in space.[47]

By launching a group of quantum-enabled satellites, China hopes to create a super-secure network that uses an encryption technique based on the principles of a field known as quantum communication. While traditional forms of encryption rely on mathematical functions that are very difficult to be reversed, scientists have revealed a far better way to transmit secret data, by utilizing encryption techniques that rely on the law of physics rather than mathematical complexity (called quantum key distribution). Without getting too technical, for the process to work, laser beams send "quantum information" held in a "quantum system" to receivers, which work together to find a protocol to secure the communication.

In a 2016 experiment, a 600-kilogram Chinese satellite was launched and a crystal at the center of the spacecraft produced pairs of entangled photons, which were used like a laser beam imbued with information. Once in orbit, the satellite sent its partners entangled photons to bases on the ground in Beijing and Vienna (Austria being a partner in the launch) to create a secret key used to access the information carried in the transmission. *The reason it cannot be hacked is because the information carried in the quantum state of a particle cannot be measured or cloned without destroying the information itself.* While, as of 2016, it could be proven that quantum encryption works in a city-sized radius (or at most between two nearby cities), China believes the atmosphere in space will allow the photons to travel further without disruption, because in space, there is nothing to attenuate light.

Quantum technology is a major focus of China's five-year economic development plan. While other space agencies have been experimenting with similar technology, none has seen the level of financial support being provided by Beijing. Although China has not disclosed how much money it has spent on quantum research, its funding for basic research, which includes quantum physics, was US$101 billion in 2015; by contrast, in 2005, it spent less than US$2 billion on quantum research. Scientists in the US, Canada, Europe, and Japan are also rushing to exploit the power of particle physics to create truly clandestine communication, but China's launch puts them far ahead of their global counterparts.[48] *As evidence that the Chinese government is peering far into the future, it plans to create an entire system of quantum-enabled, satellite-based communication that relies on entanglement.* Beijing is already well on its way to creating an Information/Industrial/Military Complex to project its power on to the world, and beyond.

Conclusion

Since establishing diplomatic relations in 1979, China and the US have experienced numerous tense episodes, such as the commencement of US arms sales to Taiwan in 1981, the Belgrade Chinese embassy bombing in 1999, and the military aircraft collision of 2001. These incidents did not result in escalatory military conflict. Bilateral relations not only survived but thrived thereafter. Decades ago, when the two countries' economic relationship was not nearly as entrenched as it is today, their leaderships desired to ratchet down tension and preserve the status quo that had proven to be the cornerstone of bilateral relations.

Since the PRC was born in 1949, there have been many opportunities for both countries to escalate tension and trigger military conflict. Neither Beijing nor Washington believed that line should be crossed. Despite the heightened tension resulting from their trade war, there remains every reason to presume that neither desires to cross that line in the future. Although the degree of tension has never been as high as it is now, there remains every reason to believe that the two countries are *not* inching toward war. It is ultimately the degree of economic pain both countries can endure, and the length of time it can be endured, that will determine the economic outcome of this trade war. There is also every reason to believe that it will not result in military conflict, but rather, mutual respect. Although the desire to continue a bilateral trading relationship that is mutually beneficial in the long-term is strong, what is unknown is how long it will take to arrive at an equilibrium, and at what cost for both countries.

What can be said with some degree of certainty is that, with the gloves now off, in every respect, America and China are about to enter a competitive relationship the likes of which the world has never seen in scope and scale. Military spending will be the centerpiece of that competition. As advanced as the incredible weaponry that has already been developed already is, a decade or two from now, the world will have entered the era of futuristic wars that will be fought by generals from behind keyboards, using robots, drones, and autonomous vehicles. China and America will both be at the forefront of that era.

Chapter 7: The Environment

Common sense, logic, and an orientation toward the well-being of future generations dictate that policy makers in both America and China would understand that, whatever their disagreements may be on a host of other issues, the two countries need to be aligned on the subject of the environment. It is surely in their mutual self-interest to work together to address this hugely consequential issue. As the world's two largest polluting nations, America and China could potentially have more positive impact via collaboration and alignment on this than on any other single issue that confronts them. It is estimated that between them, they are responsible for as much as 45% of all the ozone-depleting greenhouse gases emitted in the world today.[1]

Under Obama, the US was at the forefront of battling climate change, having undertaken numerous initiatives – including a leading role in the Paris Climate Accord in 2015. Under Trump, of course, America withdrew from the Accord and reversed decades of pro-environment government policies. Trump basically gutted much of the progress that the US had made in implementing policies designed to clean up damage that had been done to the environment in America over the course of decades, while setting the stage for a future that embraced sensitivity to the environment and concretized the government's willingness to put in place policies that would safeguard the environment for decades to come.

For example, one of the Obama era's signature policies was The Clean Power Plan, which required the energy sector to cut carbon emissions by 32% by 2030. Trump's US Environmental Protection Agency (EPA) stopped it in his first year in office, citing unfair burdens on the power sector and a "war on coal". Among the many other assaults on the environment made by the Trump administration were the loosening of regulations on toxic air pollution, rescinding methane-flaring rules, weakening fuel economy rules, revoking flood standards that accounted for sea-level rise, making changes to the Endangered Species Act, reinterpreting the Migratory Bird Treaty Act, implementing a sharp increase in logging on public lands, and bringing criminal enforcement of environmental crimes to 30-year low.[2]

For many in the US, these actions were incomprehensible and hugely irresponsible. That such a dramatic reversal of well-established policy could occur in a very short time – much of it by Executive Order and without congressional approval – made many people in America and around the world wonder just how much worse US government policy could get. Other Americans continue to question the validity of concern about climate change, even in the face of irrefutable scientific evidence to the contrary, and despite witnessing and experiencing for themselves extreme weather events that occur with regularity in America and throughout the world.

That has created an opening for China, which has been better known as the world's greatest polluter – at one point in recent history opening a new coal-fired power plant on a weekly basis – than as an emerging superpower in green energy. Although China is in the process of stepping up to the plate to become the de facto global leader of the climate change movement, it is doing so *while it remains the world's biggest carbon emitter and as its carbon emission levels continue to rise*. Much of the rest of the world does not recognize the incongruity of such a position.

China wants to become the leading voice for developing countries on the subject of climate change and carbon emissions as its greatest *offender*, promoting the concept of a dual set of standards for developed and developing countries – more stringent for developed countries and less so for developing countries. Beijing paints itself as a developing country (which enables it to adopt more lenient emission standards) and wants to be developing countries' advocate in climate change negotiations as it promotes and invests in coal-fired power plants throughout the developing world – encouraging some of the worst forms of carbon emissions in these countries, all of which are *signatories to the Paris Accord, which calls for a net global reduction by 2050!*[3]

While China has little apparent demonstrated orientation toward the Accord's targets for the world, it does seem attuned to achieving some of them for China. The CCP's 13th five-year plan[4] (which ends in 2020) targeted a reduction in fossil fuel consumption (mostly coal and gas) related to electricity generation, from 91.4% in 2010 to 85% in 2020. The plan aimed to increase solar power and improve grid connectivity at the provincial level. Once wind farms in the country's north are better connected to the national grid, it should alleviate heavy power demand in the east. Such forward-thinking policies are supported by state-backed investment funds.[5]

China is now the largest producer of solar power, after doubling its capacity in 2016,[6] and has the world's biggest solar farm, on the Tibetan plateau, with an array of four million panels. In 2017, China's Goldwind overtook America's Vestas to become the world's largest wind turbine manufacturer.[7] China has also taken the lead in the issuance of "green bonds" – funds raised by governments and corporations to address climate change and its impacts. In 2017, China also launched a market for carbon emissions trading to compete with the EU (the US has no equivalent national scheme).[8]

On the right track, but with an ulterior motive

Beijing's Made in China 2025 policy has ambitious targets for embracing next generation technologies, including rapidly expanding solar and wind power, and New Energy Vehicles (NEVs), which include plug-in hybrid and fuel cell vehicles. The Chinese government is providing subsidies to national automakers to reduce their research and development costs, with the goal of producing one million NEVs by 2020 and tripling that number by 2025.[9] Local governments have for years been granting preferential treatment to registration of NEVs over gas-driven vehicles. The national government now requires all car manufacturers to fulfill NEV quotas in order to sell cars in the country.

In 2018, China sold almost one million electric cars (representing about 4.2% of the market[10]). By comparison, the US sold under 400,000 vehicles (about 2% of the market[11]). But as with so many things about China, all is not necessarily what it may seem. It would be nice to believe that Beijing's green initiatives are truly just about cleaning China's torrid air and saving the planet; however, a review of Beijing's regulatory practices and ambitious sales targets around electronic vehicles (EVs) makes it apparent that the CCP is predominantly interested in cornering the EV market – a market in which Chinese automakers have previously struggled to dominate. By setting a goal of selling 7 million EVs by 2025, its objective is also to make several Chinese vehicle companies among the top 10 producers globally by that time.

Beijing has moved aggressively to support domestic automakers while undercutting foreign competitors – a tactic which will not be new to long-time China watchers. It has dramatically subsidized EV makers *and* consumers, invested a lot of money into research for battery technology,[12] added tariffs on foreign imports, and forced most foreign auto makers to produce cars in China as joint ventures with Chinese companies. Only Tesla was allowed to produce EVs while maintaining its IP. Even with all that government support, a number of Chinese auto makers have failed to create effective products, which prompted the government to sharply reduce its subsidies. Part of China's strategy appears to be to weed out smaller, underperforming companies in favor of a few powerful "champions" that can compete effectively internationally.[13]

EVs have had difficulty capturing the imagination of more than 1% of the global car market, but hundreds of millions of China's middle class have the resources to purchase vehicles for personal transportation, so at least part of the objective is for the Chinese government to identify a way to bring affordable, efficient EVs to urban residents. Beijing has approached this problem from a pro-business angle: By trading foreign companies' access to its market in exchange for technology transfers, China has set its own businesses up for success while pursuing an important green initiative. Beijing is very clearly betting that, in the future, it will not need to import foreign EVs, but will instead be supplying them to the rest of the world.[14]

China has long been the world's biggest exporter of coal-driven power equipment, exporting twice as much as its nearest competitor.[15] Beijing sees coal equipment exports as a solution to excess industrial capacity. As it transitions to a greener economy for the Chinese people, the CCP believes it must keep legacy coal manufacturers afloat, because the Chinese coal and steel industries, which depend on coal production, supports approximately 12 million Chinese jobs.[16] Chinese companies have constructed hundreds of coal-fired power plants abroad, many of which are in countries such as Egypt and Pakistan that burned little to no coal before the Chinese got there. Chinese coal plant developers are driving energy investments that make it impossible to limit global warming to safe levels. Based on their current practices, these companies, and the Chinese state-owned banks and institutions that support them, will have directly contributed toward significantly worsening global warming.

Xi stated in 2019 that the BRI must be green and sustainable,[17] but much of what Beijing is providing to the countries that form part of the BRI is just the opposite. The CDB and China EXIM have financed power plants in 38 countries since 2013, nearly half of which are fossil fuel-based. Most Chinese-financed, coal-fired power plants built overseas use low-efficiency, subcritical coal technology, which produces some of the highest emissions of any form of power generation, resulting in increased national emission levels. The story is even worse in countries where China has intensified its activities.

In Pakistan, for example, where Beijing has focused massive amounts of BRI spending through the China-Pakistan Economic Corridor, China has financed so many coal-fired plants that the country's power investments are more than twice as emissions-heavy as Pakistan's electric grid was in 2012. And not only does much of the BRI pass through ecologically sensitive parts of the world, but nearly all of China's non-fossil fuel power projects in the BRI were neither wind nor solar, but hydroelectric dams, which come with steep environmental costs to land, animals, and people.[18]

America may not exactly be the best guardian of the world's environment, but it is also not on a global crusade to build infrastructure that is inconsistent with its own environmental philosophy and standards. *What Beijing is doing is keeping its development banks, commercial banks, construction firms, and engineering firms busy while exporting a lot of dirty technology in the process (and spreading "debt trap diplomacy" around the world, with many of the countries it is exporting this dirty technology to being unable to actually pay for it).* Beijing is, in essence, leveraging environmentally and socially harmful infrastructure projects in exchange for diplomatic capital designed to counter America's Indo-Pacific military presence, while attempting to give itself a competitive advantage over the US in important emerging markets.[19] Beijing-backed coal projects are, for instance, enabling the CCP to broaden its defense cooperation with Islamabad while simultaneously helping to degrade its environment.[20] Pakistan's leaders – and leaders in other developing countries where Beijing is doing the same thing – either do not see the connection, or are too addicted to Chinese money to object to Beijing's approach to crafting a strong bilateral relationship.

Environmental protection and the BRI

The BRI has an Ecological and Environmental Cooperation Plan[21] which states that cooperation on environmental protection is a fundamental requirement for the BRI, and that such cooperation is vital for a green transformation of China's economy. The plan states that it is crucial that BRI-related projects comply with the environmental standards that China aspires to at home. Clearly, they do not always do so. In 2017, the Chinese government published several additional guiding policies designed to promote BRI sustainability, such as "Guidance on Promoting Green Belt and Road" and "Vision and Actions on Energy Cooperation in Jointly Building Silk Road Economic Belt and 21st Century Maritime Silk Road". These documents specifically state that BRI projects will be used to advance the Paris Accord and the UN's 2030 Sustainable Development Goals.

At the Second Belt and Road Forum, in 2019, attendees from all over the world issued a joint communique with 283 deliverables,[22] many of which focused on promoting green and socially sustainable development through BRI projects. A variety of initiatives were launched, including two focused on maximizing the efficiency of lighting and cooling to reduce energy use, and on building sustainable cities. Are these objectives even close to being reached?

Some 38 BRI countries have a target of installing 644 gigawatts of renewable energy between 2020 and 2030, which could require up to $644 billion in investment. Chinese banks and state lenders have proposed funding up to 120 of those gigawatts with new coal-fired power plants,[23] accounting for up to 26% of global coal capacity under development outside China. From 2014 to 2017, 91% of loans made by six major banks in China to BRI energy projects were used to finance power projects that utilize fossil fuels. A new coal plant has an average economic life of more than 30 years. Constructing such plants commits developing nations to increased emissions and high levels of air pollution for decades into the future. Coal-fired power plants are also at high risk of becoming stranded assets as the price for renewables only continues to drop.

The BRI is not solely a conveyor belt for coal, however. China is also exporting renewables abroad, its commercial banks have become active in the space, and it has provided the financing, engineering, construction, and/or equipment for several of the largest solar projects in the world- including the NOOR CSP complex in Morocco and the Mohammed bin Rashid Al Maktoum Solar Park in the UAE (both BRI projects). Several noteworthy wind farms have been built as part of the initiative as well, including the Dawood Wind Farm in Pakistan.

Apart from increased financing costs because of high perceived risk in many of the countries of the BRI, there is also an absence of policy support to encourage much of the required renewable energy investment. A big part of the reason why wind and solar have taken off in China is the subsidies the government provides to make renewable energy prices competitive with coal. Many of the countries in the BRI do not have the tariffs, carbon credit markets, or other financial mechanisms required to achieve a viable renewable marketplace.[24] Given the resources and sophistication required to create such a marketplace, that is likely to remain an unachievable goal for many developing countries for a long time to come. If China were smart, it would work with the MDBs to create the enabling environment to support such domestic environments as part of the BRI grand plan. As of now, any such ambition will remain exclusively the domain of Chinese financial and developmental institutions.

<u>The Arctic as an extension of the BRI</u>

As the Arctic gradually melts, China is attempting to expand its influence to the north. For Beijing, the incentives in doing so are access to additional sources of energy and faster shipping routes. Every summer since 2014, Chinese cargo ships have made their way through a new passage that officials in Beijing refer to as the Polar Silk Road, and Chinese crews have been drilling for gas in the Kara Sea, off Russia's northern coast. China's ambitions in the Far North mirror its ambitions everywhere else – the Arctic is no exception.

China is pouring money into the region, investing billions into extracting energy from beneath the permafrost on the Yamal Peninsula in northern Russia, drilling for gas in Russian waters alongside the Russian company Gazprom, and prospecting for minerals in Greenland. Chinese ships are sailing the Northern Sea Route, with the state-owned China Ocean Shipping Company having sent cargo vessels across the Arctic multiple times since 2014. The northern route has cut 10 days off a trip from Asia to Europe compared with conventional routes through the Indian Ocean and the Suez Canal. Climate change is opening up that shipping lane for longer periods each year.

The burgeoning partnership between China and Russia is meeting both countries' objectives in the Arctic. Russia needs Chinese investment to extract natural resources under the permafrost and monetize its long Arctic coast, so Moscow's previous wariness about engaging in competition in the Arctic has given way to renewed collaboration with Beijing to compete with the West. Putin is personally cultivating investments from Chinese companies in energy and transport infrastructure across the Arctic expanse of Russia. In 2019, Putin and Xi proposed linking the thawing Northern Sea Route in Russian waters with the BRI, specifically referring to the new route as a "competitive link" to Asia to Europe.

Beijing knows that as the retreat of sea ice continues, larger portions of the Arctic will become navigable, making it more difficult for Russia to rule the waters of the Far North.[25] That is an opportunity for China to do what it does best and pick up the slack from Moscow in the Arctic as it has done from Washington elsewhere in the world. In this case, Russia is happy to play along, as the narrative works well for both nations from a geopolitical and geostrategic perspective. Russia needs the cash, China needs the natural resources, and they both need each other to counter America's own global ambitions. It remains to be seen whether this marriage of convenience will last, but in the interim, neither country is wasting time trying to capitalize on one of the most serious side effects of global warming.

China has gone to great lengths to try to create alternatives and comparative advantages in global trade in the recent past. One of the best examples is in Nicaragua. In 2013, a Chinese company teamed up with Nicaraguan President Ortega to revive an old idea – create an alternative to the Panama Canal that would traverse through Nicaragua. As soon as the Nicaraguan legislature approved construction of a trans-oceanic canal through the country, a draft agreement was signed between a Hong Kong registered company and the government. The government and the project's developers saw the project as economically transformational for Nicaragua, the region, and global consumers, who in theory stood to benefit from reduced shipping costs.

They apparently did not consider the fact that the proposed 155-mile-long waterway would be three times longer than the Panama Canal, would cost an incredible $40 billion to construct, and would take an estimated 11 years to build, at the same time that the Panama Canal had finished doubling its own capacity to accommodate larger ships and heavier traffic. The developers believed that, in the decades to come, shippers would mostly prefer to transport their cargo on super-sized ships and that, despite doubling its capacity, the appeal of the Panama Canal would eventually wane. While true that, at the time, some supertankers and military vessels were already too large to pass through even the expanded Panama Canal, the number of such vessels would surely not be sufficient to justify such capital expenditure, and it would undoubtedly take decades of heavy use of such a canal to ever recoup the original investment.[26]

The very idea that a Chinese investor would ignore all this and commit funding to pursue such a pie-in-the-sky project is illustrative of the lengths some Chinese entities are willing to go in order to grab a piece of global commerce, even if it may make little commercial sense, and regardless of the impact it may have on the environment. It remains to be seen how much commercial sense China's Arctic ambitions make, or the impact it may have on the environment, but as Beijing has proven many times in the past, a project's internal rate of return is sometimes less important than an initiative's contribution toward the CCP's grander ambitions. In this case, Beijing sees a rare opportunity to kill several birds with one stone.

<u>China's environmental crisis and its spread to the rest of the world</u>

The roots of the Chinese government's negative impacts on its own land and resources started centuries ago, when Dynastic leaders who consolidated territory and developed China's economy exploited natural resources in ways that contributed to famines and natural disasters. The situation China finds itself in today is the result of a philosophy and policy choices toward the environment that were made over the course of centuries. Modern China did not even really begin to develop institutions devoted to the care of its environment until the 1972 UN Conference on the Human Environment was created.

Since then, air pollution mitigation has become a crucial political challenge for the CCP. China overtook the US as the world's largest emitter of greenhouse gases in 2007 and was responsible for 28% of global emissions by 2017.[27] China is also the world's largest coal consumer and has been for many years. The share of coal in the country's total energy mix was 68.5% in 2012, but Chinese researchers expect the total share of coal in the mix to drop to 40.5% by 2035 as renewable, nuclear, and natural gas capacity and usage continues to increase rapidly.

The government intends to have more than 60% of the Chinese population living in cities by 2020, up from 36% in 2000 (53.7% of the population in 2015 already lived in urban areas). China is home to 18% of the world's population but has only 7% of its fresh water sources. Overuse and contamination have produced severe shortages, with nearly 70% of the country's water supplies dedicated to agriculture and 20% used in the coal industry. Approximately two-thirds of China's roughly 660 cities suffer from water shortage. Industry along China's major water sources has polluted water supplies. In 2014, groundwater supplies in more than 60% of major cities were categorized as "bad to very bad", when more than a quarter of China's key rivers were judged to be unfit for human contact. The absence of waste removal and proper processing in many parts of the country has exacerbated the problem.

When combined with negligent farming practices, overgrazing, and the effects of climate change, the water crisis has turned much of China's arable land into desert.

The impact of such degradation on the environment, its impacts on the Chinese economy, and its potential to contribute to social instability have all gotten the attention of the CCP, which is now devoting hundreds of billions of dollars to turning the situation around. China has committed to hit its peak carbon emissions and have renewables account for 20% of its energy mix by 2030. China began a national cap-and-trade program in 2017 and the country is now one of the biggest investors in renewables. Chinese firms continue to invest in and partner with international companies to develop renewable energy technologies. Beijing's response to China's environmental crisis has triggered some optimism about the future,[28] not only in China but in the scores of countries in which its global investments proliferate, and it is either leaving, or has already left behind, a legacy more reminiscent of it pre-environmental enlightenment era.

A good example of this is the 1500-megawatt Coca Codo Sinclair hydroelectric facility, the largest energy project in Ecuador's history. It was designed to produce an average of 8.6 gigawatt hours of electricity per year, supplying approximately 44% of the country's electricity needs. Engineered and constructed by Chinese firms, just 2 years after it became operational in 2016 more than 7,000 cracks had appeared in the dam's machinery because of substandard steel and inadequate welding by energy giant, Sinohydro. In addition, the dam's reservoir became clogged with silt, sand, and trees and the only time engineers attempted to run the facility at full power, it shook violently and shorted the national electricity grid.

Coca Codo Sinclair was built even though previous Ecuadorian governments had rejected the idea because a volcano was located nearby, and a major earthquake had decimated oil infrastructure in the area in 1987. In fact, the volcano had been erupting with some regularity ever since the sixteenth century. An independent review of the project in 2010 warned that the amount of water in the region to power the dam had not been studied for nearly 30 years. A Chinese diplomat in Ecuador admitted that the Chinese government had doubts about the project and failed to pay sufficient attention to environmental concerns, but neither Beijing nor Quito chose to address these issues because it would have caused a multi-year delay in commencing the project. Inadequate safety measures led to the deaths of more than 100 workers, the dam displaced more than a million people, and the resulting environmental damage was considerable.[29]

According to a study published in 2018,[30] developing countries are especially susceptible to environmental degradation as a result of enhanced trade and investment because they have such weak environmental regulations and enforcement mechanisms (often hampered by rampant corruption). Western governments have increasingly encouraged developing countries to protect their environments through trade agreements. The North American Free Trade Agreement was the first US trade agreement to include legally binding environmental conditions. But China has historically not pushed its trade and investment partners to strengthen their own environmental protections, which implies that trading or investing intensively with China is especially likely to generate high levels of pollution in developing countries.

The study's author investigated whether trade with China affected sulfur dioxide emissions and environmental illnesses in 58 Latin American and sub-Saharan African countries from 2001 to 2010. He measured sample countries' trade volume in US dollars as a share of their GDP, then applied statistical measures to determine whether trade with China correlated to two relevant indicators of pollution: sulfur dioxide emissions and a framework[31] developed by researchers at Yale. The findings showed that *pollution levels in many developing countries rose in tandem with trade to China.*

The degree of overall environmental impact of trading with China appeared to depend on host country government characteristics. Those countries with a high quality of governance,[32] did not experience heightened air pollution or environmental illness despite trading at high levels with China. For countries with strong governance-such as Chile, Gambia, and Tanzania, which scored near the top of the rankings-trading with China had little impact on sulfur dioxide emissions and environmental public health. By contrast, trading intensively with China worsened air quality in countries such as the Democratic Republic of Congo, Liberia and Paraguay, which all ranked among the worst in terms of governance.

China has the ability to positively impact the degree to which it influences environmental change in the developing world, should it choose to, by either helping to improve host country governance or pushing for stronger domestic environmental laws. The US and other Western countries already tend to do this because they have become incentivized of their own accord, or because of the active lobbying efforts of non-governmental organizations and environmentalists.[33] Beijing appears to slowly be coming to the conclusion that it is ultimately in its own interests to ensure that the same type of environmental awakening that is in the process of occurring in China occurs in the countries it is actively engaged with in the developing world. The Chinese government already does so when participating in investments in conjunction with the MDBs; why, then, should it not do so on its own?

China's environmental maturation

At the conclusion of the 2009 Copenhagen climate talks, which were considered to be a failure, most of the blame went to China, which had not only rejected imposing climate targets for itself at the time, but also refused to allow any other country to agree to binding targets. Some who attended the conference believed that China wanted to weaken the climate regulation regime at the time in order to avoid the risk that it might be called on to be more ambitious in the years to come. The Copenhagen meeting illustrated that a profound shift in global geopolitics was already under way. It had already been apparent to many that this would be China's century, but multilateral environmental governance was not only not a priority in 2009, it has been viewed by Beijing as a hindrance to China's future freedom of action.[34]

When the time for decisions had arrived at the talks, the Chinese delegates had hidden away in a meeting with their allies, so Obama was forced to barge in uninvited in an attempt to arrive at any type of agreement. Fast forward to 2018, when the latest series of climate talks were being held in Poland, and it looked as if, once again, the talks were about to fail. It says a lot that the first world leader UN General Secretary Guterres' decided to call to attempt to get them back on track was Xi. This time, it was the US and a handful of oil producing nations which had refused to acknowledge the latest science on climate change. What a difference a decade can make. Xi likes to be perceived as being the adult in the room.

For many years, China had been a recalcitrant participant in global climate negotiations, with Chinese negotiators consistently reminding the world of a familiar narrative-that China was, after all, just a poor developing nation, unable to compromise its future growth by having to atone for the environmental sins of the developed world. Beijing had allied itself with the G77 bloc of developing nations to advocate for agreements with different standards for nations based on their development status. The US had long advocated against China's self-classification as a developing nation, stating publicly that doing so amounted to neglect of its obligations as the world's largest polluter. As has already been noted, China characterizes itself as a developing nation when it is convenient to achieve a given set of objectives and wants the world to believe it is a developed nation to achieve other sets of objectives.

The US and other nations have pushed for independent verification of nations' self-reported greenhouse gas emissions and efforts to reduce them. China has historically been reluctant to agree to any such measures, which has undercut the enforcement of climate agreements that typically rely on collective international pressure to keep countries in line, rather than on the imposition of sanctions. Without uniform and verifiable data from all parties, validating compliance becomes much weaker. The issue came to a head in Poland, when delegates were tasked with developing firm guidelines for the Paris Accord that would outline exactly how nations were to comply with the commitments they made in 2015 (the Paris Accord had been widely criticized for being "toothless" because there were no verification mechanisms, nor any penalties for non-compliance).

Ultimately, China, the US, and the rest of the world agreed to a detailed set of reporting requirements for emissions and commitments that each country made in Paris, which included regular reporting verified by teams of experts during in-country and virtual compliance checks. All nations are bound by the same set of standards. So, what led to China's shift toward becoming a major diplomatic force on climate change and in agreeing to greater transparency? Its attitude gradually shifted since 2009 due to a realization that it is in its own interests to modify its own behavior and constructively participate in environmental negotiations, rather than obstructing them. Beijing came to admit that it had in the past published erroneous emissions data. Though many governments continue to see China's climate targets as too relaxed, at least the data it reports will now be verifiable.[35] It took a while, but as a part of its maturation process, Beijing's approach to the environment shifted from one of intransigence toward being a thoughtful shepherd of the environment.

Competition and collaboration in climate change

Future bilateral relations between China and the US will certainly be marked by competition in a whole host of arenas, and a bit of cooperation, in what might be construed as an era of "coopetition", wherein both sides seek to lead in some sectors, pull back in others, and attempt to do both at the same time in a few selected spaces. Climate change may well be one of the segments where Beijing and Washington may agree that there is simply too much at stake for everyone involved to get caught up in a turf war or muscle flexing exercise.

Much will depend on whether either government decides to provide government subsidies designed to spur technological innovation specifically to capture segments of the green or renewable marketplaces, which have become multi-hundred billion-dollar businesses. The application of Chinese government subsidies could result in flooding the global market with cheap sources of energy while stifling incentives for companies in developed countries to continue to innovate. As an example, the heavily subsidized development of solar panels in China basically destroyed production capacity in the US and around the world.[36]

Collaborating on the environment is a far more sensible approach. Former Chinese Premier Rongji signed the very first environmental protection memorandum of collaboration between the Chinese and US environmental protection agencies in 1999. The memorandum spurred 10 collaborative sub-projects and was also the first practical environmental protection collaboration since the signing of the two nations' technology collaboration memorandum in 1979. The first sub-project was a sulfur dioxide gas emissions trading program. China subsequently implemented several policies to promote its environmental protection by referencing similar US policies and experiences, such as a pollution emissions trading platform, a penalty system, creating a green supply chain, and an emissions permit system.

Presidents Obama and Xi had jointly issued three climate change-related agreements, set the stage for the success of the Paris Accord, and ultimately encouraged other developments in the international climate change arena, and between both nations. In May 2017, China's Ministry of Environmental Protection (MEP) visited the US EPA National Enforcement Investigation Center to conduct a survey in preparation for establishing a Chinese national environmental enforcement support agency. During Trump's first visit to China as president in 2017, he was accompanied by corporate representatives from 11 energy and environment corporations. Trump and Xi signed the US-China Collaboration Agreement, which included text regarding energy and environmental protection cooperation-so exchanges and collaboration in the energy and environment sectors remain a primary focus of both countries' strategic development.[37]

The collaboration between the EPA and MEP constitutes one of the Agency's most significant bilateral relationships. It has expanded the quality of environmental protection expertise at both organizations and has equipped China to achieve significant milestones in the development and implementation of its environmental protection programs, policies, and laws. There are six areas of cooperation:

1. The EPA's Office of Research and Development has joined forces with China's Ministry of Science and Technology on joint research to better assess emissions and their impacts, improve mitigation practices and technologies, and enhance sustainability. Areas of shared research have included water sustainability, computational toxicology, technologies for soil and ground water remediation, air pollution monitoring, and motor vehicle emissions;

2. The EPA has met with national and provincial air quality and air management specialists in Beijing;

3. The US-China Green Ports and Vessels Initiative allows both countries to share best practices, tools, and technologies to assess and reduce emissions of air pollutants and black carbon from ports and vessels to help achieve sustainable economic growth;

4. The EPA collaborates with the MEP to support US equipment and technology for groundwater and soil environmental sampling

5. The two entities jointly released China's Water Pollution Prevention and Control Action Plan to tackle water pollution through science and technology, economic and industrial transformation, and stronger coordination and public participation. This included water quality testing, promoting clean water technologies, and chemicals and mercury management; and

6. The EPA shares best practices to manage soil and hazardous waste pollution through workshops, study tours, and information exchange.

The EPA also works with the Chinese government to strengthen compliance with and enforcement of environmental laws.[38] So, here is an example of common sense trumping political considerations for the common good. It is hoped that this type of collaboration will become more commonplace between the two nations in other areas of international concern, that the EPA/MEP partnership can be expanded even further, and that it will not fall victim to the political process.

<u>Are democracies better at fighting climate change than dictatorships</u>?

Anyone who has studied China knows that many of the rules that would apply in Western democracies do not necessarily (or, rather, necessarily do not) apply to the Chinese government. When it decided several decades ago to add a series of massive ring roads to make it easier to maneuver around Beijing, it forcibly relocated city residents who were unfortunate enough to be in the way out of their homes and bulldozed them to make room for the new freeways. When it wanted to build the Three Gorges Dam in the 1990s, it didn't ask for permission from impacted provincial and local governments, it just told them what they were supposed to do, and they did it.

By contrast, democracies sometimes agonize over seemingly simple decisions. Decision-making bodies often ask questions such as whether residents were properly compensated when being forcibly relocated, if protocol had been strictly followed in the decision-making process, or whether the requirements of vested interests were taken into consideration. As a result, democracies often become paralyzed and do not have the stomach to make difficult decisions, which is the reason why, at times, so little appears to get done. Thomas Friedman is fond of noting that it took China's Teda Construction Group 32 weeks to build a world-class convention center from the ground up in China-including giant escalators on every corner-while it took a repair crew near his Maryland home 24 weeks to repair two tiny escalators, each containing 21 steps.[39]

Sometimes democracies, and everything that goes with them, cannot get out of their own way, and very little can get accomplished. If something does get done, it often takes far longer than it should have, costs a lot more than it should have, and may not even have been properly completed. The partisanship on display in the US Congress is a perfect example of this. Dictatorships and authoritarian governments often excel at getting things done, and well, even if their tactics may be highly objectionable.

Which begs the question, is the stewardship of climate change better off in the hands of China or the US? In a variety of areas, China may have started off behind, but acquired technology, improved it, and then ended up leading in the very same sector in which it was disadvantaged to begin with. Beijing's previously mentioned display of high-tech weaponry during the 70th anniversary of the CCP is a good example of this. Now, it is leading the way with its stealthy hypersonic nuclear-armed drones and other advanced weapons. Never mind that it purloined some the technology required from the American and other militaries – just look at the results!

The CCP first included climate change in its planning process in 1990. Since then, the government's policy output has been prolific, including a national climate change program and a renewable energy law. By 2017, China had cut the amount of carbon dioxide emitted per unit of GDP by 46% when compared with 2005, three years ahead of schedule. Since it is the world's largest polluter, the choices Beijing makes will be critical in deciding whether the world has a chance of keeping temperature rises to no more than 1.5°celsius. Coal use must fall sharply; only China can make that happen. Despite the fact that China is by far the biggest manufacturer and user of solar technology, it remains the single largest consumer of coal.

After a two-year pause in breaking ground for new coal-fired power stations, in 2018, China began construction of 28 gigawatts of new coal-fired power capacity. The total capacity under construction (235 gigawatts) will boost Chinese coal power by a quarter. And up to a quarter of the BRI's energy projects will be coal-fired power plants. The 136 countries participating in the BRI account for 28% of global carbon emissions (*excluding* China, of course). Without decarbonization, that ratio would rocket to 66% by 2050.[40]

Authoritarian environmentalism may excel at producing policies but may not be any better than democratic environmentalism at producing good outcomes. Policy driven by bureaucratic and technocratic elites, with little or no input from non-governmental organizations (NGOs) or civil society can be a real problem. Consider that China's provincial governments may lie about their coal-use figures in order to make themselves look "clean" when they may in fact be among the biggest polluters in the world. Some of the Chinese-backed hydropower projects along Southeast Asia's rivers have taken a terrible toll on peoples' livelihoods, wildlife, and water flows.

When earthquakes, typhoons, and flooding occur, as they do frequently in China, the CCP springs into action. It knows its legitimacy is on the line.[41] When it wants to get something done, it knows very well how to do so. If we were to take the very best and the very worst that democracies and dictatorships have to offer on the subject of climate change stewardship, we would probably be well advised to embrace both and reject both. China and the US have both done a good job of making decent progress on this subject. It is now imperative that they both step up to the plate and continue to work together to salvage what is left of our planet.

Unless something were to change, the US will be the only country in the world that is no longer part of the Paris Accord on climate change, as of November 2020, which means it will no longer be bound by its provisions. Even when that occurs, it will not change the fact that China's emission levels are not projected to fall again until 2025. While it has pledged to reach peak emissions by 2030 at the latest, it continues to burn more coal than any other nation, as it continues to swiftly export its coal technologies to developing nations.[42] As the US cedes its leadership position on climate change, is China really ready to take its place? And, is it willing to stand up to the scrutiny required to assume that position?

The short answer is yes. For Xi, clean energy is not just about fighting climate change and cleaning up the world's environment; it's about economic competitiveness, and we know what kind of motivator that is for China's government. If Beijing wanted to, it could quickly ramp up its existing initiatives and surpass many of the expectations the world has of it in assuming the leadership position on climate change. If China continues to fully implement the policies that it already has in place to cut coal consumption – and really moves on its energy efficiency efforts – the nation could cap its coal consumption in the early 2020s.

In addition to its aggressive approach to green investments, China has also retooled its climate diplomacy. As the US retrenches, China is taking its seat at the leadership table. When the Paris Accord was negotiated in 2015, China was roundly criticized for demanding to be treated like a developing country and be allowed to continue to increase its emissions until 2030. With its peak levels now projected to be reached by 2025, it can take credit for taking action and moving swiftly in the direction many think it should have been going in the first place. It is also, of course, positioning itself as the natural heir to the US as the global leader on climate change, based on its recent actions.[43]

Since China has basically already taken the reins on leading the climate change movement at the national level, it will do a good job, for it does not like criticism-particularly when it happens to be justified. Xi will, in all likelihood, actually use the climate change movement to help modify prevailing opinion of some of China's past (and ongoing) environment-related sins. If the US *has* to rescind its position, and if China *has* to become its replacement, at least it may end up benefitting the world, in the end, for once China has a firm grip on the reins, it will not let go, and will want to earn accolades for prompting dramatic progress on the climate change issue. It could turn out that China will do a better job than the US would have. That would be a good thing for everyone, including the US.

Chapter 8: COVID-19

<u>Globalization in Reverse</u>

In 2020, America and China both suffered severe economic distress as a result of the SARS-CoV-2 virus (COVID-19) outbreak, the worst pandemic to hit the world since 1918. The virus set records for serious economic decline, health impacts, and supply chain interruptions around the world. Within weeks the pandemic – which began in Wuhan, China – quickly spread around the world, leaving America as the most severely impacted nation in terms of infection and deaths. COVID-19 harshly impacted numerous bilateral relationships Beijing had with the rest of the world, whether in terms of trade, investment, diplomacy, and basic trust.

It also made many businesses and governments question whether the global trade and investment regime Beijing has crafted over the past three decades – in which the world has become dependent upon China as its trading and manufacturing epicenter – would be sustainable going forward. When times were good, they profited handsomely and there was not perceived to be much reason to question what they were doing, where, and how. During the pandemic, the reverse became true. Even if some businesses *had* questioned a China-centric business model following the similarly China-induced outbreak of Severe Acute Respiratory Syndrome (SARS) in 2002/2003, most did not alter their manufacturing protocols after it subsided.

A decade ago, China had already established itself as having near monopoly status on the manufacture of a whole range of products the world rapidly consumes. By 2011, 91% of all personal computers, 80% of all air conditioners, 74% of global solar cells, 71% of cell phones, and 60% of all cement were manufactured in China.[1] As of 2020, the world's largest 1,000 companies (or their suppliers) owned more than 12,000 factories, warehouses, and other facilities in COVID-19-quarantined areas of China,[2] which meant that they could not operate these facilities during the quarantine and were forced to find alternate means of supplying their businesses.

Some of those companies will have had backup suppliers outside of China, but many did not, and many of those that did have backups may not have been incident-ready to seamlessly transition to an alternate supply chain. What the virus made abundantly clear, by virtue of how quickly national and global economies were shut down in short order, is that business interruption planning has largely been inadequate on local, national, and global bases. Even the multilateral organization charged with ensuring global health – the World Health Organization (WHO) – provided a lackluster response to the virus.

It was never really a smart idea to devote so many critical resources to a single source (China). Having done so, many firms became blinded by their decision, perhaps recognizing too late that it could take a decade (or more) to become profitable in China, if they were to become profitable at all by operating there, given Beijing's draconian approach to foreign trade and investment management. Many of them endured operational restrictions in China that they would never have endured at another investment destination, by virtue of China's population size and importance. Beijing knew this and played them like a fiddle.

The compact made between Beijing and foreign businesses all came crashing down. At the very least, those businesses that were caught flat-footed will now ensure that they have alternative means of operation outside China, should they choose to continue to operate there. But many foreign businesses will now choose to either establish or enhance manufacturing operations outside of China. That may well change the very nature of how businesses think about China going forward and, with it, succeed in shifting global manufacturing toward multiple geographical "epicenters" of operation in the future.[3]

Increased economic nationalism and protectionism are sure to be byproducts of the pandemic. Prior to the Great Recession in 2008/2009, global companies were drawn to China because of its comparatively cheap labor and domestic market size. But China's labor has not been so cheap for a while now. Average hourly wages rose to $3.60 per hour in 2016, a 64% over 2011, more on par with countries such as Portugal and South Africa, and more than five times what hourly manufacturing wage earners typically make in India. In some developing countries, such as Sri Lanka, hourly factory wages remain less than a dollar.[4] After factoring in relative productivity levels, by 2016, China was already just 4 percent less expensive to operate in than the US.[5]

This raises the question, why are American companies still there? The answer, not surprisingly, boils down to the lure of 1.4 billion consumers and the world's largest and rapidly growing middle class. The rules of the game that Beijing established in the 1990s endure: the best way to ensure access to those consumers is to establish a manufacturing operation in China. That works until Beijing makes operating there so difficult and costly – by virtue of the rules and regulations it enforces to gradually ensure that Chinese managers run these firms and Chinese companies eventually dominate or take over firms with sensitive technology – that businesses have little choice but to leave. Many of those firms that have chosen *not* to establish a manufacturing base in China have found it rather difficult to gain access to the market.

Global value chains account for roughly three-quarters of all global trade. Their growth stagnated following the Great Recession, resulting in the fragmentation of international production into a greater number of moving parts, which has served to accelerate the decoupling process away from China. Once a full-fledged recovery from COVID-19 is under way, growth in digital trade, more remote working patterns, less complex supply chains, and more environmentally sustainable operational practices that are more resilient to systemic shocks, are likely to rule the day.[6] The biggest net loser of all this is likely to be China.

Deflection and Deception

The CCP knew just how high the stakes were when it finally acknowledged that another SARS-type virus had been unleashed in China. That meant three things: 1) That it would execute a unified governmental response; 2) That it would crush dissent; and 3) That it would lie to its people and the world about when the virus broke out, how it broke out, and how bad the carnage inside China had been. Officially, the Chinese government maintained that the source of the virus required expert scientific opinion, rather than speculation. Yet, no reputable epidemiologist ever produced any evidence that the coronavirus came from anywhere other than China. Beijing had hoped to escape responsibility for its initial cover-up of the outbreak in December 2019 and January 2020, which ended up costing the world precious time to create a containment strategy and compile medical resources.

I was living in Singapore when the SARS outbreak occurred and I know from first-hand experience just how devastating it was to individuals, businesses, and governments throughout Asia. COVID-19 turned out to be SARS on steroids. At that time, the CCP was similarly accused of a lack of transparency and deception about the origin and impact of SARS. Why did the CCP believe that doing so would end up benefitting anyone – least of all themselves and the Chinese people – and why had so few lessons apparently been learned as a result of responding to the SARS outbreak?

In the case of COVID-19, at the beginning of December 2019, around the time the first cases of the virus were to have been documented in China, Beijing had failed to grasp the significance of the initial outbreak and had muzzled and punished the Chinese doctor (Li Wenliang) who first tried to warn Beijing that the virus was a previously unknown and deadly strain of SARS. On December 31st, China's National Health Commission dispatched the first group of experts to Wuhan and formally alerted the WHO. By that time, there were already more than 100 cases in Wuhan. Surely, by that time, President Xi would have known what was transpiring.

Chinese health authorities insisted that the virus did not spread from human-to-human contact until January 20th, when Xi decided to go public with news of the virus. But even then, he did not order a lockdown in Wuhan until three days later. This occurred at the worst possible time because, by then, some 5 million people had already left the city to travel throughout China in anticipation of the coming Chinese New Year. It was too late to try to contain the virus, but that did not stop Xi from personally contacting world leaders with a benign narrative to the situation, stating that his personal intervention had prevented a catastrophe.[7]

The CCP then unleashed a tsunami of media releases stating that determining the origin of the virus would be difficult and that it did not necessarily originate in China. The WHO played right along. Late in January, WHO director general Tedros Adhanom Ghebreyesus sat next to President Xi in Beijing and offered effusive praise of Xi's and the CCP's transparency and management of the outbreak. Quite apart from the many concerns that have been expressed about the wisdom and efficacy of the WHO following its poor response to the West African Ebola crisis in 2014-2017, Mr. Ghebreyesus's eyebrow raising public statements about the Chinese government's response raised question about his, and the Organization's, own transparency and allegiances.

According to the WHO's website, its total funding is just over $6 billion. The US is the largest national contributor to the WHO's budget, at approximately 15%. The next largest national contributor is the UK, at about 7%. By contrast, Chinese funding of the WHO jumped 58% between 2014 and 2019, from $12 million to $19 million,[8] which amounts to just 0.23% of the Organization's budget.[9] That did not stop Beijing from exerting influence and punching well above its weight in the WHO.

A Chatham House Report[10] noted that the WHO is highly politicized and bureaucratic and is dominated by medical staff seeking medical solutions to what are often social and economic problems. It added that staff are often too timid to approach controversial issues, too overstretched, and too slow to adapt to change. If any multilateral organization needs to be nimble and sure footed, it is the WHO, which relies on its member states to provide the essential data necessary to make critical decisions impacting the lives of millions of people around the world. Given its COVID-19 performance, and the same during the SARS outbreak in 2002-2003, that the WHO relied on Beijing to provide that information was particularly dangerous.

The fact that the Ethiopian government is Marxist, that Ghebreyesus was its former Health Minister, that China is Ethiopia's largest foreign investor, and that China had plans to build a new African Center for Disease Control in Addis Ababa, apparently prompted Ghebreyesus to walk a tight rope between demanding accurate and timely information from Beijing versus upsetting Xi and the CCP. This, despite the fact that, during the SARS epidemic, the Chinese government also did not report the outbreak for months and refused to provide access to WHO experts.

The WHO did not declare a global health emergency for COVID-19 until January 30th, 2020 – at least two months after the outbreak first began and more than a week after it had been confirmed that human-to-human contact was a source of infection. Days earlier, Ghebreyesus had been in Beijing extolling the virtues of Xi's response to the virus. But Xi did not even begin to quarantine the Chinese population outside of Wuhan until early February, and Ghebreyesus did not declare a global pandemic until March 11th, after 114 countries had *already* experienced infections from the virus.[11]

According to the WHO's 2017 Pandemic Influenza Risk Management guidelines,[12] the director general may make a declaration of a pandemic based on his/her risk assessment – but there were no specific guidelines for what constituted a pandemic, when a pandemic should be declared, or how nations should universally respond. That clearly needs to change.

As if to play along on cue, when asked at the time by a China Global Television Network reporter whether the virus could have originated outside of China, Michael Ryan, the executive director for WHO's Health Emergencies Program, replied that "the disease can emerge anywhere" and that "coronaviruses are a global phenomenon."[13] His response ended up framing the government's subsequent narrative that the virus could have emerged anywhere. By March, the Ministry of Foreign Affairs (MFA) was routinely stating that the source of the outbreak had yet to be determined, despite the fact that the 1957 Asian Flu[14] and 1968 Hong Kong flu (both pandemics), the 1977 "Russian" flu, the 1996 H5N1 flu, SARS, and the 2009 H1N1 flu had *all* emanated from China.[15] That COVID-19 had originated in China should have been a surprise to no one. China's MFA then embarked on a weeks-long media rampage stating that the source of the virus could not be determined.[16]

Bat Research

In 2004, the WHO determined that an outbreak of SARS had been caused by two separate leaks at the Chinese Institute of Virology in Beijing. The Chinese government said at the time that the leaks were a result of "negligence". It is a remarkable coincidence that the Wuhan Institute of Virology was researching Ebola and SARS-associated coronaviruses in bats before the pandemic outbreak, and that in the month when Wuhan doctors were treating the first patients of COVID-19, the Institute announced in a hiring notice that a large number of new bat viruses had been discovered and identified. [17] In November[18] and December[19] 2019 the Wuhan Institute for Virology posted job openings for scientists to research the relationship between the coronavirus and bats. And a scientific paper published by the South China University of Technology in February 2020[20] stated that "the coronavirus probably originated from a laboratory in Wuhan" and that safety levels needed to be reinforced in high risk biohazardous laboratories in China.

There was much speculation at the outset about whether there was an animal link or the virus had been crafted and then escaped from China's only BSL-4 (biosafety laboratory) - the Wuhan National Biosafety Laboratory, located very near epicenter of the outbreak. While maintaining that the source of the virus could not be determined, the Chinese government had - simultaneously and since the beginning of the outbreak - crafted a narrative that the virus had originated at the Wuhan seafood market. However, the first documented cases of the virus had no direct link to the market. A February 2020 study in Lancet[21] study showed that about a third of the first 41 confirmed infected patients had no direct exposure to the animal market. Among them was the first known patient, whose symptoms reportedly began appearing December 1.

The notion that it was a secretly developed biological weapon was quickly debunked. The New England Journal of Medicine noted at the time that the virus's ribonucleic acid sequences closely resembled those of viruses that exist in bats and that epidemiologic information implicates a bat-origin virus infecting unidentified animal species sold in China's live-animal markets.[22] The Washington Post similarly reported that US intelligence found no evidence that the coronavirus was created in a laboratory as a potential bioweapon and that scientific research demonstrated that the virus originated in bats.[23]

However, based on scientific evidence, it is worth noting that Chinese government researchers had previously isolated more than 2,000 new viruses - including deadly bat coronaviruses – at the BSL-4 laboratory. The Chinese video "Youth in the Wild — Invisible Defender"[24] records researchers engaged in the casual handling of bats containing deadly viruses. The film boasts that China had taken the lead in global virus research since the outbreak of the bat-originated[25] virus that caused SARS. In the months prior to the Covid-19 outbreak, several Chinese state media outlets had praised the virus research being done in Wuhan by Tian Junhua, a leader in bat virus research.[26] Mr. Tian worked for the office of decontamination and biological disease vector prevention and control within the Wuhan Center for Disease Control (CDC). He had gathered thousands of bats for research work on bat viruses since 2012.

The most plausible theory is that COVID-19 mutated from bats that infected animals and people at Wuhan's wild animal market. But, if true, did the transmission occur naturally or via a link to the lab. Chinese state media outlets revealed that Mr. Tian had once failed to wear protective gear in a cave and came into contact with bat urine. To avoid contracting a disease, he self-quarantined for 14 days—the same period recommended for people exposed to the new COVID-19 strain. Could he, or another Chinese scientist working with bats, have been patient zero? It was widely believed in 2002 that the SARS virus had jumped from a bat to an intermediate host that infected a person at a food market in China. But two studies since then since then – from Nature magazine in 2013[27] and the NIH in 2017[28] - strongly suggested that SARS may have transitioned directly from a bat to a human.

Biosecurity researcher Richard Ebright, a Rutgers University professor at the Waksman Institute of Microbiology, noted by March 2020 that COVID-19 was 96.2% similar to a bat virus discovered by the Wuhan Institute of Virology in 2013 and studied at the Wuhan CDC. He believes that the virus could have jumped naturally from animal to human, but also *could have escaped from the lab*. Until the COVID-19 outbreak, all but two coronaviruses in China were studied at biosafety level-2 (BSL-2) facilities, with significantly lower levels of safeguards — not the high-security BSL-4 laboratory at the Wuhan Institute of Virology.

Virus collection, culture, isolation or animal infection at BSL-2 laboratories with a virus having the transmission characteristics of the outbreak virus pose high risk of accidental infection of a lab worker, and from the lab worker to the public.[29] Horseshoe bats are believed to have been the source of the virus, but these bats are not native to the Wuhan area, nor were they sold at the Wuhan seafood market - but *both* the Wuhan Institute of Virology and that Wuhan Center for Disease Control and Prevention had conducted research on horseshoe bats.

It is also worth noting that in April 2020, as China started to open its economy following months of lockdown, British news sources reported that some of the stalls at China's wild animal markets were reopening, and were, astonishingly, once again, selling bats. Some Chinese consumers prefer to eat animals that were recently alive and to see them killed in person so as to be certain that they were freshly killed. This is due in part to the fact that meat tastes better when it is fresh, but also the desire to avoid unknown sources of food as a result of China's sometimes questionable food sourcing and delivery system. The SARS outbreak, which was also attributed to live animal markets, did not prompt the Chinese government to shut down these markets — a multi-billion dollar business in China. Apparently, neither will COVID-19.

What became crystal clear during the crisis is that we should not listen to what the Chinese government says, but rather, observe what it does or does not do. In this case, while continuing to proclaim that there was no real problem in January 2020 — month two of the outbreak for China — the government was busy quarantining tens of millions of its citizens and curtailing travel in and outside of the country. The most seasoned Sinologist or most novice observer of Chinese affairs really did not need to know anything more than that. The CCP's willingness to attempt to blatantly disregard and deny reality was truly noteworthy and spoke volumes about the lengths it will go to in order to craft a narrative aligned with its own warped version of reality.

America's Response: Ignorance, Delusion, Denial, and Unpreparedness

President Trump and his administration's response to COVID-19 was less sinister than the CCP in orientation but equally abysmal in terms of crafting a narrative that revealed a warped reality, based on a combination of ignorance, delusion, denial, and a lack of preparedness. Trump displayed utter ignorance – especially in the early days of the outbreak in America – stating in February 2020 that there were about 15 cases in the US, the result of a single traveler from China, and that the number of infected individuals would soon dwindle down to zero.[30] Only someone completely divorced from the reality of the virus would have uttered such an imbecilic statement. It was then that Americans truly understood just how ill prepared Trump was to navigate the country through the crisis.

Messaging out of the White House had been an absolute disaster, starting with the president and trickling down to the various cabinet members, department heads, and other sources of information at the federal level. Delusion on the president's part, misinformation (whether deliberate or otherwise) from other federal officials, a preoccupation with political correctness, and a predilection to pander to the president's political base, had combined to create a muddled, discombobulated mess in response to the virus.

It didn't take long for many of America's governors, mayors, and corporate CEOs to realize that they would not be gaining any divine guidance from the Trump administration about what to do, or when to do it, in response to the virus. While, by March, most of the nation's governors had issued stay at home orders, an astonishing number of governors had still failed to do so – three months after the first cases became apparent in the US. And in every case, those lockdown orders were voluntary, since there was no way to actually enforce them. Unlike in China, the sanctity of governmental decrees became dependent upon citizens' willingness to comply. Fortunately, most Americans understood what was at stake and stayed home.

As bad as the government's messaging was, its level of preparedness for a pandemic was atrocious. Despite the fact that several prior administrations (from Bush to Obama to Trump) had plans in place to address a pandemic or bioterrorism event, based on its response to an actual pandemic, the American government appeared never to have contemplated the issue prior to the arrival of COVID-19.

For example, in 2004, George W. Bush had signed into law Project BioShield, to protect Americans against biological, chemical, radiological, or nuclear attack. It had allocated $5.6 billion over 10 years for countermeasures against anthrax, smallpox, and other chemical, biological, radiological, and nuclear agents. Development of medical countermeasures had been accelerated by the NIH, a national network of regional Centers of Excellence for Biodefence was established, and the Food and Drug Administration (FDA) was supposed to make treatments speedily available in emergency situations.[31] Yet the NIH, FDA, Department of Homeland Security, Department of Health and Human Services, and a host of other government agencies failed to communicate, collaborate, or respond effectively.

In 2015, government scientists estimated that a severe flu outbreak infecting 20-30% of the US population would require at least 1.7 billion N95 respirator masks. In 2006, the US Congress had provided supplemental funds to add 104 million N95 masks and 52 million surgical masks, in an effort to prepare for a flu pandemic (well below that which was likely to be necessary). Following the H1N1 influenza outbreak in 2009, under Obama, – which triggered a nationwide shortage of masks and caused a two- to three-year backlog of orders for the N95s – the stockpile distributed about three-quarters of its inventory but failed to replenish the supply.[32] The US continued to rely on foreign sources of supply of personal protective equipment for much of its needs; in addition, there has been an overreliance on foreign sources of critical drugs.

Also in 2015, a Bipartisan Commission on Biodefense[33] produced more than 30 recommendations for what the US government should do to become better prepared for biological threats. In 2016, the Commission received a grant of just $1.3 million from an NGO[34] to continue its work, and in 2018, $2.5 million more from the same NGO.[35] It did not receive official US government financial support and the government failed to follow through on virtually any of the recommendations made by the Commission – an indication of the continued lack of focus on the subject.

Shortly after taking office in 2017, Trump disbanded the White House's National Security Council Directorate for Global

Health Security and Biodefense – an important link in the national preparedness chain. In 2018, the Trump administration did commence a National Biodefense Strategy designed to enhance national biodefense capabilities. It established a governance structure composed of federal agencies to collect and assess data on their biodefense activities and to identify gaps. But the US Government Accountability Office found that there were no clear or detailed processes for joint decision-making, including how agencies would identify opportunities to leverage resources, or who would make and enforce decisions. It concluded that, in the absence of clearly documented methods for enterprise-wide decision-making, the effort ran the risk of failing to adopt a strategic, enterprise-wide approach that would meaningfully enhance national defense capabilities.[36]

Contrary to the attempted launch of the Strategy, the Trump administration's repeated calls to cut the budget for the Centers for Disease Control and Prevention, the NIH, and other public health agencies made it evident that the ability to respond to pandemics was clearly not going to be a priority. His administration certainly contributed to the deficient American response to the virus but, in truth, successive American administrations have failed in unison to adequately prepare for such a calamity.

What America Can Learn from China's Response

During the depths of the Great Recession, China acted like the bastion of fiscal conservatism. Its currency did not go into free fall (as so many of the world's major currencies did), its companies did not collapse en masse (as so many Western firms did), and it ended up weathering the storm in relatively good shape. Similarly, in fairness to Beijing, once it decided to get serious about containing the COVID-19, it did so with gusto and significant positive results.

The Chinese government should rightly be criticized for its initial slow response, lack of transparency, and punishment of whistle blowers and truth tellers when the virus first erupted. Had it responded differently, the world's nations would have had even more time to anticipate the arrival of the virus, and to act more expeditiously in the attempt to thwart its spread on their shores and to save lives. At the same time, it should be acknowledged that, during a pandemic with profound economic, social, and health impacts, there really is no room for a lot of discussion, worrying about political correctness, or walking on eggshells at the risk of offending individuals or businesses. What is required is swift, bold action. This gave the Chinese government a tremendous advantage in terms of actually implementing a plan to combat the virus. So did a willingness and capability to devote vast resources and a draconian approach (when necessary) toward resolving the problem.

China did a number of things differently than the US. Wenzhou, on China's southeast coast, is an example: when, in January 2020, the city confirmed its first case of COVID-19, three steps were taken immediately:

1. Suspected and confirmed patients were centralized in designated hospitals for treatment;

2. All returnees from Wuhan were Identified and investigated using big data and persuaded to observe a14-day home quarantine; and

3. Individuals who had been exposed to a confirmed COVID-19 patient were medically observed.

When the disease kept spreading, Wenzhou moved to heavier-handed measures that included blocking transport in and out of the city, closing down places of public gathering, setting up inspection stations at major locations and screening entrants for temperature, using phone data and in-person screenings at city entrances to track and investigate individuals at risk of infection, rapidly transferring the ill to designated medical facilities, transferring critically ill patients to a designated hospital for intensive care, and tracking down patients' contacts.[37] By contrast, in the US, many hospitals had a mix of infected and non-infected patients, big data did not tend to be used to track patient movements, and neither extensive contact tracing nor widespread medical screening was performed on a routine basis throughout states or the country.

Many governments outside of China, including the US, were, and remained, poorly prepared to address a pandemic as it progressed. Too few had resources specifically earmarked to be applied to pandemics, many have been too slow to address the virus, and many performed poorly in mobilizing resources. Although the rest of the world had up to 2 months' notice that the virus would be coming to their shores, too few governments took even rudimentary steps to prepare for its eventuality.

The Chinese government has a real advantage in times of crisis: it can act with force, swiftly and effectively; it has the ability to keep track of nearly all of its citizens; and, as a leader in AI, it can deploy electronic and drone technology to enforce its edicts. Beijing has proven repeatedly that it has the ability to deploy massive human, monetary, and physical resources as no other nation can. Too many other nations cannot say any of that. The Chinese government also has the advantage of having practiced long-term planning for decades, which makes preparedness for natural disasters much easier to achieve.

The legacy of the virus, and the Chinese government's reaction to it, represented a stark clash between the Chinese and American systems of government. As was also the case during the Great Recession, China seemed much better prepared to manage the crisis and weather the storm. By contrast, America's government appeared feeble and inept, underscoring its woeful, ongoing unpreparedness for the virus's onslaught and the enormous challenges it faced in executing its laggard response.

If there could be a "winner" in all this, it was Xi Jinping, who sat unimpeachably astride the country's machinery of state, backed by China's state-owned enterprises and banking system as core constituents in the country's fight to recover economically. In the early days of the pandemic, America could only look on with awe at Xi's domestic hold on power. As Xi rode a surge in the country's soft power, confident that his government's response to the virus successfully stopped its inexorable march across China, Trump maintained his deluded sense of unreality, leading America into an economic, social, and health abyss.[38]

Cooperation, Competition, or Coopetition?

Former Swedish Prime Minister Carl Bildt noted, as the virus engulfed Europe, that COVID-19 was the first great crisis of the post-American world.[39] He meant that, in the Trump era, as the world was learning to function without American engagement and leadership, the outbreak was the first real instance when the world was forced to maneuver through the crisis without a global leader. China had an opportunity to fill that void but, as a result of its actions, many around the world were wondering if it would ever be capable of assuming the mantle of leadership.

The manner in which the American and Chinese governments reacted to the pandemic offers some insights into how their bilateral relationship would evolve in the future, and its potential impact on the rest of the world. The virus only served to accentuate the many differences between the two governments, ensuring a prolongation of the trade war and a continuation of the fissure between them more generally. Both governments pursued divergent paths during and following the commencement of the outbreak – the Chinese government continuing to deny, obfuscate, and fail to be transparent about what was really happening in China, and the US government displaying all of its actions, inactions, and failings for the world to see on a daily basis.

This left many of the world's people bewildered and yearning for some alternative to either government. In an environment in which Sino/US relations were at their lowest ebb since the Mao era, the question became, was there some other alternative? The answer was "no". The world had only two realistic choices. Perhaps the solution would be for both governments to find a way to cooperate with each other, and the world, to battle a common enemy. But with Trump at the helm in America, expectations were low about what Washington might do to help *any* other country. The US did make some high profile contributions to the UN, other aid agencies, and selected countries (including China) in the early days of the pandemic, but far less in scope and scale than China assisted after it endured the initial wave of the virus in the first quarter of 2020.

COVID-19 induced numerous instances of the Chinese government stepping up to the plate to assist other pandemic-stricken nations, from sharing the genetic code of the virus early on with scientists and researchers to providing personal protection and medical equipment deliveries to countries around the world. For example, after its own viral peak had been reached, Beijing sent 1,000 ventilators to New York.[40] India, long a major foe of China's, was allowed to purchase much needed ventilators and masks from Beijing to address its own lockdown. However, doing so revealed quality issues in Chinese-manufactured medical products. For example, the Netherlands ended up recalling thousands of masks imported from China, and Spain complained about defective imported test kits supplied by a Chinese manufacturer.[41]

But Beijing's timely sequencing of the novel coronavirus genome, and its subsequent rapid release to the world, permitted a massive global research effort to begin. Only two weeks following the release of the genome, scientists at America's NIH were able to validate how the virus entered cells. The vaccine trial that subsequently began in America was the fastest that had ever occurred. The data collected and shared by Chinese physicians enabled the first estimates of the virus's transmissibility to be made and epidemiologic models of infection to be modeled by governments around the world. They also provided the first set of data leading to estimates of fatality rates, which led to the creation of models to predict the scope, spread, and severity of the disease.

That said, it did not take long for Beijing and Washington to turn the pandemic into a contest to be seen by the global community as the world's leading humanitarian force, sparring over the air waves to be perceived as the leader in providing foreign aid to nations and assistance to global aid agencies. At a governmental level, the two nations appeared incapable of engaging in genuine cooperation, but that did not stop entities on both sides of the Pacific from identifying ways to cooperate. The Harvard Medical School teamed up with Chinese doctors to form the Harvard-Guangzhou Institute, to understand the basic biology of the virus and accelerate development of better diagnostics and treatments.[42]

The pandemic raised serious questions about just how cooperative either could or would become toward the other in times of crisis. Presumably, when it is in both of their interests, they would find a way to do so, even during their trade war, and while Trump was at the helm in America. With almost any other occupant of the White House, that task would have to be considered an easier lift in the future. But for the duration of 2020, and possibly the succeeding four years (if Trump is re-elected), the fissure between Beijing and Washington would, more likely, endure and even worsen, as progress on bilateral trade talks stalled in the wake of COVID-19, their economies become more distressed, and the global economy faltered.

The Need for New Codes of Conduct

Among the many lessons that will have been learned following the COVID-19 pandemic is the need for some new codes of conduct for what nations should do in the event of a pandemic, how to better marshal resources, and how to achieve better collaboration internationally. There are, of course, numerous examples of global collaboration following calamities, key examples being the creation of the UN, International Monetary Fund, and World Bank following World War II. Many other multilateral organizations were created in the decades that followed, all in response to enduring global needs.

One area in which the COVID-19 pandemic has amply demonstrated an increased need for collaboration is that of biological weapon defense. The Biological Weapons Convention (BWC) has 147 member states and prohibits them from developing, producing, stockpiling, or otherwise acquiring equipment to deliver biological agents. But that has not prevented some of the world's most weapons-capable nations from doing just that.

Approximately 50 nations remain outside the scope of the Convention; in addition, the BWC has no verification measures to ensure compliance. It has been clear for decades now that some member states have either violated the Convention or operated illegal bioweapons programs. The BWC charter should therefore be updated to add compliance and enforcement provisions. The pandemic should incentivize those nations that have not joined to do so, as well as motivate member nations to put some teeth into the Convention.

COVID-19 also served to emphasize how politicized the WHO has become and how inadequate its response to the virus was. The idea that more than 100 nations can have cases of a virus without the WHO declaring a pandemic, and that there are no specific guidelines for what constitutes a pandemic, when a pandemic should be declared, or how nations should universally respond, must change. Going forward, specific guidelines should be established for what constitutes a pandemic, when it should be declared, and how nations should respond.

It is worth noting, also, that there was a marked increase in hacking, phishing attempts, and online threats as the virus progressed around the world, emphasizing how vulnerable many governments, businesses, and individuals remain to hacking and cyber warfare. That is especially true when much of the world is working from home, businesses are under financial distress, and fewer resources are devoted to robust cybersecurity. There is a compelling case to be made for the creation of a World Cybersecurity Organization (WCO) to provide much needed focus on identifying threats, sharing information about the latest hacking techniques, distributing software updates, and sending teams of specialists to address incidents that threaten national economies and their security as needed.

The WCO's mandate could include crafting a set of universal laws designed to combat cybercrime and hacking. That may be the only way to commence the badly needed effort to create a set of globally applicable laws to fight it. Such laws might also entail coming to agreement about what would constitute a crime, as well as having a common agreement on how jurisdiction would be applied and enforced.

These three recommendations are illustrative of the enormous task that awaits the world's nations once the spread of the virus has abated and a vaccine found. The objective is to establish a proactive footing, mindful that it is only a matter of time until another robust response is required of the global community. The world's nations should never again be caught flat-footed. Creating new multilateral organizations and enhancing the ability of existing organizations to respond to future calamities more meaningfully should be considered minimal responses to the COVID-19 pandemic.[43]

Implications for Sino/US Relations

As the world's nations and its multilateral organizations were focused squarely on the pandemic, once China had turned the corner in addressing it at home, the government wasted no time seeking to capitalize on the virus to its maximum benefit. It took advantage of all the turmoil and uncertainty to raise its profile in the South China Sea, for example. By April 2020, it was conducting military drills and deploying large-scale military assets to the area, with the objective of both rallying the Chinese people around the flag and exploiting America's and Asian nations' weakened condition. This was done while simultaneously moving forward in exploiting hydrocarbon resources from the seabed, seeking to drive a diplomatic wedge between Washington and its transatlantic allies, and expanding its strategic and economic footprint around the world.[44]

Ever since 1784, when the first American merchant ship landed in China to trade ginseng for tea, both sides have cycled through what the author John Pomfret has called "rapturous enchantment followed by despair,"[45] but their union has always been based on mutual benefit. Eight American Presidents – from Nixon through to Obama – have deployed a strategy of engagement, based on the conviction that embracing China politically and economically would eventually make it more liberal. As the decades progressed, successive American governments had to have realized that Beijing was never going to become the liberal bastion they desired. So, despite that, and China's flagrant abuses of IP and human rights, the strategy of engagement resulted in the creation of the largest trading relationship in the world.

Now, given Trump's desire to produce a forced uncoupling, both nations are on a path toward becoming permanent adversaries. Many in Washington see Beijing as an existential menace, worthy of the same bellicose response America had toward the Soviet Union for decades. Many in Beijing view Washington as relentlessly trying to inhibit China's inevitable rise to become a global power, making the Chinese leadership worried that America's historical support of popular uprisings around the globe[46] might result in an uprising among the Chinese people, domestic instability being the thing the CCP fears most. Trump's decision to spurn engagement with Beijing has enabled Xi and the CCP to rally the Chinese people around the flag. Trump's bellicosity is thus seen as a "gift" to be used to maximum benefit. It is, and will remain, questionable whether the Chinese government would necessarily respond favorably to a change in tone from the American government.

The truth is that the Chinese and American governments have both made big mistakes – in reacting to the virus and in governing their countries. Many of China's failings have been well catalogued in this chapter and book. America's failings under Trump include not creating a widely shared prosperity in the US and promoting widespread animosity abroad. Such failures lend credence to the notion that autocracy may ultimately be preferable to liberal democracy. But the death of decency and competence in the main Western governments matters beyond that – the pandemic is a global moral challenge and the US must play a big role, for there is no real alternative.[47] Certainly not China.

Deng Xiaoping once said that "the China-US relationship can never be too good or too bad"[48] because it is too important, meaning both countries' leaders and people should be realistic about how close their bilateral relationship can be at any given point in time and they should never let their disagreements get so out of hand that they threaten general peace and prosperity. While seemingly simplistic, the quote accurately encapsulates the general nature of relations between the two nations since Richard Nixon and Mao Zedong commenced the modern bilateral relationship in 1972.

China's political orientation and national pride dictate that it pursue its own political and developmental path, and an independent foreign policy that it believes (and would like the rest of the world to believe) is ultimately aimed at achieving peace in Asia and elsewhere. Many countries in Asia, and the world, are highly skeptical about this so-called 'peaceful development', pointing to China's unilateral actions in the South China Sea as directly contrary to that objective. The Chinese government and most of its people believe that the country's actions are consistent with both recent regional history and current international law, based on their own unique perspective of history and international relations.

Part of the reason for the vastly different perspectives on this issue is a genuine belief on the part of both sides that each is right. China points to previous maps and maritime practices, which were at the time unopposed by other nations. The US (and other nations) see this as inconsistent with modern international maritime law as defined by UNCLOS, which, ironically, China has signed and ratified while the US has not. China views itself and the US as 'different, but not distant' because Confucian philosophy advocates 'accommodating divergent views'. *President Xi has repeatedly said that the Pacific Ocean is vast enough to accommodate both China and the US and has proposed a new model of international relations aimed at avoiding confrontation and conflict, and respecting one another's political systems and national interests, while pursuing joint win-win cooperation.*

That all sounds good on paper, but Beijing's actions in the South China Sea are certainly inconsistent with accommodating both countries and avoiding conflict. The question becomes whether and how Confucian philosophy may become more consistent with current international law, whether both sides can reach an understanding about how China's rise may coincide with America's gradual decline as a global power, and how China's neighbors will view ongoing territorial disputes in the future. We stand at a critical juncture. Much will depend on how far all sides are willing to reach across the table and genuinely compromise.

Maintaining equilibrium, between China and its neighbors, as well as between China and the US, will remain of paramount importance. Sino-US relations will remain the world's most important bilateral relationship for many years to come, with implications for the entire world. Both nations' people have much more to gain by maintaining a friendly and cooperative relationship with each other, rather than the other way around. It will clearly take a great degree of wisdom, an appreciation of history, and a willingness by all sides to compromise, in order to maintain mutual peace and prosperity.[49] There is clearly incongruity between what both are seeking and what either may be prepared to deliver. What differentiates this challenge from that of any other two nations is that both countries need each other in order to prosper and either of them is capable of causing insurmountable problems politically, economically, and militarily for the other.

Expect More of the Same

The US government, which was always leery of what China was, and skeptical about what it might become, now clearly views China as a strategic rival, a malevolent actor, and a rule-breaker. Socialism with Chinese characteristics, which has been a work-in-progress since the days of Mao, has now morphed into President Xi Jinping Thought, whose 14 points (with some caveats) basically boil down to the following precepts: *enforce the rule of law, strengthen national security, and ensure the perpetual omnipotence of the CCP.*

President Xi is under no illusions about what he wants China to become: an even more entrenched authoritarian state where making money is just fine as long as the omnipotence of the CCP is neither questioned nor challenged. Peaceful coexistence with the rest of the world and a common destiny is fine just as long as it occurs based on China's rules and objectives. The US government now understands what China and Xi are all about and is acting accordingly – calling Beijing out on its decades-long theft of American IP, intensive spying, and a deeply unbalanced trading relationship.

Not since the late 1940s has there been such unanimity of opinion among American law makers, the military, businesses, and citizens about who America's number one rival is. For a short time, during the 2016 presidential election, many believed it was Russia, but that has changed. Similarly, *Chinese strategists have long suspected that America was mostly interested in preventing China from reaching its true potential and surpassing the US in both economic size and power. Many Chinese see America as a hypocrite that commits all the sins it accuses China of, while poisoning the atmosphere that would otherwise give Beijing a clear path toward its destiny.*

President Trump has sought nothing less than a reordering of the global trade regime so that it was not tipped so much in Beijing's favor, but that the import and export playing field was leveled for America, and for the rest of the world in the process. Trump sees his trade war with Beijing, and the trade war he initiated with the rest of the world, as an effort to tip the balance before it is too late. It may already be too late, however. America's trade imbalances did not occur overnight but rather over the course of many decades. If the balance is to be readjusted, it will take many years – perhaps decades – for it to occur.

The Chinese government and many Chinese people believe that Trump's trade war, and other investment restrictions placed on Chinese companies, are ultimately aimed at curbing China's technological development – particularly in light of its 'Made in China 2025' strategy – to attempt to contain China's rise as a great power. This is indeed a consideration in Trump's strategy, as the race for supremacy in 5G, AI, and enhanced cyber technology heats up. The stakes are extremely high in that regard.

At its outset, from the Chinese perspective, the US was perceived as aggressive and offensive in the trade war, while China was seen as reactive, defensive, and reciprocal. Based on this, it would appear that Beijing wanted to avoid the Thucydides Trap. Similarly, there was no reason to believe that Trump desired military conflict with China. On the contrary, both countries' leadership realized what was at stake, and neither ultimately desired to derail the mutually beneficial economic relationship that buttresses the foundation of their economies.

In postwar history, there have been many opportunities for both countries to escalate tension and trigger military conflict. Beijing and Washington have always understood that this is a line neither should cross, and there is every reason to presume that neither desires to cross that line in the future. It is ultimately the degree of economic pain both countries can endure, and the length of time it can be endured, that determines the economic outcome of such trade conflicts. Mutual respect and benefit is the long-term objective. What is unknown is how long it will take to arrive at an equilibrium and at what cost for both countries.[50]

Time may be on China's side, however, for its economy was growing at more than twice the rate of the US before the outbreak of COVID-19 and has been significantly outpacing the growth of America's 'mature' economy for decades. As Beijing continues to pour massive amounts of money into advanced technologies such as AI, quantum computing, and biotechnology, the US government and many other governments are only starting to lace up their shoes and determine a course of action. Many of the new norms governing how the world's leading nations will behave in the future are only just being established.

Do America and China have any real hope of achieving a genuinely peaceful and possibly collaborative existence in the decades to come? To accomplish that, both nations must believe that they are sufficiently strong – militarily, economically, and politically – to *want* to strive toward achieving such objectives. Clearly, Washington has ramped up its game against China and raised the ante for Beijing. Given the inherent inequity in the two nations' trading relationship, and Beijing's ongoing insistence on continuing with its theft of IP and high level cyberattacks, it is up to Xi to *demonstrate* that China is willing to modify its behavior. Many in the US government will believe that when they see it.

Clearly, the Chinese government's response to the initial outbreak of COVID-19 at the beginning of 2020, its subsequent non-transparent reporting of levels of infection and death, its opportunistic military actions in the South China Sea, and its attempts to broaden the reach of its soft power as the pandemic raged throughout the globe, indicated to America and the world that not much had changed since the outbreak of SARS in 2002, in terms of how China would communicate and engage with the rest of the world. There is certainly no reason to believe that, the next time a viral outbreak originates and spreads from China (and there will be a next time, if history is any guide), the government's response will be any different. If anything, COVID-19 served to remind the world that China has repeatedly been the source of viral outbreaks and that, each time, it had been handled poorly by the Chinese government.

While the American government's response left a lot to be desired, and it was clearly deficient in a range of areas, at least the American media did a superlative job of ensuring that the government was transparent – warts and all. The Trump administration's bungled response was laid out for all to see, and Trump could not resist ensuring that he was the face of that response. That is admired by most of the world's people, many of whom have never known a free media or transparent communication from their government. It will remain a reminder, especially to the Chinese people, about the findings of that Pew poll referenced in Chapter One, which stated that most of the world's people do not want to live under a government inspired by China.

The Chinese government has broken its social contract with the Chinese people: It failed to keep them, or the nation, safe. Will COVID-19 prove to be the catalyst that leads to a tipping point between the government and its people, leading to a popular uprising and the overthrow of the CCP? While that is doubtful, it is worth remembering that just 6% of the Chinese people belong to the CCP,[51] the remaining 94% are tacit accomplices by virtue of their complicity and acquiescence to the Party and the government. That is something that is often forgotten in the narrative.

COVID-19 was disruptive of world order in virtually every way, but it failed to disrupt the well-worn pattern that has been established between America and China for nearly 50 years. With bilateral relations never having been at such a low point since the 1960s, the virus only served to ensure that frothy relations would endure for many years to come. Since Xi is in power for life, and because he re-established iron-fisted authoritarian rule in China, the only way the dynamics of Sino-American relations may change in the coming one to two decades is if an American president other than Trump is elected *and* there is consensus among the establishment in Washington that engagement may, once again, be a desired path. We may be waiting a very long time to see that.

Chapter 9: Conclusion

<u>The BRI is losing its appeal</u>

A good way to measure China's appeal to the rest of the world is to gauge the success of the BRI. As of September 2019, Beijing had signed more than 190 cooperation documents with more than 160 countries and international organizations in support of the BRI. Its cumulative investment in BRI countries had already exceeded US$100 billion, with the value of construction projects alone being valued at a staggering $720 billion. Yet, the Initiative had already begun to slow down by 2018. Beijing's overseas lending began to flatten out and the number of new overseas construction projects had notably declined. The total value of new projects spread across 61 countries had fallen 13% (to US$126 billion) in 2018 compared with the previous year, and another 7% through August 2019 (when existing contracts had also dropped another 4% for the period). In the first half of 2019, China's investment and construction activity around the world plunged by more than 50% compared with the first half of 2018; new projects had also declined precipitously.

This was due, in part, to a decline in the amount of Chinese funds available to invest in other countries. Chinese state banks had become more cautious about lending, following the commencement of the trade war with the US. Chinese SOEs were still moving car and steel capacity overseas and building new motorways and cement plants in developing economies, but on a much smaller scale compared to their 2016 investment peak. In addition, some of the Initiative's member countries (such as Myanmar, Sierra Leone, and Tanzania) became hesitant to continue borrowing large sums of money for fear of falling into the debt trap.

It seems that Beijing had also become more attuned to the flip side of debt trap diplomacy: not being paid back. The fear of balance of payments not being aligned, combined with exchange rate weakness as a result of the trade war with the US, caused a rationing of the hard currency used to make investments and finance construction. Beijing had at last come to realize that some BRI projects had led to excessive levels of debt for developing countries. Although Xi had pledged to improve project sustainability, the crucial issue became how this enhanced "sensitivity" would be implemented in practice,[1] and the impact this would have on Chinese SOEs, many of which had come to attribute much of their profitability to the BRI.

Rather than expand China's soft power, as originally intended when the Initiative was launched in 2013, the BRI appeared to be achieving the opposite in many of the countries in which it was supposed to have the greatest impact. Malaysia's presidential election in 2018 crystallized the concerns that had been building within BRI client countries about the expansion of Chinese power. Following Mahathir Mohamad's reelection as president, he criticized outgoing president Razak for having approved expensive BRI infrastructure projects that required borrowing large sums from China, which Razak had actually used to create the illusion of development, as he and his associates plundered state coffers. Upon taking office, Mohamad cancelled two of the largest Chinese projects in Malaysia – a $20 billion railroad and a $2.3 billion natural gas pipeline, citing Putrajaya's inability to pay. These were eventually reinstated, years later, on more suitable terms for Putrajaya.

The backlash was not limited to Malaysia. Pakistan received an estimated $62 billion in Chinese lending to finance large infrastructure projects – including highways, rail infrastructure, and the port at Gwadar. Islamabad's growing inability to service its international debt – which had grown considerably as a result of the receipt of Chinese loans – prompted anti-BRI sentiment in the country. Pakistan subsequently re-entered negotiations with the IMF to arrange for yet another in what had been a series of bailouts. Other countries that got into serious trouble include Kenya, the Maldives, Sri Lanka, Uganda, and Zambia. These countries must now worry not only about the costs associated with having agreed to accept BRI projects under sometimes onerous Chinese terms but about the sustainability of their debt loads and their ability to continue borrowing in international markets. Host governments are now more carefully scrutinizing BRI projects and their associated costs.

Many Chinese are also asking why the massive funds that are being devoted to the Initiative are not instead being used to address domestic issues, such as education, health care, and housing. Others in China see the BRI as positioning the country to become a global hegemon[2] – in essence, putting it into the same category as former colonial powers, and opening Beijing up to the same type of criticism it has itself leveled against the US and West. Beijing is being criticized by the very same countries that were supposed to be praising China for promoting development via BRI projects. It has learned that, just as the world no longer simply stands at attention when the US snaps its fingers, it also cannot simply dictate the terms of engagement for bilateral relations or cross-border trade and investment.

Balance of power

That said, the Chinese people are understandably proud of what their nation has achieved – and they should be – having risen from relative poverty to become a global superpower in the space of just two generations. The CCP has, rightfully, taken credit for the radical transformation of the Chinese economy and the country's many noteworthy achievements. China's spectacular economic power relative to the US surpasses the former Soviet Union's relative power by a factor of two or three. But its relative strength in military and strategic terms is harder to gauge. The US has tremendous military advantages over China, with more than 20 times as many nuclear warheads, a far superior air force, and a defense budget at least three times as high as China's.[3] It also has allies (such as Australia, Japan, and South Korea) and prospective allies (like India and Vietnam) in Asia that have substantial military capabilities of their own. China has no equivalent in Asia, or in the Western Hemisphere.

Yet, the balance of power in East Asia has clearly shifted in China's favor over the past decade. China has enough ground-based ballistic missiles, aircraft, and ships to have military superiority in its neighborhood, and its missile force is formidable enough that US air bases and aircraft carriers in the Pacific can no longer claim supremacy in the region. Beijing has the potential to surpass the US militarily in several decades, if it were to continue to devote as many financial and other resources to that task for a sustained period. China is likely to become more of a military match for the US than the former Soviet Union had ever become. While Washington ultimately buried Moscow by devoting greater and greater resources to building its military might, which Moscow could not match, that will not happen in this case, and Washington knows it.

In much the same way, Washington used to be able to brush Moscow off by noting the inherent contradictions of its ways and reveling in its belief that capitalism would inevitably trump communism. But China's version of socialism (with Chinese characteristics) is far superior to the hard-core Leninism that the Soviet Union pursued, and the CCP has been smart enough to pivot when necessary to adjust to new economic and political realities. Few would have guessed that Xi would become the strongest leader since Mao, or that nationalism would be deployed as effectively under Xi as it was under Mao to support the CCP and its objectives. Similarly, the US is using nationalism to whip up anti-Chinese sentiment, as if to prepare the American people for a long battle, though most Americans do not see it in anything other than economic terms.

The truth is that the trade war – and competition in the political, military, and technological spheres – are evidence of a potentially, even likely, permanent state of American-Sino relations. There is little reason to conclude that the gridlock that has come to characterize bilateral relations in the Trump-Xi era will either change or end any time soon. Comprehensive rivalry between the two nations has become an organizing principle of both nations' political, economic, and security policies. As a result, there has been a coalescence of opinion in Washington about the necessity of putting an end to what is seen as China's predatory commercial, industrial, and technological strategy, and its comprehensive approach to spying at all levels of American society.

It was never realistic to have imagined that China would have become the democratic, liberal, open political system that many Americans, and people from around the world, would have liked to imagine it would eventually become, but its failure to do so has made it easy for politicians of diverse persuasions to coalesce around the idea that China will never change, it is an enemy, and it must be contained and/or defeated. The problem, of course, is that, under Trump, there is even less likelihood that China will ever be "contained" because America cannot do so on its own. As was the case with the Soviet Union, it needed many allies to join together for a common purpose; America's allies are less inclined to join it in such joint ventures for as long as Trump is in power and American foreign policy remains rudderless and prone to erratic and unpredictable change.

In addition, America's win-at-all-costs approach for political, economic, foreign, military, and technology policy is obviously unsustainable and unattainable, when faced with such a formidable adversary. Trump's approach has seriously undermined US leadership, and not to America's advantage. A more accommodating, moderate approach to policy is appropriate and welcome. This does not imply that Washington should "cave" in areas of core focus and importance, but rather, when it sees a genuine opportunity to reach across the Pacific where there is alignment – such as on environmental policy – it should do so, to build a foundation for future cooperation and collaboration.

China is acting exactly as one would expect a rising global power to act, and not too differently than America did when it became a superpower: strengthening its position, spreading its influence, and building its military power. Instead of taking offense, America should be doubling down on its own ability to do the same. Many in the US Congress are acting as if China's rise was a personal challenge to their own sense of self-worth – as if, rather than two nations acting on a global stage, this was two children jockeying for position on the playground and refusing to play together in the sand box.

The thing is, China has already mastered how to play chess on the Western chess board. If America and the West aren't careful, Beijing will soon seize the advantage. It has already proven it can beat the West at portions of its own game. What if it became strong enough to not only master the rest, but to impose its own game on the rest of the world? Who would stop it from doing so? As America continues down its isolationist path – established under Obama and perfected by Trump –

what are its prospects for turning the situation around as China continues down its path of multilateralism? Not good.

It is ultimately in America's, and the world's, interest to pursue a path of genuine collaboration where it can and engage in full throttled competition where it must. America should abandon its unrealistic expectations that China will change anything about itself or its approach to engagement with the world. From the Chinese perspective, what it is doing has worked quite well. After all, China's capacity to adapt, evolve, and reinvent itself has already made it the second most important country in the world.

Americans are from Mars, the Chinese are from Venus

At the heart of the America-China divide are differences between the two nations' cultures. Culture shapes every nation's orientation to the rest of the world and the differences between American and Chinese cultures are stark. The fact that the two nations have such different cultures helps to partially explain why both governments have chosen the combative path they are on, and how they approach international relations, cross-border investment, strategic planning, and a whole host of other topics. Both nations benefit from, and create, their own distinct set of challenges, as a result of their cultures. The implications for the world are similarly stark, for choosing to be allied with one nation or the other implies the imposition of a range of obstacles in terms of accomplishing a given set of objectives.

Americans put strong emphasis on individuality and autonomy, so personal goals and motives take precedence over collective objectives. This is part of the reason why individuals are encouraged to be ambitious and helps to create their drive to succeed. Being different and wanting to make a difference are net results. The Chinese tend to base their actions more on how they will be perceived by those around them, considering how their decisions may affect their family, friends, and colleagues. For the Chinese, decisions are commonly made with the greater good in mind, as opposed to personal gain.

Americans are very direct in their manner of speaking, which can create a lot of misunderstanding or hurt feelings among Chinese people. In the US, people are encouraged to speak freely and defend their ideas. This can lead to a debate or confrontation. In response, many Chinese will nod in agreement to be polite, so as to respect and honor others' opinions. Chinese people prefer more subtle, indirect ways of expressing their thoughts and opinions. In China, individuals tend to show humility when discussing their successes. They may wish to avoid discussing their successes at all, so as to avoid humiliating others in the process. Self-promotion is generally frowned upon. By contrast, in the US, bragging is not only widely accepted, but constitutes the norm. Humility may be thought of as a weakness rather than a virtue.

The Chinese put strong emphasis on building social networks, believing in the value of building relationships ("guanxi"). They emphasize guanxi when conducting business by socializing with customers before becoming business partners. Americans value speed and efficiency in business; social interactions with business partners often occur after a relationship is established and tend to be more casual. In America, personal and professional lives are usually considered to be separate. Apart from more formal office-sponsored events, most Americans do not socialize with each other at work. In China (and elsewhere in Asia), employees are expected to have personal relationships with those they work with, fostering trust.

The Chinese tend to take things personally and have long memories for both favors and humiliations; they hate losing face and never want to be perceived as a fool or lacking self-control. This is the reason the Chinese do not usually express how they feel and keep their opinions to themselves. Americans generally express their thoughts freely, do not mind making mistakes, and consider doing so to be part of the learning process. In China, hierarchy is what dictates authority – in the family or the workplace. Those in lower ranks at work accept their place in the hierarchy and are expected to listen to instructions and obey without question. Americans have much greater fluidity at home and at work. Decisions are often made together, and it is not uncommon for managers and employees to have heated debates before arriving at a final outcome.[4]

Chinese negotiations are process-oriented; decisions require careful review and consideration and may take a long time to evolve. High-pressure tactics do not work in attempting to speed up the process. Decisions are unlikely to be made during meetings. The Chinese are shrewd negotiators, so do not expect to hit a home run on your first try – or necessarily ever. Like most things in China, business management is based upon the teachings of Confucianism, which denotes that no relationship is underpinned by equality; hierarchy rules and the most senior person in the company is viewed like a father who should be treated with unquestioned loyalty and obedience.[5] The Chinese believe that the West's ignorance of this principle of hierarchy has led to its moral degradation and increasing focus on the individual.

Taken in totality, the two countries' cultures could not be more diametrically opposed to each other's frame of reference. This is part of the reason why so little progress was made in arriving at a quick resolution to their trade war. Add in nationalism, large egos, stubbornness, being dug into a corner, and the notion of saving face, and one would be forgiven for wondering whether there can ever truly be a comprehensive, lasting solution to the trade war.

Take away the rhetoric and flag waving, and what is clear is that the trade war is imperiling both the American and Chinese economies, posing a threat to the international trading system, increasing the chances of a global recession, and making it a near certainty that their bilateral competition will continue for decades to come. The US is in the process of abandoning its 40-year policy of strategic engagement with Beijing and has embraced a yet-to-be-defined concept of strategic competition. It took decades to define what the previous period of strategic collaboration was really all about and it will take some years to truly understand all the moving parts associated with this era of strategic competition.

Weaponizing globalization

Some parts of it are already clear, however. The trade war is not really about Huawei or soybeans; rather, it is about owning the future and trying to find a way to cripple the other side's comparative advantages. It is, in some respects, an interminable game of chicken with the highest possible stakes. To better understand the point, consider the conflict over Huawei, which has relatively little to do with Trump's obsession with America's terms of trade. The American government was trying to stifle Huawei's rise as a global telecommunications giant long before Trump became America's president. It has more to do with intelligence, security, and globalization.

The American government sees companies such as Huawei, with its obscure ownership structure and ambitions for global dominance, as a threat to US national interests and an effort to dominate the global communications networks it has itself dominated for decades. In short, a battle that has been going on for decades to dominate the communication networks that are shaping the global economy has finally broken out into the open. Logistics and communication networks have transformed national manufacturing systems into vast global supply chains, radically altering how products are made and conveyed to customers. The result is that most national economies are profoundly interdependent with one other; businesses in one country rely on businesses in other countries to produce their basic components.

While these networks offer vast economic efficiencies, they can also create enormous vulnerabilities. The patterns of information and money flows, and the manner in which manufacturing is organized, mean that the networks are organized around central nodes. Payment systems and Internet providers channel massive amounts of data through a tiny number of companies. The nations that control these companies have the potential to control entire networks. *The great business networks of globalization, which support the foundations of our interconnected and interdependent world, are increasingly being weaponized by states for strategic purposes.* Powerful governments can deny other states (or actors) access to the networks that make globalization work. So, the US fears that Huawei will turn the global telecommunications system into a vast machinery of surveillance, which will compete with America's own systems and surveillance capabilities.

5G networks will connect the Internet of Things, where everything from industrial robots to smart appliances to pacemakers will have embedded interconnected mobile computers, cameras, and microphones, providing the institutions that control them to monitor everything we do every minute of the day.[6] The US security establishment fears that Beijing may ultimately develop superior monitoring capabilities over the majority of the world's people, businesses, and governments. *Every government, business, and person that agrees to use Huawei products is giving Beijing a green light to monitor everything they do – but most may not even realize it.* The same is true vis-à-vis the US, of course, but given a choice, many will prefer that America does the snooping.

The Huawei case signals *a new type of conflict in which global networks are the battlefield and global companies are strategic assets that may be deployed or destroyed*. Some aspects of the globalization process are being turned into powerful tools of coercion and surveillance, used, in part, to gain advantage over other nations and businesses. The terrain is vastly complex and constantly in a state of flux. The rules of engagement, if there are any, are currently being determined, which is one big reason why neither the US nor China have been in a rush to get to the negotiating table. They both want to try to preserve their positions before being put in a position of having to give anything up.

Both America and China *could* survive just fine if the trade conflict were to last for many more years, or in perpetuity, for that matter. They are already busy finding alternative manufacturing sources, suppliers, buyers. By the time the conflict is resolved, there will be less to talk about. Perhaps that is what China is betting on. Beijing has already said it has no intention of changing anything fundamental about how it functions, and who could blame the Chinese for having that position? If the roles were reversed, the US would surely say exactly the same thing. What incredible chutzpah Washington had for suggesting that in the first place. Doing so did not exactly create an enabling environment for meaningful conversations.

China and the world

For the past two decades, China's leaders have viewed the global landscape as yielding unprecedented strategic opportunity. The relative peace and stability that the world has enjoyed (with a few exceptions, of course) has meant that the CCP has been able to pursue its domestic and international agendas without too much risk of being interrupted. That has afforded it the ability to usher in an era of incredible prosperity, creating goodwill among the Chinese people and spreading its soft power throughout the world in the process. Globalization's continuation will support and enhance China's enduring modernization agenda. In this G-zero, multipolar world, Beijing's influence can only continue to grow, as America's political and diplomatic dysfunction continues unabated.

Xi has pursued a complex strategy of confrontation and accommodation internationally. Having expropriated the Spratly and Paracel Islands, sparred with Japan over the Senkaku Islands, and challenged any number of its Asian neighbors over oil, gas, and fishing rights, Beijing has not hesitated to flex its regional muscles. By establishing the BRI and strengthening its partnership with Russia, Beijing has created stability on its periphery while creating a foundation for permanently confronting the US from a geostrategic perspective. Beijing is running circles around the US in Africa and has established strong bilateral relations with most of the Middle East's governments. It has been proactive at the UN and among the world's MDBs, putting itself in a position to heavily influence the dialectic inside these institutions. And the AIIB and New Development Bank are poised to have real impact as they increase their lending levels, particularly in the infrastructure sector of developing countries.

Chinese strategic planners excel at separating the short-term from the long-term, the trivial from the important, and the tactical from the strategic.[7] The CCP's five-year plans have demonstrated a well-worn ability to peer into the future, identify trends, anticipate needs, and allocate resources where they are needed the most. Of course, Chinese planners had no way of anticipating the disruption that would follow Trump's election and the commencement of the trade war with America. It forced the CCP to inwardly reflect, as well as modify its strategic planning sooner than had been anticipated. In the next five-year plan, the CCP will undoubtedly chart a course that views America as a permanent enemy and self-reliance as an even greater necessity.

Domestically, the CCP has doubled down on its historical conservatism by seeking to crush dissent and implement the social credit system. The exception has been in Hong Kong, where Beijing has shown uncharacteristic restraint, knowing, undoubtedly, that if it were to have steamrolled the protesters in 2019, that would have meant the end of Hong Kong as the world has known it. Xi gets high marks for having the wisdom not to overreact and do what most people expected him to do in response. That also enabled Hong Kong's citizens to blow off some steam while giving the Hong Kong government to identify the biggest troublemakers, for future reference. It illustrated that the CCP and Xi do not necessarily implement one-size-fits-all solutions to the many challenges that plague the country. Only time will tell whether Xi has the wisdom and patience not to crack down on future protests in Hong Kong. If this had occurred anywhere else in China, he certainly would have.

Likewise, as has been discussed, Xi and the CCP deserve credit for modifying the country's approach to the environment and shifting course in some aspects of the foreign investment associated with the BRI, especially in Africa. China still has a long way to go before it can say that the days of debt trap diplomacy have ended, but it is reasonable to expect that its worst excesses are probably done. Fortunately for Beijing, it discovered relatively early on in the process that successful FDI sometimes requires more nuance, subtlety, and ethics than jackhammers or sledgehammers.

Beijing had been brazen in the manner in which it treated global investors in China and many of those investors were hard-headed and greedy enough to stay there, despite the many restrictions and outrages placed upon them. Likewise, no one forced natural resource companies, or their home nations to become so dependent upon Chinese consumption. When times were good, that worked fine, but when the Chinese economy faltered, they paid the price. The Chinese middle class has indeed risen to the occasion and helped support everything from foreign cars and films to fast food and luxury items. The lure of 1.4 billion consumers is compelling to companies from around the world, but greed has gotten the better of many of them, falling prey to dishonest joint venture partners, corrupt suppliers, or a rigged judicial system.

As for China and America, this was a fight that was a long time in the making, and it took two to tango. As was noted earlier, Trump turned out to be the messenger, but the message finally had to be delivered because previous American presidents had failed to do so. Many Americans are glad he did so, despite the pain implied as a result on both sides of the Pacific. However, it is clear that Trump not only wanted to level the playing field on trade, but reverse decades of cooperation for mutual benefit with China.

He viewed the world in stark black and white terms: America was good and China was bad. Of course, there is plenty of nuance in any bilateral relationship, but when faced with an adversary (China, in this case) that had blatantly taken advantage of the trade and investment ecosystem created by America and the West, repeatedly violated the rules that underpinned that system, and repeatedly stolen IP, that demonstrated to Trump not just ill will but a government that would stop at nothing to get what it wanted.

China brought the trade war and deterioration of bilateral relations on itself by its decades of actions in that regard, but America brought the disruption, chaos, and erratic behavior of Trump on itself and the rest of the world by electing him. Many Americans may disagree on whether they like or hate Trump, but, also as previously noted, there is broad consensus about how they feel about China. That cuts across party lines. Most Americans remain willing to endure more pain as a direct result of the trade war, because they know that doing so is the only way to ultimately change China's behavior.

The price that the world has paid for the trade war is largely incalculable, but it is worth noting that in the absence of the trade war, much of the world would likely have remained oblivious to China's tactics in the trade and investment arena until they actually experienced it for themselves. In that regard, Trump and America have done the world a service by waging the trade war, because they now know in advance what to expect and that it is within their power to refuse to accept China's terms of trade and investment. Beijing is also now more attuned to the importance of crafting transactions that are fair and meet the needs of all parties – not just China's.

Is China the right country to lead the world?

In gatherings of the world's leaders, President Xi has become accustomed to casting himself and China as natural heirs to lead the global system, but is a country that regularly violates global norms, standards, and laws really the right country to lead the world? At Xi's Davos speech in 2017,[8] he spoke of economic globalization but made no mention of the political, security, cultural, or normative aspects of globalization. He argued that China's rich history and current success qualified it to lead the trade and investment regimes that have enabled its rise but made no argument about why else it might be qualified to lead. He made no mention of China's ability or inclination to uphold established values or institutions that advance the rule of law, the free flow of information, representative government, or the social, cultural, and political pluralism that are as representative of the global system.

Xi was proposing to lead a global economic system whose principles China frequently violates with high tariffs, non-tariff barriers, a semi-closed economy, state-owned enterprises, and a willingness to use trade to punish partners for political sins, whether by banning banana imports from the Philippines or rare earth minerals to Japan. While Beijing has clearly made progress, it remains a long way from establishing the type of track record of good governance that would otherwise warrant claiming to be the natural heir of the global system. That is, until and unless it were to create an alternative global system in its own image that was accepted and utilized by the majority of the world, as the existing system is.

Xi Jinping Thought, also unveiled in 2017, consists of 14 points that summarize Xi's basic governing philosophy. It has now become required reading in Chinese schools and is representative of China's world view. They are:

1. Ensuring Party leadership over all work;

2. Committing to a people-centered approach;

3. Continuing to comprehensively deepen reform;

4. Adopting a new vision for development;

5. Seeing that the people run the country;

6. Ensuring every dimension of governance is law-based;

7. Upholding core socialist values;

8. Ensuring and improving living standards through development;

9. Ensuring harmony between humans and nature;

10. Pursuing a holistic approach to national security;

11. Upholding absolute Party leadership over the people's forces;

12. Upholding the principle of "one country, two systems" and promoting national reunification;

13. Promoting the building of a community with a shared future for mankind; and

14. Exercising full and rigorous governance over the Party.[9]

While Xi Jinping Thought touches on such topics as reform, development, the environment, and rule of law, the perpetuity of the CCP and omnipotence of China are the common underlying themes. There is no Xi Jinping Thought addressing specific global policies or the future of humanity. In fact, there are very few global challenges for which Xi has proposed his own (or China's) solutions. Rather, he (and the Chinese government) are more in the habit of signing on to initiatives that other individuals, countries, or institutions have advanced. The most noteworthy exceptions to this are the BRI and the AIIB. One can argue whether the BRI is more in China's interest or that of the rest of the world, or whether the creation of the AIIB was intended to compete with the MDBs and advance China's interests or altruistically pick up some of the slack left over by the MDBs to address the shortage of infrastructure finance capabilities within the existing system.

Xi tends to speak in platitudes at global forums, not really providing much original thought, but wanting to portray himself as wise in the process. For example, in his Davos speech, he said: "It is war, conflict, and regional turbulence that have created the refugee crisis, and its solution lies in making peace, promoting reconciliation, and restoring stability."[10] Armed with that and $5, you can head to Starbucks and buy yourself a cup of coffee. *If China wants to claim the mantle of leadership it believes it should have, it can start by making some meaningful proposals to tackle the world's most pressing problems and demonstrate that it can gain the backing of the world's leading nations to implement it.*

A 2018 report by the Clingendael Institute[11] examined case studies of Chinese leadership in human rights, development finance, and climate change. The report concluded that Chinese interests clash with those of European countries vis-à-vis the relationship between human rights and sustainable development as objectives that the UN wishes to pursue. While most European governments regard human rights (including political and civil human rights) as unconditional, China approaches human rights as conditional based on a given country's level of development. The report concluded that the UN Human Rights Council is where this contrast in interests was most visible, and it validated how the Chinese government uses UN bodies to internationalize and legitimize its own domestic interests, as well as its economic approach to development. It did so most notably by using the UN to showcase public recognition for the BRI.

Apart from publicly espousing the value of economic growth for its citizens, the Chinese government supports few other values that the world's democracies want to emulate. In reality, it has no more civilizational influence than most of the rest of the world in terms of national values, ideas, or practical solutions to the world's most intractable problems. *Much of the rest of the world not only does not trust the Chinese government but does not want to be like it*. It is almost as if the ability of the Chinese government to say that it does not wish to invade other countries is supposed to be a lottery ticket that allows it to claim moral authority over the rest of the world.

Unfortunately for Xi, he cannot change the fact that the international stage on which he wants China to play a central role already hosts actors steeped in skepticism, irony, irreverence, logic, common sense, debate, and the critical interplay of ideas, all of which are forbidden in Chinese public discourse. This is directly contrary to the CCP's concern that liberalization at home may create instability and jeopardize its rule. *How can a ruling body afraid of its own shadow possibly expect that the rest of the world would be interested in emulating its governing style, or believe that it is itself prepared to assume a leadership role in a world seeking to embrace debate, rather than make it illegal?*

That is a quality the US possesses in great quantity. *Say what you will about the slippery slope the US government has been on since Trump came to power, it has a rich history of promoting creative thought, running head-first into particularly uncomfortable subjects, and encouraging robust debate internally and among its allies and partners.* The world's nations know that Trump, and what he stands for, has a limited shelf life. Once he leaves the scene, America is sure to be perceived as having briefly lost its senses and will come charging back into the mainstream of global thought and debate. *China has entered the arena crippled by its own ideology*, but with a clear sense of its interests, capabilities, and strategy.[12] Ultimately, the US is better equipped to lead the world. It knows that, and so does much of the rest of the world. Someone had better tell China.

<u>Will the future be a transaction-driven landscape</u>?

English remains the world's predominant language, the US is (for now) the world's largest economy, the dollar is its reserve currency, Google is the world's primary search engine, and Facebook is the largest social media platform. But in 30 years, Beijing's ability to project its soft and hard power will be greatly enhanced. This decade, China will become the world's largest economy and parents around the world will ensure that their children speak Mandarin (if they do not already). Once the Chinese government makes the yuan fully convertible, it could well become the world's reserve currency. Given the growth in the number Chinese speakers, it could well be Baidu that becomes the world's predominant search engine and Weibo that supplants Facebook. The growth in the Chinese middle class, already larger than the US, will help ensure that China weans itself of overdependence on exports to sustain growth and becomes increasingly self-reliant for economic development.

If Xi has his way, it will be China that becomes the world's center of gravity just a decade from now. The coming Chinese world order is likely to be devoid of the kinds of checks and balances we have taken for granted in the postwar system. Rather, *it is more likely to be akin to a transaction-driven landscape where the strongest party rules, and the weak are considered collateral damage.* This transformation has already begun, and as it is occurring, the US and many other countries are essentially asleep at the wheel. As domestic crisis upon crisis piles up, the world's leading Western economies continue to turn their attention inward, preoccupied with political and economic issues at home and functioning with unipolar blinders on. Many of the world's leaders fail to see all that Beijing is doing or appreciate the implications for the future.

Not since the modern liberal order was born in the 1940s has the world had to grapple with the possibility of its demise. Just at a time when the world is in need of the stability and good governance it has had the luxury of relying upon for decades, it must contemplate transitioning to a world order not of the West's choosing. Clearly, the era of US hegemony is coming to an end. Will the global institutions it was so instrumental in creating become less relevant and influential with time? Will Beijing be successful in crafting new institutions derived from a Chinese footprint? If so, will good governance and rule of law be consistent with such organizations? Only time will tell, of course.

What is certain is that Beijing's realization of the Chinese century is sure to be infused with precepts and applications that are uniquely Chinese. The world has yet to fully contemplate all that this portends, but Xi wants to achieve a pathway that guarantees the supremacy of China and the CCP throughout this century and beyond. He is likely to do just that, for he has a vision not only for how China reigns supreme in the economic, political, diplomatic, technological and, eventually, military arena, but also how it gets there.

That is certainly more than can be said for the US at this juncture, much less of other Western powers that appear to be sitting on the sidelines as Beijing smashes barrier after barrier for how things are *supposed* get done. Xi deserves credit for having a vision of the future and for acting swiftly and decisively to achieve it-whether in the area of technology (where China is outspending Silicon Valley to achieve AI supremacy), building the world's largest navy by number of ships, landing a probe on the dark side of the moon as evidence of its growing strength in the field of science, or seeking to influence the world's media. China is engaged in a multi-pronged effort to become influential in a wide spectrum of areas of global importance.

Will Beijing's tendency to elbow its way to the front of the line, find a way to get more or less whatever it wants from the world's poorest and weakest nations, and at times ignore the rule of international law yield to a kinder, gentler China in the future that shows evidence of a respect for the established international order and well-worn rules of the road? The current international system did not come about quickly, or by accident. It was established as a result of a deliberate effort to be transparent and inclusive, placing a premium on governance and the rule of law. If China really wants to achieve top-tier rankings in the areas it considers important-and do so in a manner that helps ensure its longevity – it should seek to enhance, rather than supplant, the very world order that has enabled it to rise to become the global power it already is.[13]

Every nation must make a choice

The America-China divide has created a mammoth dilemma for many of the world's nations-should they ally themselves with Washington, with Beijing, or hedge their bets and become allied with both? For some countries, this will be an easy choice to make, having already been allied with one or the other, or being able to easily decipher which is more closely aligned with their own values and objectives, or would be the likeliest to help them reach their long-term goals. For others, ideology will be a central component of the decision-making process. And for the rest, it may boil down to which country will be easiest to work with or is the most likely to come out on top when the dust settles. However, as is almost always the case in attempting to predict the future, few will get it right, and if they do get it right, it won't be for very long.

At issue is not simply the idea of selecting a "winner ", for we are witnessing a fundamental change in how the world works. In the end, this is not about who purchases the most iron ore or builds the best high-speed train in the shortest amount of time. If that were the case, picking a winner would be easy. Rather, this is a race between two nations to control the world-a race in which both nations will achieve a level of success, not in *every* aspect of *everything*, but vis-à-vis the systems based upon which the world functions.

America has reigned supreme for 75 years, having been the world's dominant superpower since 1945, and having either designed, or been instrumental in designing, many elements of the world's postwar economic and political systems. While it seems unlikely that these systems will simply evaporate as China continues its inexorable rise, they are being, and will continue to be, weakened as a result of inertia, inherent contradictions, America's own actions, or those of China. Perhaps some combination of all of them will contribute to a gradual replacement or modification of the organs of multilateral power. Either way, you can be sure that America will be trying to prop them up just as China will be working to either strengthen its own position within the existing system or replace it with one better to its liking.

This race is a marathon, not a sprint. Both America and China *need* the other to continue in the role of primary enemy. Doing so serves a very useful purpose, enabling their leaders to whip up nationalist frenzy at a moment's notice, serving as a rallying point to build up even further their respective militaries, and diverting attention away from domestic problems.

While every dominant power naturally resists falling off, or being pushed off, of its pinnacle, many powers throughout history have thrived without being on top. Since America cannot, and will not, remain the dominant global power indefinitely, its leaders should begin to ponder what happens when China becomes the largest economy, has the biggest military power, and assumes the role of most generous aid donor. That day will eventually come. When it does, what is to say that America *cannot* be a successful number two? Isn't it probable, after all, that being number two should simply serve to make Americans even more competitive, innovative, and entrepreneurial?

One could certainly argue that America and China are holding a gun to each other's heads – and that of a large part of the world for that matter – by engaging in this race. It is, however, a race that neither has "chosen", but rather that has been thrust upon them. Each has the ability to negatively or positively influence each other's economies, and that of every other nation in the world. Yet, both countries seem more intent on "winning" (whatever that means) than in finding mutually acceptable solutions to the plethora of challenges facing each of them, and the world. When they do eventually decide to reach across the Pacific to get serious about arriving at solutions, it will take compromise, creativity, and humility to get there. Both nations possess these qualities in spades. Hopefully, one of them will be thoughtful enough to suggest to the other that they find a way to compromise, lock arms, and start heading in the same direction.

In the absence of that, the world will be forced to endure many more decades of sparring between the two goliaths, with an uncertain outcome. It is reasonable to assume that, at least for the 2020s, unfriendly competition will dominate the landscape, as America grapples with its gradual (in part, self-imposed) decline on the world stage and China continues to gain its footing as a rising power. The Thucydides Trap (wherein the declining power and rising power clash militarily) is not inevitable in this instance, at least in part because of the stakes involved, but also because of the changing nature of warfare. Nor is a scenario wherein both countries decide to become allies. Rather, as previously noted, a period of coopetition is more likely. In short, we should expect more of the same type of bilateral relationship that has emerged during the Trump era to endure-especially since both countries, and the world, have become oddly accustomed to this state of affairs in such a short time.

So, each nation, international business, and set of consumers must inevitably make a choice about whether to maintain or change the nature of their alliances with America and/or China. The choices they make about whether to become allied with Washington or Beijing (or both) will contribute mightily to the ultimate outcome of this race. The two governments will slug it out in the global corridors of power, in the military arena, and their own bilateral competition to achieve cyber and AI supremacy, but the rest will be up to everyone else.

America is likely to regain its international footing after the Trump era ends, which could dramatically change the nature of this race. Based on the cycles of American history, the isolationism that marked the Obama and Trump eras is likely to be replaced by a return to interventionism, or, at a minimum, to active engagement and cooperation with its many allies. Although Beijing is in the process of establishing its own plethora of allies around the world, it will be some time before the depth of its alliances comes close to matching Washington's. But anyone who doubts China's resolve to reassume its position as the world's leading nation is bound to be daunted by the ferocity, and competency, with which it pursues that objective.

Notes

Chapter 1

[1] "China Foreign Exchange Reserves," Summary, *Trading Economics*, https://tradingeconomics.com/china/foreign-exchange-reserves, accessed August 27, 2019.
[2] "United States Foreign Exchange Reserves," Summary, *Trading Economics*, https://tradingeconomics.com/united-states/foreign-exchange-reserves, accessed August 27, 2019.
[3] Richard Wike, Bruce Stokes, Jacob Poushter, Laura Silver, Janell, Fetterolf, and Kat Devlin, "Methodology," *Pew Research Centre*, Global Attitudes & Trends, https://www.pewresearch.org/global/2018/10/01/methodology-u-s-image/, accessed August 30, 2019.
[4] Argentina, Australia, Brazil, Canada, France, Germany, Greece, Hungary, Indonesia, Israel, Italy, Japan, Kenya, Mexico, Netherland, Nigeria, Philippines, Poland, Russia, South Africa, South Korea, Spain, Sweden, Tunisia, UK.
[5] "China GDP Annual Growth Rate," Summary, *Trading Economics*, https://tradingeconomics.com/china/gdp-growth-annual, accessed August 31, 2019.
[6] Daniel Wagner, "China Cannot Have It Both Ways," *Lobelog*, February 5, 2018, https://lobelog.com/china-cannot-have-it-both-ways/, accessed Dec. 9, 2019.
[7] Laura Hillard and Amanda Shendruk, "Funding the United Nations: What Impact do U.S. Contributions have on UN Agencies and Programs?" Council on Foreign Relations, *ForeignAffairs.com*, April 2, 2019, https://cfr.org/article/funding-united-nations-what-impact-do-us-contributions-have-un-agencies-and-programs, accessed August 31, 2019.
[8] Xinhua, "China Rises to 2nd Largest Contributor to UN Budget," *ChinaDaily.com*, http://www.chinadaily.com.cn/a/201812/24/WS5c20a231a3107d4c3a0028c1.html, accessed August 31, 2019.

[9] "Security Council-Veto List," *United Nations Dag Hammarskjold Library,* https://research.un.org/en/docs/sc/quick, accessed August 31, 2019.

[10] "US funding to the United Nations System: Overview and Selected Policy Issues," *Congressional Research Service,* April 25, 2018, https://www.everycrsreport.com/files/20180425_R45206_a4c337a4e66b3487f0088c2c065e8ed25305d097.pdf, accessed September 1, 2019.

[11] United Nations, "Chapter XV: The Secretariat," *Charter of the United Nations,* United Nations, https://www.un.org/en/sections/un-charter/chapter-xv/index.html, accessed September 1, 2019.

[12] "Soviet Presence in the UN Secretariat, Report of the US Senate Select Committee on Intelligence, United States Senate," May 1985, p. 2, https://www.intelligence.senate.gov/sites/default/files/publications/9952.pdf, accessed September 1, 2019.

[13] "CCTV Interview with Wu Hongbo," World Uyghur Congress, *Facebook,* April 25, 2019, https://www.facebook.com/watch/?v=649658305496919, accessed September 1, 2019.

[14] Brett Schaefer, "How the U.S. Should Address Rising Chinese Influence in the United Nations," *The Heritage Foundation,* Aug. 20, 2019, https://www.heritage.org/global-politics/report/how-the-us-should-address-rising-chinese-influence-the-united-nations, accessed September 1, 2019.

[15] Press Release: The South China Sea Arbitration, The Hague, July 12, 2016, https://assets.documentcloud.org/documents/2990864/Press-Release-on-South-China-Sea-Decision.pdf, accessed September 1, 2019.

[16] Susan Ratcliffe, ed., *Oxford Essential Quotations,* 4th ed., Oxford University Press, 2016, https://www.oxfordreference.com/view/10.1093/acref/9780191826719.001.0001/q-oro-ed4-00008130, accessed September 1, 2019.

[17] James Petras, "China: Rise, Fall, and Reemergence as a Global Power: The Lessons of History, *Global Research,* Oct.

10, 2019, https://www.globalresearch.ca/china-rise-fall-and-re-emergence-as-a-global-power-2/29644, accessed September 2, 2019; see also John Hobson, *The Eastern Origins of Western Civilization* (Cambridge University Press, 2004.

[18] Michael McFaul, "China is Winning the Ideological Battle with the US," *The Washington Post*, July 23, 2019, https://www.washingtonpost.com/opinions/2019/07/23/china-is-winning-ideological-battle-with-us/?noredirect=on, accessed September 1, 2019.

[19] Chaorong Wang, "5 Countries that Provide the Largest Foreign Aid," *The Borgen Project*, March 14, 2018, https://borgenproject.org/five-countries-that-give-the-largest-foreign-aid/, accessed September 1, 2019.

[20] United Nations, "How We are Funded," *United Nations Peacekeeping,* https://peacekeeping.un.org/en/how-we-are-funded, accessed September 1, 2019.

[21] Carlos Martinez, "Is China the New Imperialist Force in Africa?," *Invent the Future*, Oct. 8, 2018, https://www.invent-the-future.org/2018/10/is-china-the-new-imperialist-force-in-africa/#fn:43, accessed December 17, 2019.

[22] Ibid.

[23] Mogopodi Lekorwe, Anyway Chingwete, Mina Okuru, and Romaric Samson, "China's Growing Presence in Africa Wins Largely Positive Popular Reviews," *Afrobarometer,* Dispatch No. 122, October 24, 2016, http://afrobarometer.org/sites/default/files/publications/Dispatches/ab_r6_dispatchno122_perceptions_of_china_in_africa1.pdf, accessed December 17, 2019.

[24] Daniel Wagner, "China and Neocolonialism in Africa," *International Policy Digest*, Feb. 18, 2019, https://intpolicydigest.org/2019/02/18/china-and-neocolonialism-in-africa/, accessed December 17, 2019. (See Daniel Wagner, *China Vision*, Kindle Direct Publishing, February 16, 2019, p. 89).

[25] Josh Rogin, "Commentary: Congress Demands Answers on AP's Relationship with Chinese State Media," *The Bulletin,* Dec. 27, 2018, https://www.bendbulletin.com/opinion/commentary-congress-demands-answers-on-ap-s-relationship-with-

chinese/article_7a1f469d-48a1-545b-8d8d-aa534979230c.html, accessed December 17, 2019.

[26] Ryan Woo and Ben Blanchard, "China Aims to 'Optimise' Spread of Controversial Confucius Institutes," February 23, 2019, https://uk.reuters.com/article/uk-china-education/china-aims-to-optimise-spread-of-controversial-confucius-institutes-idUKKCN1QD00X, accessed December 17, 2019.

[27] Rachelle Peterson, "Outsourced to China," *National Association of Scholars*, July 12, 2017, https://www.nas.org/blogs/dicta/outsourced_to_china, accessed December 17, 2019.

[28] Joshua Kurlantzick, "As China Extends Its Reach Abroad, When Does Influence Become Interference?" *World Politics Review,* January 8, 2018, https://www.worldpoliticsreview.com/articles/23935/as-china-extends-its-reach-abroad-when-does-influence-become-interference, accessed December 17, 2019.

[29] The Economist, "How China Could Dominate Science," *The Economist,* Jan. 12, 2019, https://www.economist.com/leaders/2019/01/12/how-china-could-dominate-science, accessed December 17, 2019.

[30] The Economist, "Can China Become a Scientific Superpower?" *The Economist,* Jan. 12, 2019, https://www.economist.com/science-and-technology/2019/01/12/can-china-become-a-scientific-superpower, accessed December 17, 2019.

[31] Daniel Wagner, "China is Waging a Silent Media War for Global Interest," *The National Interest*, September 19, 2019, https://nationalinterest.org/feature/china-waging-silent-media-war-global-influence-81906, accessed September 19, 2019.

Chapter 2

[1] Mark J. Perry, "The Trade War's Winners don't Include Us…," *AEI*, September 5, 2019, http://www.aei.org/publication/the-trade-wars-winners-dont-include-us/, accessed September 7, 2019.

[2] Andrew Lescaleia, "The Winners and Losers of the US-China Trade War," *Atlantic Council*, August 13, 2019, https://www.atlanticcouncil.org/blogs/new-atlanticist/the-

winners-and-losers-of-the-us-china-trade-war, accessed September 7, 2019.

[3] Laura Silver, Kat Devlin, and Christine Huang, "U.S. Views of China Turn Sharply Negative Amid Trade Tensions," *Pew Research Center*, August 13, 2019, https://www.pewresearch.org/global/2019/08/13/u-s-views-of-china-turn-sharply-negative-amid-trade-tensions/, accessed September 5, 2019.

[4] Salvatore Babones, "China's Middle Class is Pulling up the Ladder Behind Itself," *FP*, February 1, 2018, https://foreignpolicy.com/2018/02/01/chinas-middle-class-is-pulling-up-the-ladder-behind-itself/, accessed September 5, 2019.

[5] "Bush: 'You Are Either With Us, Or With The Terrorists' – 2001-09-21," *OA*, October 27, 2009, https://www.voanews.com/archive/bush-you-are-either-us-or-terrorists-2001-09-21, accessed September 5, 2019.

[6] "Record Number of Americans Hold Passports," *VOA*, January 18, 2018, https://blogs.voanews.com/all-about-america/2018/01/18/record-number-of-americans-hold-passports/, accessed September 6, 2019.

[7] "The Ten Most Popular International Vacations by Americans," *World Atlas*, 2019, https://www.worldatlas.com/articles/the-10-most-popular-international-vacations-by-americans.html, accessed September 6, 2019.

[8] Shan Jie, "Record Number of Chinese, US Tourists Visit Each Other's Countries in 2016," *Global Times,* January 11, 2017, http://www.globaltimes.cn/content/1028161.shtml, accessed September 5, 2019.

[9] Gary Stoller, "Mexico: Where More Americans are Murdered than in All Foreign Countries Combined," *Forbes*, February 21, 2018, https://www.forbes.com/sites/garystoller/2018/02/21/mexico-where-more-americans-are-murdered-than-in-all-other-countries-combined/#55f372fcde37, accessed September 5, 2019.

[10] "United States Population," *Worldometers*, https://www.worldometers.info/world-population/us-population/, accessed September 5, 2019.

[11] Matt Schievenza, "How Humiliation Drove Modern Chinese History," *The Atlantic*, October 25, 2013, https://www.theatlantic.com/china/archive/2013/10/how-humiliation-drove-modern-chinese-history/280878/, accessed September 4, 2019.

[12] "The People's Republic of China," *Office of the United States Trade Representative*, https://ustr.gov/countries-regions/china-mongolia-taiwan/peoples-republic-china, accessed September 6, 2019.

[13] Alan Rappaport, "Chinese Money in the U.S. Dries Up as Trade War Drags On," *The New York Times*, July 21, 2019, https://www.nytimes.com/2019/07/21/us/politics/china-investment-trade-war.html, accessed September 6, 2019.

[14] M. Szmigiera "Direct Investment Position of the United States in China from 2000 to 2018," *Statista,* September 2, 2019, https://www.statista.com/statistics/188629/united-states-direct-investments-in-china-since-2000/, accessed September 6, 2019.

[15] Mel Gurtov and Mark Seldon, "The Dangerous New US Consensus on China and the Future of US-China Relations,"*The Asia-Pacific Journal*, August 17, 2019, reprinted on truthout.org, https://truthout.org/articles/the-dangerous-new-us-consensus-on-china-and-the-future-of-us-china-relations/, accessed September 7, 2019.

[16] "Statistics," *Harvard International Office*, http://www.hio.harvard.edu/statistics, accessed September 6, 2019.

[17] Jeffrey A. Bader, "U.S.-China Relations: Is it Time to End the Engagement?" *Brookings*, September 2018, https://www.brookings.edu/research/u-s-china-relations-is-it-time-to-end-the-engagement/, accessed September 6, 2019.

[18] David Himbara, "Trump Administration Cuts Aid to Africa by 35 Percent," *Medium.com*, Oct. 12, 2017, https://medium.com/@david.himbara_27884/trump-administration-cuts-aid-to-africa-by-35-percent-a4276581594e, accessed September 6, 2018.

[19] Anna Fifield, "China Pledges $60 Billion in Aid and Loans to Africa, No 'Political Conditions Attached'," *The Washington Post*, September 3, 2018, https://www.washingtonpost.com/world/china-pledges-60-

billion-in-aid-and-loans-to-africa-no-strings-
attached/2018/09/03/a446af2a-af88-11e8-a810-
4d6b627c3d5d_story.html, accessed September 6, 2019.
[20] "U.S. Imports from Saudi Arabia of Crude Oil and
Petroleum Products," Petroleum & Other Liquids, *U.S Energy
Information Administration*, November 27, 2019,
https://www.eia.gov/dnav/pet/hist/LeafHandler.ashx?n=PET&
s=MTTIMUSSA2&f=M, accessed September 6, 2019.
[21] Paul Ausick, "Why China Imports Much More Saudi Oil
Than the US," *24/7 Wallst,* August 15, 2019,
https://247wallst.com/energy-economy/2019/08/15/why-china-
imports-much-more-saudi-oil-than-the-us/, accessed
September 6, 2019.
[22] World Economic Forum, "Global Competitiveness Index
4.0," The Global Competitiveness Report 2018, *World
Economic Forum,* 2018, http://reports.weforum.org/global-
competitiveness-report-2018/competitiveness-rankings/,
accessed September 7, 2019.
[23] Michael Nacht, Sarah Laderman, and Julie Beeston,
"Strategic Competition in China-U.S Relations," *Cgsr.llnl.gov,*
October, 2018,
https://cgsr.llnl.gov/content/assets/docs/CGSR_livpaper5.pdf,
p. 120, accessed September 7, 2019.
[24] Judah Grunstein, "The U.S. Should base its China Strategy
on Competitive Cooperation, Not Containment," *World Politics
Review,* April 17, 2019,
https://www.worldpoliticsreview.com/articles/27765/the-u-s-
should-base-its-china-strategy-on-competitive-cooperation-
not-containment, accessed September 7, 2019.
[25] Thomas Callender, "Completing the Pivot to Asia," *The
National Interest,* July 7, 2019,
https://nationalinterest.org/feature/completing-pivot-asia-
65526, accessed September 7, 2019.
[26] Daniel Wagner, "China, the US, and Realistic
Expectations," *Lobe Log,* February 25, 2019,
https://lobelog.com/china-the-us-and-realistic-expectations/,
accessed September 7, 2019.

Chapter 3

[1] Daniel Wagner, "In an era of disruption, China is positioning itself as the next foreign policy leader," *south China Morning Post,* May 21, 2019, https://www.scmp.com/comment/insight-opinion/article/3010962/era-disruption-china-positioning-itself-next-foreign-policy, accessed September 10, 2019.

[2] Adam Taylor, "Why US allies aren't rushing to back Trump's China trade war," *Washington Post*, May 14, 2019, https://www.washingtonpost.com/world/2019/05/14/why-us-allies-arent-rushing-back-trumps-china-trade-war/, accessed September 1, 2019.

[3] Daniel Wagner, "China is the net beneficiary of global disruption," *The Business Times,* September 4, 2019, https://www.businesstimes.com.sg/opinion/china-is-the-net-beneficiary-of-global-disruption, accessed September 10, 2019.

[4] Mathew Mcadam, Jonathan Rogers, and Daniel Wagner, "China plays fast catch-up with the global ESG wave," *The Business Times,* August 23, 2019, https://www.businesstimes.com.sg/opinion/china-plays-fast-catch-up-with-the-global-esg-wave, accessed September 11, 2019.

[5] Scott Moore, "China's Belt and Road and the World's Water Resources," *Reconnecting Asia*,February 6, 2019,https://reconnectingasia.csis.org/analysis/entries/blue-belt-and-road/, accessed September 15, 2019.

[6] Scott Moore and Michelle Melton, "China's Pivot on Climate Change and National Security," *Lawfareblog,* April 2, 2019, https://www.lawfareblog.com/chinas-pivot-climate-change-and-national-security, accessed September 15, 2019.

[7] "What Are Rare Earths?" *Rare Earth Technology Alliance,* http://www.rareearthtechalliance.com/What-are-Rare-Earths, accessed September 11, 2019.

[8] Daniel Wagner, "China, Rare Earth Minerals, and Nuclear Options," *International Policy Digest,* May 30, 2019,https://intpolicydigest.org/2019/05/30/china-rare-earth-minerals-and-nuclear-options/, accessed September 11, 2019.

[9] Daniel Wagner, "China and Neocolonialism in Africa," *International Policy Digest,* February 18, 2019,

https://intpolicydigest.org/2019/02/18/china-and-neocolonialism-in-africa/, accessed September 12, 2019.
[10] Daniel Wagner and Dr. Theodore Karasik, "The Maturing Saudi-Chinese Alliance," *Eurasiareview*, April 8, 2010, https://www.eurasiareview.com/08042010-the-maturing-saudi-chinese-alliance/, accessed September 13, 2019.
[11] Daniel Wagner, "China's Rise in the Middle East," *Inside Arabia,*February 23, 2019, https://insidearabia.com/china-rise-middle-east/, accessed September 12, 2019.
[12] Daniel Wagner, "China, the South China Sea, and misplaced national pride," *SundayGuardianLive,* February 23, 2019, https://www.sundayguardianlive.com/opinion/china-south-china-sea-misplaced-national-pride, accessed September 12, 2019.
[13] Daniel Wagner, "Amid China's port buying spree, Europe needs to ensure its own interests are protected too," *SouthChinaMorningPost,* March 28, 2019, https://www.scmp.com/comment/insight-opinion/article/3003642/china-needs-eu-buy-belt-and-road-plan-and-eu-needs-bargain, accessed September 12, 2019.
[14] Daniel Estrin and Emily Feng, "There's A Growing Sore Spot In Israeli-U.S. Relations: China," *npr,* September 11, 2019, https://www.npr.org/2019/09/11/757290503/theres-a-growing-sore-spot-in-israeli-u-s-relations-china accessed September 12, 2019.
[15] Amos Harel, "Israel Is Giving China the Keys to Its Largest Port – and the U.S. Navy May Abandon Israel ," *Haaretz,* September 17, 2018, https://www.haaretz.com/israel-news/.premium-israel-is-giving-china-the-keys-to-its-largest-port-and-the-u-s-navy-may-abandon-israel-1.6470527, accessed September 12, 2019.
[16] Charlie Campbell, "Xi Jinping's Party Congress Speech Leaves No Doubts Over His Leadership Role," *Time,* October 18, 2017,https://time.com/4986999/xi-jinping-china-19th-congress-ccp/, accessed September 14, 2019.
[17] Abraham Denmark, "A New Era of Intensified U.S.-China Competition," *Wilsoncenter,* January 4, 2018, https://www.wilsoncenter.org/blog-post/new-era-intensified-us-china-competition, accessed September 14, 2019.

[18] Daniel R. Coats, "Worldwide Threat Assessment of U.S. Intelligence Community," *dni.gov,* January 29, 2019, https://www.dni.gov/files/ODNI/documents/2019-ATA-SFR---SSCI.pdf, p. 25, accessed September 14, 2019.
[19] Ryan Hass and Mira Rapp-Hopper, "Responsible competition and the future of U.S.-China relations," *Brookings.edu,* February 6, 2019, https://www.brookings.edu/blog/order-from-chaos/2019/02/06/responsible-competition-and-the-future-of-u-s-china-relations/, accessed September 14, 2019.
[20] Paul Heer, "Rethinking U.S. Primacy in East Asia," *The National Interest,* January 8, 2019, https://nationalinterest.org/blog/skeptics/rethinking-us-primacy-east-asia-40972, accessed September 14, 2019.

Chapter 4

[1] Stephen Johnson, "China will overtake the U.S. as world's top economy in 2020, says Standard Chartered Bank ," *BigThink,* January 14, 2019, https://bigthink.com/politics-current-affairs/china-worlds-biggest-economy-2020, accessed September 19, 2019.
[2] Ha Jimming and Adam S. Posen, "US-China Economic Relations: From Conflict to Solutions—Part I," *Peterson Institute For Intanational Economics,* June, 2018, https://www.piie.com/publications/piie-briefings/us-china-economic-relations-conflict-solutions-part-i, pp. 43-52, accessed September 18, 2019.
[3] Gregory Messenger, "The public–private distinction at the World Trade Organization: Fundamental challenges to determining the meaning of "public body"," *International Journal of Constitutional Law,* March 13, 2017, https://academic.oup.com/icon/article/15/1/60/3068317, accessed September 18, 2019.
[4] Ha Jimming and Adam S. Posen, "US-China Economic Relations: From Conflict to Solutions—Part I," *Peterson Institute For Intanational Economics,* June, 2018, https://www.piie.com/publications/piie-briefings/us-china-economic-relations-conflict-solutions-part-i, pp. 22-30, accessed September 18, 2019.

[5] WTO, "Disputes by member," *World Trade Organization,* https://www.wto.org/english/tratop_e/dispu_e/dispu_by_count ry_e.htm, accessed September 18, 2019.

[6] USTR, "2018 USTR Report to Congress on China's WTO Compliance," *United States Trade Representative,* February, 2019, https://ustr.gov/sites/default/files/2018-USTR-Report-to-Congress-on-China%27s-WTO-Compliance.pdf, pp. 2-3, accessed September 18, 2019.

[7] USTR, "2018 USTR Report to Congress on China's WTO Compliance," *United States Trade Representative,* February, 2019, https://ustr.gov/sites/default/files/2018-USTR-Report-to-Congress-on-China%27s-WTO-Compliance.pdf, pp. 2-3, accessed September 18, 2019.

[8] Xinhua, "China's Position on the China-US Economic and Trade Consultations," *English.Gov.Cn,* June 2, 2019, http://english.www.gov.cn/archive/white_paper/2019/06/02/co ntent_281476694892692.htm, accessed September 18, 2019.

[9] Bloomberg Business, "In Full: China's White Paper on US Economic and Trade Talks," *Bloomberg,* June 2, 2019, https://www.bloomberg.com/news/articles/2019-06-03/read-the-full-china-white-paper-on-u-s-economic-and-trade-talks, accessed September 19, 2019.

[10] Martin Wolf, "The Looming 100-Year China-US Conflict," *Financial Times*, June 4, 2019, https://www.ft.com/content/52b71928-85fd-11e9-a028-86cea8523dc2, accessed September 17, 2019.

[11] Associated Press, "Six in 10 Americans hold dim view of China amid trade war, survey shows," *South China Morning Post,* August 14, 2019, https://www.scmp.com/news/china/article/3022671/six-10-americans-hold-dim-view-china-amid-trade-war-survey-shows, accessed September 19, 2019.

[12] Mark Murray, "Support for free trade reaches new high in NBC/WSJ poll," *nbcnews,* August 18, 2019, https://www.nbcnews.com/politics/meet-the-press/support-free-trade-reaches-new-high-nbc-wsj-poll-n1043601, accessed September 19, 2019.

[13] USTR, "The People's Republic of China," *United States Trade Representative*, https://ustr.gov/countries-

regions/china-mongolia-taiwan/peoples-republic-china, accessed September 20, 2019.

[14] Cliff White, "Tariffs changing shopping habits of US consumers ," *Seafoodsource,* August 16, 2019, https://www.seafoodsource.com/news/foodservice-retail/tariffs-changing-shopping-habits-of-us-consumers, accessed September 21, 2019.

[15] Jennifer Pak, "Are consumers in China changing their spending habits? ," *MarketPlace,* January 11, 2019, https://www.marketplace.org/2019/01/11/china-consumers-changing-spending-habits/, accessed September 21, 2019.

[16] Oxford Economics, "Understanding the US-China Trade Relationship," *Oxford Economics,* January, 2017, https://www.uschina.org/sites/default/files/Oxford%20Economics%20US%20Jobs%20and%20China%20Trade%20Report.pdf, accessed September 20, 2019.

[17] Joshua P. Meltzer and Neena Shenai, "The US-China economic relationship: A comprehensive approach," *Brookings,* February, 2019, https://www.brookings.edu/wp-content/uploads/2019/02/us_china_economic_relationship.pdf accessed September 20, 2019.

[18] Beth Ann Bovino, Shaun Roache, and Sylvain Broyer, " The U.S. – China Trade War: The Global Economic Fallout," *S & P Global,* May 22, 2019, https://www.spglobal.com/en/research-insights/articles/the-u-s-china-trade-war-the-global-economic-fallout, accessed September 20, 2019.

[19] Patricia Buckley and Rumki Majumdar, "The services powerhouse: Increasingly vital to world economic growth," *Deloitte,* July, 2018, https://www2.deloitte.com/us/en/insights/economy/issues-by-the-numbers/trade-in-services-economy-growth.html, accessed September 22, 2019.

[20] Tatiana Lacerda Prazeres, "Services are the hidden side of the US-China trade war," *World Economic Forum,* September 20, 2019, https://www.weforum.org/agenda/2019/09/us-china-trade-war-disrupting-services/, accessed September 21, 2019.

[21] Paul Wiseman, "China's investment in US drops 83% amid growing mistrust," *AP News,* May 8, 2019,

https://www.apnews.com/d3009cef73e24479ac53e8ad968eff
cd, accessed September 21, 2019.

[22] Heather Somerville, "Chinese investment in U.S. startups
peaks but 'tremendous uncertainty' ahead," *Reuters:
Thomson Reuters,* May 8, 2019,
https://www.reuters.com/article/us-china-us-venture/chinese-
investment-in-u-s-startups-peaks-but-tremendous-uncertainty-
ahead-idUSKCN1SE0AF, accessed September 21, 2019.

[23] Jamie Wang, Tarik Abdel-Meguid, and Tina Zheng, "New
Law Significantly Expands CFIUS Jurisdiction and Mandates
Declaration to CFIUS for Certain Transactions," *White and
Williams,*September 6, 2018,
https://www.whiteandwilliams.com/resources-alerts-New-Law-
Significantly-Expands-CFIUS-Jurisdiction-and-Mandates-
Declaration-to-CFIUS-for-Certain-Transactions.html,
accessed September 21, 2019

[24] Gordon Orr, "What can we expect in China in 2019?"
McKinsey & Company, December, 2018,
https://www.mckinsey.com/featured-insights/china/what-can-
we-expect-in-china-in-2019, accessed September 21, 2019.

[25] Evelyn Cheng, "China's overseas investment drops in 2017
for the first time on record," *CNBC,* September 28, 2018,
https://www.cnbc.com/2018/09/28/chinas-overseas-
investment-drops-for-the-first-time-on-record.html, accessed
November 10, 2018.

[26] Stephen Goldsmith and Daniel Wagner, "FDI with Chinese
Characteristics," *Huffpost,* May 25, 2011,
https://www.huffingtonpost.com/stephen/fdi-with-chinese-
characte_b_759903.html, accessed November 10, 2018.

[27] Daniel Wagner and Stephen Goldsmith, FDI Intelligence,
October/November 2010, pp. 78-79.

[28] https://www.weforum.org/agenda/2018/02/the-future-global-
order-will-be-managed-by-china-and-the-us-get-used-to-it/,
accessed November 12, 2018.

[29] Bloomberg, "The FIX:The Bloomberg Fixed Income
Exchange," *Bloomberg,*
https://www.bloomberg.com/markets/fixed-income, accessed
September 22, 2019

[30] Eswar Prasad Monday, "Which country is better equipped
to win a US-China trade war?," *Brookings, August 12, 2019,*

https://www.brookings.edu/opinions/which-country-is-better-equipped-to-win-a-us-china-trade-war/, accessed September 22, 2019.
[31] Paul Craig Roberts, "What Globalism Did Was to Transfer the US Economy to China," *Global Research,* August 21, 2019, https://www.globalresearch.ca/globalism-transfer-us-economy-china/5686832, accessed September 22, 2019.

Chapter 5

[1] The China Senior Analyst Group, "A New Great Game – China, the U.S. and Technology," *S&P Global*, 2019, https://www.spglobal.com/en/research-insights/featured/a-new-great-game-china-the-u-s-and-technology, accessed September 23, 2019.
[2] Sumner Lemon, "China gets access to Microsoft source code," *InforWorld,* March 3, 2003, https://www.infoworld.com/article/2681548/china-gets-access-to-microsoft-source-code.html, accessed September 23, 2019.
[3] Daniel Wagner, "China races to reign supreme in Artificial Intelligence," *SundayGuardianLive,* January 26, 2019, https://www.sundayguardianlive.com/world/china-races-reign-supreme-artificial-intelligence, accessed September 23, 2019.
[4] Framingham Mass, "Smartphone Shipments Experience Deeper Decline in Q1 2019 with a Clear Shakeup Among the Market Leaders, According to IDC," *IDC,* April 30, 2019, https://www.idc.com/getdoc.jsp?containerId=prUS45042319, accessed September 26, 2019.
[5] Katharina Buchholz, "Which Countries Have Banned Huawei?," *Statista,* August 19, 2019, https://www.statista.com/chart/17528/countries-which-have-banned-huawei-products/, accessed September 23, 2019.
[6] Daniel Wagner, "Huawei Will Damage American Security and Prosperity," The National Interest, April 4, 2019, https://nationalinterest.org/blog/skeptics/huawei-will-damage-american-security-and-prosperity-50727, accessed September 23, 2019.
[7] "The world's Top Innovators 2009-10," *Global Innovation Index,* 2010,

https://www.globalinnovationindex.org/userfiles/file/GII-2009-2010-Report.pdf, accessed September 24, 2019.

[8] "Rankings," *Global Innovation Index*, 2015, https://www.wipo.int/edocs/pubdocs/en/wipo_pub_gii_2015-intro5.pdf, accessed September 24, 2019.

[9] "Global Innovation Index 2019: India Makes Major Gains as Switzerland, Sweden, U.S., Netherlands, U.K. Top Ranking; Trade Protectionism Poses Risks for Future Innovation," *WIPO,* July 24, 2019, https://www.wipo.int/pressroom/en/articles/2019/article_0008.html, accessed September 24, 2019.

[10] James Andrew Lewis, "Technological Competition and China," *CSIS*, November 30, 2018, https://www.csis.org/analysis/technological-competition-and-china, accessed September 23, 2019.

[11] Geoffrey Garrett, "The "Trade War" is Really About the Future of Innovation," *Wharton Magazine*, https://whartonmagazine.com/blogs/the-trade-war-is-really-about-the-future-of-innovation/, accessed September 24, 2019.

[12] McKinsey & Company, "The China Effect on Global Innovation," *McKinsey Global Institute,* October, 2015, https://www.mckinsey.com/~/media/McKinsey/Featured%20Insights/Innovation/Gauging%20the%20strength%20of%20Chinese%20innovation/MGI%20China%20Effect_Executive%20summary_October_2015.ashx, accessed September 24, 2019.

[13] Jon Cohen, "China's CRISPR push in animals promises better meat, novel therapies, and pig organs for people," *ScienceMag,* July 31, 2019, https://www.sciencemag.org/news/2019/07/china-s-crispr-push-animals-promises-better-meat-novel-therapies-and-pig-organs-people, accessed September 24, 2019.

[14] Joe Palca, "China Expands Research Funding, Luring U.S. Scientists And Students," NPR,November 27, 2018, https://www.npr.org/sections/health-shots/2018/11/27/669645323/china-expands-research-funding-luring-u-s-scientists-and-students, accessed September 25, 2019.

[15] Kathleen McLaughlin, "Science is a major plank in China's new spending plan," *ScienceMag,* March 7, 2016, https://www.sciencemag.org/news/2016/03/science-major-plank-china-s-new-spending-plan, accessed September 25, 2019.

[16] Shelly Fan, "Wait, What? The First Human-Monkey Hybrid Embryo Was Just Created in China," *SingularityHub,* August 13, 2019, https://singularityhub.com/2019/08/13/wait-what-the-first-human-monkey-hybrid-embryo-was-just-created-in-china/, accessed September 25, 2019.

[17] Jon Cohen, "To feed its 1.4 billion, China bets big on genome editing of crops," *ScienceMag,* July 29, 2019, https://www.sciencemag.org/news/2019/07/feed-its-14-billion-china-bets-big-genome-editing-crops, accessed September 25, 2019.

[18] Bloomberg News, "Farming the World: China's Epic Race to Avoid a Food Crisis," *Bloomberg,* May 22, 2017, https://www.bloomberg.com/graphics/2017-feeding-china/, accessed September 25, 2019.

[19] Marc Prosser, "Inside China's Play to Become the World's CRISPR Superpower," *SingularityHub,* August 18, 2019, https://singularityhub.com/2019/08/18/inside-chinas-play-to-become-the-worlds-crispr-superpower/, accessed September 23, 2019.

[20] "China vs USA: who leads the CRISPR race?," *mycrispr.blog,* February 28, 2018, https://mycrispr.blog/2018/02/28/china-vs-usa-who-leads-the-crispr-race/, accessed September 25, 2019.

[21] Daniel R. Coats, "Worldwide Threat Assessment of U.S. Intelligence Community," *dni.gov,* January 29, 2019, https://www.dni.gov/files/ODNI/documents/2019-ATA-SFR---SSCI.pdf, accessed September 25, 2019.

[22] "Statistics," *nsf.gov,* 2019, https://www.nsf.gov/statistics/2019/nsf19321/overview.htm, accessed September 25, 2019.

[23] Niv Elis, "Trump calls for cutting National Science Foundation funding by $1 billion," *TheHill,* March 11, 2019, https://thehill.com/homenews/administration/433507-trump-

proposes-cutting-national-science-foundation-budget-by-billion-dollars, accessed September 25, 2019.

24 Teddy Ng and Jane Cai, "China's funding for science and research to reach 2.5 per cent of GDP in 2019," *South China Morning Post,* March 10, 2019, https://www.scmp.com/news/china/science/article/2189427/chinas-funding-science-and-research-reach-25-cent-gdp-2019, accessed September 25, 2019.

25 Dmitriy Frolovskiy, "China's Education Boom," *The Diplomat*, December 29, 2017, https://thediplomat.com/2017/12/chinas-education-boom/, accessed September 25, 2019.

26 Ezekiel Emanuel, "Amy Gadsden and Scott Moore, How the US Surrendered to China on Scientific Research," *Wall Street Journal*, April 19, 2019, https://www.wsj.com/articles/how-the-u-s-surrendered-to-china-on-scientific-research-11555666200, accessed September 23, 2019.

27 "PISA 2015 Worldwide Ranking – average score of math, science and reading," *FactsMaps,* http://factsmaps.com/pisa-worldwide-ranking-average-score-of-math-science-reading/, accessed September 25, 2019.

28 Ezekiel Emanuel, "Amy Gadsden and Scott Moore, How the US Surrendered to China on Scientific Research," *Wall Street Journal*, April 19, 2019, https://www.wsj.com/articles/how-the-u-s-surrendered-to-china-on-scientific-research-11555666200, accessed September 23, 2019.

29 Larry Diamond and Orville Schell, "Chinese Influence & American Interests; Promoting Constructive Vigilance, " *Hoover Institute Press,* October 24, 2018, https://www.hoover.org/sites/default/files/research/docs/chineseinfluence_americaninterests_fullreport_web.pdf, pp. 121-129, accessed September 24, 2019.

30 Joshua Philipp, "Actually, We Probably Shouldn't Let China Spy On Us," *The Epoch Times,* April 24, 2019, https://www.theepochtimes.com/actually-we-probably-shouldnt-let-china-spy-on-us_2891506.html, accessed September 25, 2019.

[31] Joshua Philipp, "Exclusive: How Hacking and Espionage Fuel China's Growth", *The Epoch Times*, September 10, 2015, http://www.theepochtimes.com/n3/1737917-investigative-report-china-theft-incorporated/, accessed July 21, 2017.

[32] Daniel Wagner, "China races to reign supreme in Artificial Intelligence," *SundayGuardianLive,* January 26, 2019, https://www.sundayguardianlive.com/world/china-races-reign-supreme-artificial-intelligence, accessed September 29, 2019.

[33] "Research and Development (R&D) - Gross Domestic Spending on R&D - OECD Data," *The OECD*, 2019, https://data.oecd.org/rd/gross-domestic-spending-on-r-d.htm accessed September 6, 2018.

[34] Jeff Desjardins, "Innovators wanted: these countries spend the most on R&D," *World Economic Forum,* December 18, 2018, https://www.weforum.org/agenda/2018/12/how-much-countries-spend-on-r-d, accessed September 26, 2019.

[35] Shankar Narayanan, "Top 10 Cloud Computing Companies,"*1redDrop,* January 7, 2019, https://1reddrop.com/2019/01/07/top-10-cloud-computing-companies/, accessed September 26, 2019.

[36] Will Knight, "Inside the Chinese Lab That Plans to Rewire the World with AI," *MIT Technology Review, MIT Technology Review*, March 10, 2018, https://www.technologyreview.com/s/610219/inside-the-chinese-lab-that-plans-to-rewire-the-world-with-ai/ accessed July 19, 2018.

[37] Sarah Zhang, "China's Artificial-Intelligence Boom," *The Atlantic, Atlantic Media Company*, February 27, 2017, https://www.theatlantic.com/technology/archive/2017/02/china-artificial-intelligence/516615/ accessed March 4, 2018.

[38] "Why China's AI Push Is Worrying," *The Economist, The Economist Newspaper*, July 27, 2017, https://www.economist.com/news/leaders/21725561-state-controlled-corporations-are-developing-powerful-artificial-intelligence-why-chinas-ai-push accessed March 4, 2018.

[39] "Central Huijin Investment," *Wikipedia*, Wikimedia Foundation, August 30, 2018, accessed September 5, 2018, https://en.wikipedia.org/wiki/Central_Huijin_Investment.

40 "State Administration of Foreign Exchange," Wikipedia, Wikimedia Foundation, August 30, 2018, accessed September 5, 2018, https://en.wikipedia.org/wiki/State_Administration_of_Foreign _Exchange
41 "China Investment Corporation," 2018. Wikipedia. Wikimedia Foundation. August 26, 2018. Accessed September 5, 2018, https://en.wikipedia.org/wiki/China_Investment_Corporation
42 Paul Mozur and Jane Perlez, "China Bets on Sensitive U.S. Start-Ups, Worrying the Pentagon," The New York Times, The New York Times, March 22, 2017, accessed March 4, 2018, https://www.nytimes.com/2017/03/22/technology/china-defense-start-ups.html
43 Tom Simonite, "China Targets Nvidia's Hold on Artificial Intelligence Chips," Wired, Conde Nast, November 20, 2017, accessed March 4, 2018, https://www.wired.com/story/china-challenges-nvidias-hold-on-artificial-intelligence-chips/
44 Phil Stewart, "U.S. Weighs Restricting Chinese Investment in Artificial Intelligence," Reuters, Thomson Reuters, June 14, 2017, accessed March 4, 2018, https://www.reuters.com/article/us-usa-china-artificialintelligence/u-s-weighs-restricting-chinese-investment-in-artificial-intelligence-idUSKBN1942OX
45 "Silicon Valley Gets Queasy about Chinese Money," The Economist, August 09, 2018, accessed August 11, 2018, https://www.economist.com/business/2018/08/09/silicon-valley-gets-queasy-about-chinese-money
46 Tom Simonite, "The Trump Administration Can't Stop China From Becoming an AI Superpower," Wired, Conde Nast, June 30, 2017, Accessed March 4, 2018. https://www.wired.com/story/america-china-ai-ascension/
47 Gregory Allen and Elsa B. Kania, "China Is Using America's Own Plan to Dominate the Future of Artificial Intelligence," Foreign Policy, Foreign Policy, September 8, 2017,accessed March 4, 2018, http://foreignpolicy.com/2017/09/08/china-is-using-americas-own-plan-to-dominate-the-future-of-artificial-intelligence/
48 *Artificial Intelligence: Implications for China*, PDF, McKinsey Global Institute, April 2017, accessed March 4, 2018,

https://www.mckinsey.com/~/media/McKinsey/Featured%20In
sights/China/Artificial%20intelligence%20Implications%20for
%20China/MGI-Artificial-intelligence-implications-for-
China.ashx
[49] *Findings of the Investigation Into China's Acts, Policies, and
Practices Related to Technology Transfer, Intellectual
Property, and Innovation Under Section 301 of the Trade Act
Of 1974*, PDF, Executive Office of the President of the United
States, March 22, 2018, accessed April 4, 2018,
https://ustr.gov/sites/default/files/Section%20301%20FINAL.P
DF, p. 67.
[50] Echo Huang, "Chinese Investment in the US Skyrocketed
Last Year," Quartz, Quartz, January 3, 2017, accessed March
4, 2018, https://qz.com/876693/chinese-investment-in-the-us-
skyrocketed-in-2016/
[51] "Why Does Everyone Hate Made in China 2025?" n.d.,
Council on Foreign Relations, Council on Foreign Relations,
accessed March 4, 2018, https://www.cfr.org/blog/why-does-
everyone-hate-made-china-2025

Chapter 6

[1] "TWs Top Ten Export Destinations," Ministry of Economic
Affairs, Bureau of Foreign Trade,
https://www.trade.gov.tw/english/Pages/Detail.aspx?nodeID=
94&pid=651991&dl_DateRange=all&txt_SD=&txt_ED=&txt_K
eyword=&Pageid=0, accessed September 30, 2019.
[2] "TWs Top Ten Import Sources," Ministry of Economic
Affairs, Bureau of Foreign Trade,
https://www.trade.gov.tw/english/Pages/Detail.aspx?nodeID=
94&pid=651992&dl_DateRange=all&txt_SD=&txt_ED=&txt_K
eyword=&Pageid=0, accessed September 30, 2019.
[3] Clarence J. Bouchat, US Land Power in the South China
Sea, US Army War College, Strategic Studies Institute, July
2017,
https://publications.armywarcollege.edu/pubs/3350.pdf, pp. vi-
viii, accessed September 27, 2019.
[4] Office of the Secretary of Defense, *Annual Report to
Congress: Military and Security Developments Involving the
People's Republic of China 2019*, May 2, 2019,

https://media.defense.gov/2019/May/02/2002127082/-1/-1/1/2019_CHINA_MILITARY_POWER_REPORT.pdf, accessed September 27, 2 019.

[5] Kathy Gilsinan, "How the U.S. Could Lose War with China," *The Atlantic*, July 25, 2019, https://www.theatlantic.com/politics/archive/2019/07/china-us-war/594793/, accessed September 27, 2019.

[6] "U.S. Military Spending From 2000 to 2018," *Statista*, https://www.statista.com/statistics/272473/us-military-spending-from-2000-to-2012/, accessed October 1, 2019.

[7] "DoD Releases Fiscal Year 2019 Budget Proposal," PDF, https://comptroller.defense.gov/Portals/45/Documents/defbudget/fy2019/fy2019_Press_Release.pdf, accessed October 1, 2019.

[8] Eric Heginbotham, et al., *The U.S.-China Military Scorecard*, PDF, *Rand Corporation*, 2015, https://www.rand.org/content/dam/rand/pubs/research_reports/RR300/RR392/RAND_RR392.pdf, accessed September 29, 2019.

[9] "Military Expenditure (% of GDP) – China, United States," *The World Bank*, data.worldbank.org/indicator/MS.MIL.XPND.GD.ZS?locations=CN-US, accessed September 10, 2019.

[10] "Gross Domestic Product, Fourth Quarter and Annual 2018 (Initial Estimate)," BEA, July 26, 2019, https://www.bea.gov/news/2019/initial-gross-domestic-product-4th-quarter-and-annual-2018, accessed September 10, 2019.

[11] "Military Expenditure (% of GDP) – China, United States," *The World Bank*, data.worldbank.org/indicator/MS.MIL.XPND.GD.ZS?locations=CN-US, accessed September 10, 2019.

[12] "China GDP," *Trading Economics*, 2019, https://tradingeconomics.com/china/gdp, accessed September 10, 2019.

[13] Oriana Skylar Mastro and Ely Ratner, "China is Gaining on the United States. What Are We Doing About It?" *Politico Magazine*, Feb. 9, 2018, https://www.politico.com/magazine/story/2018/02/09/china-

united-states-donald-trump-216955, accessed September 29, 2019.

[14] Travis Tanner and Wang Dong, eds., U.S.-China Relations in Strategic Domains, NBR Special Report #57, *The National Bureau of Asian Research*, April 2016, https://www.nbr.org/wp-content/uploads/pdfs/publications/special_report_57_us-china_april2016.pdf, pp. 109-119, accessed September 27, 2019.

[15] Aaron Mehta, "How the US and China Collaborated to get Nuclear Material out of Nigeria – and Away from Terrorist Groups," *Defense News*, defensenews.com, Jan. 14, 2019, https://www.defensenews.com/news/pentagon-congress/2019/01/14/how-the-us-and-china-collaborated-to-get-nuclear-material-out-of-nigeria-and-away-from-terrorist-groups/.

[16] R.C. Porter, "America's Hidden Role in Chinese Weapons Research," *Fortuna's Corner,* March 30, 2017; https://fortunascorner.com/2017/03/30/americas-hidden-role-in-chinese-weapons-research-many-scientists-have-returned-to-china-after-working-at-los-alamos-and-other-top-u-s-research-laboratories/, accessed September 27, 2019.

[17] Porter, accessed September 27, 2019.

[18] Ana Swanson and Keith Bradsher, "White House Considers Restricting Chinese Researchers Over Espionage Fears," *New York Times*, April 30, 2018, https://www.nytimes.com/2018/04/30/us/politics/trump-china-researchers-espionage.html, accessed September 28, 2019.

[19] Andrew Liptak, "The US Air Force has a new weapon called THOR that can take out swarms of drones," *Theverge,* June 21, 2019, https://www.theverge.com/2019/6/21/18701267/us-air-force-thor-new-weapon-drone-swarms, accessed September 30, 2019.

[20] James Stavridis, "China's military buildup is worry for neighbors and warning for US," *Nikkei Asian Review*, October 1, 2019, https://asia.nikkei.com/Opinion/China-s-military-buildup-is-worry-for-neighbors-and-warning-for-US?utm_source=Fareed%27s+Global+Briefing&utm_campaign=57c428f05a-EMAIL_CAMPAIGN_2019_09_30_10_02&utm_medium=ema

il&utm_term=0_6f2e93382a-57c428f05a-83726697, accessed October 1, 2019.

[21] Missile Defense Project, "DF-41 (Dong Feng-41 / CSS-X-20)," *Missile Threat,* August 12, 2016, https://missilethreat.csis.org/missile/df-41/, accessed September 30, 2019.

[22] Benedict Brook and AP, "China set to unveil Dongfeng-41 nuclear weapon at military parade commemorating 70 years of Communist rule," *News,* October 1, 2019, https://www.news.com.au/technology/innovation/military/china-set-to-unveil-dongfeng41-nuclear-weapon-at-military-parade-commemorating-70-years-of-communist-rule/news-story/359b936d65e3f172c8ef641d85142e2d, accessed October 1,2019.

[23] Benedict Brook and AP.

[24] Missile Defense Project, "China Tests New DF-17 with Hypersonic Glide Vehicle," *Missilethreat,* January 4, 2018, https://missilethreat.csis.org/china-tests-new-df-17-hypersonic-glide-vehicle/, accessed September 30, 2019.

[25] Chu Wen, "CCP Parade: Two Latest Drone Exposure Technology Strikes Super Beautiful," *Dwnews,* September 16, 2019, http://news.dwnews.com/china/news/2019-09-16/60149326.html, accessed September 30 2019.

[26] "China's Anniversary Parade Reveals New Weapons That Will Influence U.S. Strategies, " *MoonofAlabama,* October 1, 2019, https://www.moonofalabama.org/2019/10/chinas-anniversary-parade-reveals-new-weapons-that-will-influence-us-strategies.html, accessed October 2, 2019.

[27] Brad Lendon, "China is preparing to show off some incredible weaponry. Here's what it could be," *CNN,* September 27, 2019, https://edition.cnn.com/2019/09/27/asia/china-military-parade-analysis-preview-intl-hnk/index.html?no-st=1569742471, accessed September 29, 2019.

[28] Andrew S. Erickson, "China's Massive Military Parade Shows Beijing is a Missile Superpower," *TheNationalInterest,* October 1, 2019, https://nationalinterest.org/blog/buzz/chinas-massive-military-parade-shows-beijing-missile-superpower-84731?utm_source=Fareed%27s%20Global%20Briefing&utm_campaign=3cca99bfff-

EMAIL_CAMPAIGN_2019_10_01_08_51&utm_medium=ema
il&utm_term=0_6f2e93382a-3cca99bfff-
83726697&page=0%2C1, accessed October 2, 2019.
[29] Ibid.
[30] "Annual Report to Congress: Military and Security
Developments Involving the People's Republic of China
2019," *Media.Defense,* May 2, 2019,
https://media.defense.gov/2019/May/02/2002127082/-1/-
1/1/2019%20CHINA%20MILITARY%20POWER%20REPOR
T%20(1).PDF, accessed September 30, 2019.
[31] Ryan Browne, "Top US general says Google 'is indirectly
benefiting the Chinese military'," *CNN,* March 14, 2019,
https://www.cnn.com/2019/03/14/politics/dunford-china-
google/index.html, accessed September 30, 2019.
[32] Ryan Browne, "Pentagon says China's military using
espionage to steal secrets," *CNN,* May 3, 2019,
https://www.cnn.com/2019/05/02/politics/china-pentagon-
report/index.html, accessed September 30, 2019.
[33] Joshua Philipp, "US Navy Cruisers and Destroyers Look to
Ditch Lenovo Servers," *The Epoch Times*, May 7, 2015,
http://www.theepochtimes.com/n3/1348839-us-navy-cruisers-
and-destroyers-look-to-ditch-lenovo-servers/.
[34] "Defense Budget Overview: United States Department of
Defense Fiscal Year 2020 Budget Request,"
Comptroller.Defense, March, 2019,
https://comptroller.defense.gov/Portals/45/Documents/defbud
get/fy2020/fy2020_Budget_Request_Overview_Book.pdf,
accessed September 30, 2019.
[35] Michael T. Klare, "The US Military Is Preparing for a New
War," *The Nation,* June 5, 2019,
https://www.thenation.com/article/us-military-is-preparing-for-
new-wars-china-russia/, accessed September 30, 2019.
[36] Ryan Browne, "Pentagon launches development agency
seen as key to future Space Force," *CNNPolitics,* March 13,
2019, https://www.cnn.com/2019/03/13/politics/pentagon-
space-force-agency/index.html, accessed September 30
2019.
[37] Philipp, Joshua, "China Covers Up Anti-Satellite Test,
Again", *The Epoch Times*, August 3, 2014, accessed July 26,

2017, http://www.theepochtimes.com/n3/838700-china-covers-up-anti-satellite-test-again/.
[38] "Active protection system", *Wikipedia*, https://en.wikipedia.org/wiki/Active_protection_system, accessed July 26, 2017.
[39] Kania Elsa B., "The PLA's Potential Breakthrough in High-Power Microwave Weapons", *The Diplomat*, March 11, 2017 ,http://thediplomat.com/2017/03/the-plas-potential-breakthrough-in-high-power-microwave-weapons/, accessed July 26, 2017.
[40] Philipp Joshua, "China Makes Advances in Space Lasers, Microwave Weapons", *The Epoch Times*, March 22, 2017, http://www.theepochtimes.com/n3/2234510-china-advances-assassins-mace-warfare-program/, accessed July 26, 2017.
[41] Gertz Bill, "How China's Mad Scientists Plan to Shock America's Military: Super Lasers, Railguns, and Microwave Weapons", *The National Interest*, March 10, 2017, http://nationalinterest.org/blog/the-buzz/how-chinas-mad-scientists-plan-shock-americas-military-super-19737, accessed July 26, 2017.
[42] Philipp, Joshua, "World Powers Are Preparing for Space Warfare", *The Epoch Times*, September 6, 2015, http://www.theepochtimes.com/n3/1741095-world-powers-are-preparing-for-space-warfare/, accessed July 26, 2017.
[43] Mike Wall, "China Makes Historic 1st Landing on Mysterious Far Side of the Moon," *Space,* January 3, 2019, https://www.space.com/42883-china-first-landing-moon-far-side.html, accessed September 30, 2019.
[44] Li Zheng, "Space: A New Frontier for Sino-American Cooperation," *ChinaUsFocus,* January 29, 2019, https://www.chinausfocus.com/energy-environment/space-a-new-frontier-for-sino-american-cooperation, accessed September 27, 2019.
[45] Robert Hackett, "Google Claims 'Quantum Supremacy,' Marking a Major Milestone in Computing," *Fortune,* September 20, 2019, https://fortune.com/2019/09/20/google-claims-quantum-supremacy/, accessed September 23, 2019.
[46] Elsa B. Kania and John Costello, "Quantum Hegemony? China's Ambitions and the Challenge to U.S. Innovation

Leadership," *Cnas,* September 12, 2018, https://www.cnas.org/publications/reports/quantum-hegemony, accessed September 23, 2019.
[47] Whigham Nick, "China sets new record for quantum entanglement to build new communication network," *News.com*, June 19, 2017, http://www.news.com.au/technology/science/space/china-sets-new-record-for-quantum-entanglement-en-route-to-build-new-communication-network/news-story/e528da0cf68b2e63bbe093cab49ec507, accessed October 5, 2019.
[48] Twinkle Ghosh, "China takes major step in creating a global network for quantum communication," *The Indian Telegraph,* August 16, 2016, https://theindiantelegraph.com.au/china-takes-major-step-creating-global-network-quantum-communication/, accessed October 5, 2019.

Chapter 7

[1] "Pollution By Country 2019," *World Population Review,* October 24, 2019, http://worldpopulationreview.com/countries/pollution-by-country/, accessed October 31, 2019.
[2] Sarah Gibbens, "15 ways the Trump administration has changed environmental policies," *National Geographic,* February 1, 2019, https://www.nationalgeographic.com/environment/2019/02/15-ways-trump-administration-impacted-environment/, accessed October 8, 2019.
[3] Leslie Hook and Lucy Hornby, "China Emerges as Powerbroker in Global Climate Talks," *Financial Times,* Nov. 16, 2018, https://www.ft.com/content/7c1f16f8-e7ec-11e8-8a85-04b8afea6ea3, accessed October 5, 2019.
[4] Jorrit Gosens, Tomas Kåberger, and Yufei Wang, "China's next renewable energy revolution: goals and mechanisms in the 13th Five Year Plan for energy," *Wiley Online Library,* June 26, 2017, https://onlinelibrary.wiley.com/doi/full/10.1002/ese3.161, accessed October 5, 2019.

[5] Charles Street, "The US Needs to Take Back Climate Leadership," *China Us Focus,* August 16, 2019, https://www.chinausfocus.com/energy-environment/the-us-needs-to-take-back-climate-leadership, accessed October 5, 2019.

[6] Jon Fingas, "China is now the biggest producer of solar power," *engadget,* February 5, 2017, https://www.engadget.com/2017/02/05/china-becomes-biggest-solar-energy-producer/, accessed October 5, 2019.

[7] Joshua S. Hill, "Goldwind Edges Out Vestas As World's Leading Wind Turbine Supplier," *Cleantechnica,* May 19, 2016, https://cleantechnica.com/2016/05/19/goldwind-edges-vestas-worlds-leading-wind-turbine-supplier/, accessed October 5, 2019.

[8] Mark Jones, "How the US and China compare on action against climate change," *Worldeconomicforum,* June 27, 2017, https://www.weforum.org/agenda/2017/06/how-china-and-us-compare-on-climate-action/, accessed October 5, 2019.

[9] Godfrey Yeung, " 'Made in China 2025': the development of a new energy vehicle industry in China," *tadfonline,* September 5, 2018, https://www.tandfonline.com/doi/full/10.1080/23792949.2018.1505433, accessed October 5, 2019.

[10] Bart Demandt, "China car sales analysis 2018 – brands," *Carsalesbase,* January 20, 2019, http://carsalesbase.com/china-car-sales-analysis-2018-brands/, accessed October 5, 2019.

[11] Steven Loveday, "December 2018 U.S. EV Sales Recap: Over 360K Secured!" *insideevs,* January 7, 2019, https://insideevs.com/news/341825/december-2018-us-ev-sales-recap-over-360k-secured/, accessed October 5, 2019.

[12] "Electric cars: China's battle for the battery market," *Financial Times,* https://www.ft.com/content/8c94a2f6-fdcd-11e6-8d8e-a5e3738f9ae4?mhq5j=e5, accessed October 5, 2019.

[13] Keith Bradsher, "China's Electric Car Push Lures Global Auto Giants, Despite Risks," *The New York Times,* September 10, 2017,

https://www.nytimes.com/2017/09/10/business/china-electric-cars.html?_r=1, accessed October 5, 2019.

[14] Zach Montague, "China's Electric Vehicle Plan Is a Bid to Lead the World," *China Us Focus,* October 27, 2017, https://www.chinausfocus.com/energy-environment/chinas-electric-vehicle-plan-is-a-bid-to-lead-the-world, accessed October 5, 2019.

[15] Kara Sherwin, "China Is Outsourcing Its Pollution," *Foreign Policy,* December 7, 2016, https://foreignpolicy.com/2016/12/07/china-is-outsourcing-its-pollution/, accessed October 5, 2019.

[16] Kevin Yao and Meng, "China expects to lay off 1.8 million workers in coal, steel sectors," *Reuters: Discover Thomas Reuters,* February 29, 2016, https://www.reuters.com/article/us-china-economy-employment-idUSKCN0W205X, accessed October 5, 2019.

[17] Brenda Goh and Cate Cadell, "China's Xi says Belt and Road must be green, sustainable" *Reuters: Discover Thomas Reuters,* April 25, 2019, https://www.reuters.com/article/us-china-silkroad/chinas-xi-says-belt-and-road-must-be-green-sustainable-idUSKCN1S104I, accessed October 5, 2019.

[18] "Environment & Energy Congressional Round-Up | December 6 - December 17," *EESI,* December 20, 2019, https://www.eesi.org/articles/view/exploring-the-environmental-repercussions-of-chinas-belt-and-road-initiative, accessed December 21, 2019.

[19] Sagatom Saha, "China's Belt and Road Plan Is Destroying the World," *The National Interest,* August 18, 2019, https://nationalinterest.org/feature/chinas-belt-and-road-plan-destroying-world-74166, accessed October 5, 2019.

[20] Ibid.

[21] "The Belt and Road Ecological and Environmental Cooperation Plan," *Ministry of Ecology and Environment,* May, 2017, http://english.mee.gov.cn/Resources/Policies/policies/Framew orkp1/201706/t20170628_416869.shtml, accessed October 5, 2019.

[22] "Joint Communique of the Leaders' Roundtable of the 2nd Belt and Road Forum for International Cooperation," *Belt and Road Forum,* April 27, 2019,

https://www.fmprc.gov.cn/mfa_eng/zxxx_662805/t1658766.sh
tml, accessed October 5, 2019.
[23] Christine Shearer, Melissa Brown, and Tim Buckley, "China
at a Crossroads: Continued Support for Coal Power Erodes
Country's Clean Energy Leadership," *Institute For Energy
Economics and Financial Analysis,* January, 2019,
http://ieefa.org/wp-content/uploads/2019/01/China-at-a-
Crossroads_January-2019.pdf, accessed October 5, 2019.
[24] Lily Hartzell, "Greening the Belt and Road," *China Us
Focus,* August 6, 2019,
https://www.chinausfocus.com/energy-environment/greening-
the-belt-and-road, accessed October 5, 2019.
[25] Somini Sengupta and Steven Lee Myers, "Latest Arena
for China's Growing Global Ambitions: The Arctic," *New York
Times*, May 24, 2019,
https://www.nytimes.com/2019/05/24/climate/china-
arctic.html, accessed October 2, 2019
[26] Daniel Wagner, "China, Nicaragua, and the Canal: Global
Shipping with Chinese Characteristics," *Huffington Post*, June
13, 2013,
https://www.huffingtonpost.com/daniel-wagner/china-
nicaragua-and-the-c_b_3436149.html, accessed October 5,
2019.
[27] "How is China managing its greenhouse gas emissions?"
China Power, July 19, 2018, updated March 7, 2019;
https://chinapower.csis.org/china-greenhouse-gas-emissions/,
accessed October 6, 2019.
[28] Eleanor Albert and Beina Xu, "China's Environmental
Crisis," *Council on Foreign Relations,* January 18, 2016,
https://www.cfr.org/backgrounder/chinas-environmental-crisis,
accessed October 6, 2019.
[29] Nicolas Casey and Clifford Krauss, "It Doesn't Matter if
Ecuador Can Afford This Dam. China Still Gets Paid," *The
New York Times*, Dec. 24, 2018,
https://www.nytimes.com/2018/12/24/world/americas/ecuador
-china-
dam.html?rref=collection%2Fspotlightcollection%2Fchina-
reach, accessed October 6, 2019.
[30] Jonas Gamso, "Environmental policy impacts of trade with
China and the moderating effect of governance," *Wiley Online*

Library, June 7, 2018,
https://onlinelibrary.wiley.com/doi/abs/10.1002/eet.1807,
accessed October 6, 2019.

[31] "Global metrics for the environment," *EPI,*
https://epi.envirocenter.yale.edu/, accessed October 6, 2019.

[32] "Data," *QOG,* https://qog.pol.gu.se/data, accessed October 6, 2019.

[33] Jonas Gamso, "Is China worsening the developing world's environmental crisis?" *The Conversation,* August 22, 2018, https://theconversation.com/is-china-worsening-the-developing-worlds-environmental-crisis-100284, accessed October 6, 2019.

[34] Mark Lynas, "How do I know China wrecked the Copenhagen deal? I was in the room," *The Guardian,* December 22, 2009, https://www.theguardian.com/environment/2009/dec/22/copenhagen-climate-change-mark-lynas, accessed October 6, 2019.

[35] Lily Hartzell, "A Shift in Climate Strategy: China at the COP 24," *China Us Focus,* January 25, 2019, https://www.chinausfocus.com/energy-environment/a-shift-in-climate-strategy-china-at-the-cop-24, accessed October 6, 2019.

[36] Mathew Petti, "U.S.-China Competition Meets the Climate Challenge," *The National Interest,* August 1, 2019, https://nationalinterest.org/feature/us-china-competition-meets-climate-challenge-70651, accessed October 6, 2019.

[37] Zhang Jianyu, "The evolution of US-China collaboration on environmental protection," *EDF,* November 8, 2017, http://blogs.edf.org/climatetalks/2017/11/10/the-evolution-of-us-china-collaboration-on-environmental-protection/, accessed October 7, 2019.

[38] "EPA Collaboration with China," *EPA,* https://www.epa.gov/international-cooperation/epa-collaboration-china, accessed October 7, 2019.

[39] "Thomas Friedman: Making America Great Again," *Wbur,* October 5, 2011, https://www.wbur.org/onpoint/2011/10/05/thomas-friedman, accessed October 7, 2019.

[40] Lili Pike, "Belt and Road countries will make or break the Paris Agreement," *The Third Pole,* September 24, 2019, https://www.thethirdpole.net/en/2019/09/24/belt-and-road-countries-will-make-or-break-the-paris-agreement/, accessed October 8, 2019.

[41] "Are dictatorships better than democracies at fighting climate change?" *The Economist*, September , 21, 2019, https://www.economist.com/asia/2019/09/19/are-dictatorships-better-than-democracies-at-fighting-climate-change?utm_source=Fareed%27s+Global+Briefing&utm_ca mpaign=81033659e8-EMAIL_CAMPAIGN_2019_09_25_09_53&utm_medium=ema il&utm_term=0_6f2e93382a-81033659e8-83726697, accessed October 13, 2019.

[42] Peter Bittner, "Is China Ready to Fill the US Leadership Void on Climate Change?" *China Us Focus,* December 12, 2018, https://www.chinausfocus.com/energy-environment/is-china-ready-to-fill-the-us-leadership-void-on-climate-change, accessed October 7, 2019.

[43] Luiza Ch. Savage, "The U.S. left a hole in leadership on climate. China is filling it," *Politico,* August 15, 2019, https://www.politico.com/story/2019/08/15/climate-china-global-translations-1662345, accessed October 7, 2019.

Chapter 8

[1] Matt Schiavenza, "China's Dominance in Manufacturing – in One Chart, *The Atlantic*, August 5, 2013; https://www.theatlantic.com/china/archive/2013/08/chinas-dominance-in-manufacturing-in-one-chart/278366/, accessed March 31, 2020.

[2] Tom Linton and Bindiya Vakil,"Coronavirus is Proving We Need More Resilient Supply Chains," *Harvard Business Review*, March 5, 2020; https://hbr.org/2020/03/coronavirus-is-proving-that-we-need-more-resilient-supply-chains, accessed March 31, 2020.

[3] Daniel Wagner, "Coronavirus Threatens China's Global Trade and Investment Regime, *Fair Observer*, March 5, 2020; https://www.fairobserver.com/region/asia_pacific/coronavirus-

covid-19-china-global-trade-manufacturing-investment-regime-news-16443//, accessed March 31, 2020.

[4] Sophia Yan, " 'Made in China' isn't so cheap anymore, and that could spell headache for Bejing," *CNBC,* Feb. 27, 2017; https://www.cnbc.com/2017/02/27/chinese-wages-rise-made-in-china-isnt-so-cheap-anymore.html, accessed March 31, 2020.

[5] Sophia Yan, " 'Made in China' Labor is not actually that cheap," *CNN Business,* March 17, 2016; https://money.cnn.com/2016/03/17/news/economy/china-cheap-labor-productivity/index.html, accessed April 16, 2020.

[6] James Crabtree, "Coronavirus will send globalization into reverse," Nikkei Asian Review, March 25, 2020; https://asia.nikkei.com/Opinion/Coronavirus-crisis-will-send-globalization-into-reverse, accessed March 31, 2020.

[7] Bradley A. Thayer and Lianchao Han, "What did China's Xi Jinping know, and when did he know it?" *The Hill*, March 4, 2020; https://thehill.com/opinion/international/490258-what-did-chinas-xi-jinping-know-and-when-did-he-know-it, accessed March 31, 2020.

[8] World Health Organization, "Statement of Account, China, as of 31 December, 2019," *World Health Organization*; https://www.who.int/about/finances-accountability/funding/account_statement/chn_en.pdf?ua=1, accessed March 31, 2020.

[9] World Health Organization, "Contributors," *World Health Organization;* http://open.who.int/2018-19/contributors/contributor; accessed March 31, 2020.

[10] Charles Clift, "What's the World Health Organization For?" *Chatham House*, May 21, 2014; https://www.chathamhouse.org/publication/what-s-world-health-organization, accessed March 31, 2020.

[11] Daniel Wagner, "China's Influence Dampens International Response to Coronavirus Outbreak," *Fair Observer*, February 24, 2020; https://www.fairobserver.com/region/asia_pacific/china-coronavirus-outbreak-covid-19-who-international-response-news-16661/, accessed March 31, 2020.

[12] World Health Organization, *Pandemic Influenza Risk Management, World Health Organization*, May, 2017;

https://www.who.int/influenza/preparedness/pandemic/PIRM_
update_052017.pdf, accessed March 31, 2020.
[13]David Gitter, Sandy Lu, Brock Erdahl, "China Will Do
Anything to Deflect Coronavirus Blame," *FP*, March 30, 2020;
https://foreignpolicy.com/2020/03/30/beijing-coronavirus-
response-see-what-sticks-propaganda-blame-ccp-xi-jinping/,
accessed April 6, 2020.
[14] Kara Rogers, "1957 Flu Pandemic," *Encyclopedia
Britannica*, March 26, 2020;
https://www.britannica.com/event/Asian-flu-of-1957, accessed
April 6, 2020.
[15] Edwin D. Kilbourne, "Influenza Pandemics of the 20th
Century," *Emerging Infectious Diseases*, 12:1 (Jan, 2006), 9–
14, doi: 10.3201/eid1201.051254;
https://www.ncbi.nlm.nih.gov/pmc/articles/PMC3291411/;
accessed April 6, 2020.
[16] Gitter, et al.
[17] https://www.nationalreview.com/2020/04/coronavirus-china-
trail-leading-back-to-wuhan-labs/; accessed April 6, 2020.
[18] http://www.whiov.cas.cn/105341/; accessed April 6, 2020.
[19]

http://www.whiov.cas.cn/105341/201912/t20191224_5471634
.html; accessed April 6, 2020.
[20]

https://web.archive.org/web/20200214144447/https:/www.res
earchgate.net/publication/339070128_The_possible_origins_
of_2019-nCoV_coronavirus; accessed April 6, 2020.
[21]

https://www.sciencedirect.com/science/article/pii/S014067362
0301835?via%3Dihub; accessed April 6, 2020.
[22]

https://www.nejm.org/doi/full/10.1056/NEJMp2002106?query=
TOC; accessed April 6, 2020.
[23] https://www.washingtonpost.com/opinions/global-
opinions/how-did-covid-19-begin-its-initial-origin-story-is-
shaky/2020/04/02/1475d488-7521-11ea-87da-
77a8136c1a6d_story.html; accessed April 6, 2020.
[24] https://www.youtube.com/watch?v=_txYMXL9NJ0;
accessed April 6, 2020.

[25] https://www.ncbi.nlm.nih.gov/pmc/articles/PMC3291347/; accessed April 6, 2020.

[26] Ibid.

[27] https://www.nature.com/articles/nature12711; accessed April 9, 2020.

[28] https://www.ncbi.nlm.nih.gov/pmc/articles/PMC5708621/; accessed April 9, 2020.

[29] https://www.washingtontimes.com/news/2020/mar/30/china-researchers-isolated-bat-coronaviruses-near-/; accessed April 6, 2020.

[30] Rem Reider, "Trump's Statements About the Coronavirus," *FactCheck.org,* March 19, 2020; https://www.factcheck.org/2020/03/trumps-statements-about-the-coronavirus/, accessed April 9, 2020.

[31] Fred Charatan, "Bush signs law to protect US from bioterrorism," *BMJ*, 329:7460 (July 31, 2004), 250, doi: 10.1136/bmj.329.7460.250-b; https://www.ncbi.nlm.nih.gov/pmc/articles/PMC498057/; accessed April 9, 2020.

[32] Rebeccah Heinrichs, "The Truth about the National Security Council's Pandemic Team," *National Review,* April 1, 2020; https://www.nationalreview.com/2020/04/coronavirus-truth-national-security-council-pandemic-team/, accessed April 9, 2020.

[33] Bipartisan Commission on Biodefense; https://biodefensecommission.org/, accessed April 9, 2020.

[34] Global Biodefense, "Blue Ribbon Study Panel on Biodefense Receives 1.3M Grant," *Global Biodefense,* Sept. 22, 2016; https://globalbiodefense.com/2016/09/22/blue-ribbon-study-panel-biodefense-receives-1-3-million-grant/, accessed April 9, 2020.

[35] Aaron Martin, "Blue Ribbon Study Panel on Biodefense awarded $2.5 million grant," *Homeland Preparedness News,* Feb. 16, 2018; https://homelandprepnews.com/stories/26837-blue-ribbon-study-panel-biodefense-awarded-2-5-million-grant/, accessed April 9, 2020.

[36] United States Government Accountability Office, *National Biodefense Strategy,* February 2020;

https://www.gao.gov/assets/710/704698.pdf, accessed April 9, 2020.

[37] Linhui Ruan et al., "New measures for COVID-19 response: a lesson from the Wenzhou experience," *Clinical Infectious Diseases,* April 3, 2020, doi.org/10.1093/cid/ciaa386; https://academic.oup.com/cid/advance-article/doi/10.1093/cid/ciaa386/5815716, accessed April 9, 2020.

[38] Daniel Wagner and Jonathan Rogers, "China's coronavirus success shows up poor pandemic preparedness in the rest of the world," *South China Morning Post,* April 9, 2020; https://www.scmp.com/comment/opinion/article/3078848/chinas-coronavirus-success-shows-poor-pandemic-preparedness-rest#comments, accessed April 9, 2020.

[39] Susan B. Glasser, "The Coronavirus is the World's Only Superpower," *The New Yorker.* April 2, 2020; https://www.newyorker.com/news/letter-from-trumps-washington/the-coronavirus-is-the-worlds-only-superpower; accessed April 6, 2020.

[40] Jennifer Peltz, Amy Forliti, and David Rising, "New York gets Chinese ventilators; Trump wants more thanks," *AP News*, April 4, 2020; https://apnews.com/24b8b30cbc11c43a19e7e7aff69e4044, accessed April 6, 2020.

[41] Neha Dasgupta, Aditya Kalra, "Facing shortages, India bets on China for swift ramp-up of protective health gear: sources," *Reuters*, March 31, 2020; https://www.reuters.com/article/us-health-coronavirus-india-equipment/facing-shortages-india-bets-on-china-for-swift-ramp-up-of-protective-health-gear-sources-idUSKBN21I0OM, accessed April 6, 2020.

[42] Graham Allison, Christopher Li, "In War Against Coronavirus: Is China Foe—or Friend?" *The National Interest*, March 27, 2020; https://nationalinterest.org/feature/war-against-coronavirus-china-foe%E2%80%94or-friend-138387?page=0,1, accessed April 6, 2020.

[43] Forthcoming in *Diplomatic Courier.*

[44] Richard Javid Heydarian, "China seizes Covid-19 advantage in South China Sea," *Asia Times,* April 1, 2020;

https://asiatimes.com/2020/04/china-seizes-covid-19-advantage-in-south-china-sea/, accessed April 9, 2020.

[45] Edward Wong, "In the History of U.S.-China Relations, a Pattern of Enchantment and Despair," *The New York Times, Nov. 24, 2016;* https://www.nytimes.com/2016/11/24/world/asia/china-us-history-john-pomfret.html?_r=2, accessed April 12, 2020.

[46] Evan Osnos, "The Future of America's Contest with China," *The New Yorker,* January 6, 2020; https://www.newyorker.com/magazine/2020/01/13/the-future-of-americas-contest-with-china, accessed April 9, 2020.

[47] Martin Wolf, "The Tragedy of Two Failing Superpowers," *Financial Times*, March 31, 2020; https://www.ft.com/content/ea1563e8-725f-11ea-ad98-044200cb277f, accessed March 31, 2020.

[48] Sun Xi, "US-China trade war: toward the Thucydides Trap?" *Asia Times*, July 30, 2018; http://www.atimes.com/us-china-trade-war-toward-the-thucydides-trap/.

[49] Daniel Wagner and Sun Xi, "Realistic expectations must guide China-US relations," *South China Morning Post,* Aug. 7, 2016; https://www.scmp.com/comment/insight-opinion/article/1999600/realistic-expectations-must-guide-china-us-relations.

[50] Daniel Wagner and Sun Xi, "Will China, US fall into Thucydides Trap?" *The Sunday Guardian Live,* July 28, 2018; https://www.sundayguardianlive.com/opinion/will-china-us-fall-thucydides-trap.

[51] C. Textor, "Chinese Communist Party (CCP) members as a share of the Chinese population from 2008 to 2018," *Statista*, Sept. 23, 2019; https://www.statista.com/statistics/250090/share-of-chinese-communist-party-ccp-members-in-chinese-population/, accessed April 11, 2020.

Chapter 9

[1] Cissy Zhou, "China slimming down Belt and Road Initiative as new project value plunges in last 18 months, report shows," *South China Morning Post,* October 10, 2019, https://www.scmp.com/economy/global-economy/article/3032375/china-slimming-down-belt-and-road-initiative-new-project, accessed October 11, 2019.
[2] Christopher Balding, "Why Democracies Are Turning Against Belt and Road," *AIInstitute,* October, 2018, https://alinstitute.org/images/Library/DemocraciesTurningAgainstBeltandRoad.pdf, accessed October 13, 2019.
[3] Odd Arne Westad, "The Sources of Chinese Conduct-Are Washington and Beijing Fighting a New Cold War?," *Foreignaffairs,* September, 2019, https://www.foreignaffairs.com/articles/china/2019-08-12/sources-chinese-conduct, accessed October 13, 2019.
[4] Jude Tan, "7 Differences between Chinese and American Culture," *Goldstarteachers,* May 15, 2015, https://goldstarteachers.com/7-differences-between-chinese-and-american-culture/, accessed October 12, 2019.
[5] "你好! (Hello!) and Welcome to our Guide to Chinese Culture, Customs, Business Practices & Etiquette," *Commisceo-global,* https://www.commisceo-global.com/resources/country-guides/china-guide, accessed October 12, 2019.
[6] Henry Farrell and Abraham Newman, "Weaponized Globalization: Huawei and the Emerging Battle over 5G Networks," *GlobalAsia,* September 26, 2019, http://www.globalasia.org/v14no3/cover/weaponized-globalization-huawei-and-the-emerging-battle-over-5g-networks_henry-farrellabraham-newman, accessed October 13, 2019.
[7] Kevin Rudd, "The Trade War, Economic Decoupling, and Future Chinese Strategy Towards America," *AsiaSociety,* June 13, 2019, https://asiasociety.org/policy-institute/trade-war-economic-decoupling-and-future-chinese-strategy-towards-america, accessed September 21, 2019.
[8] "Full Text of Xi Jinping keynote at the World Economic Forum," *America.cgtn,* January 17, 2017, https://america.cgtn.com/2017/01/17/full-text-of-xi-jinping-

keynote-at-the-world-economic-forum, accessed September 5, 2019.

[9] Goh Sui Noi, "19th Party Congress: Xi Jinping outlines new thought on socialism with Chinese traits," *The Straits Times,* October 18, 2017, https://www.straitstimes.com/asia/east-asia/19th-party-congress-xi-jinping-outlines-new-thought-on-socialism-with-chinese-traits, accessed September 5, 2019.

[10] "President Xi's speech in Davos in full," *CGTN,* January 18, 2017, https://news.cgtn.com/news/324d544f34457a6333566d54/share_p.html, accessed September 5, 2019.

[11] Maaike Okano-Heijmans, Etienne Béchard, Louise van Schaik, and Vishwesh Sundar, "A United Nations with Chinese characteristics?," *Clingedael,* December, 2018, https://www.clingendael.org/sites/default/files/2018-12/China_in_the_UN_1.pdf, accessed September 5, 2019.

[12] Robert Daly, "China and the United States are Equals. Now What?," *WilsonCenter,* November 17, 2017, https://www.wilsoncenter.org/article/china-and-the-united-states-are-equals-now-what, accessed September 5, 2019.

[13] Daniel Wagner, "The Coming Chinese World Order," *FairObserver,* February 19, 2019, https://www.fairobserver.com/region/asia_pacific/china-rising-new-world-order-us-trade-war-news-16521/, accessed October 14, 2019.

269

INDEX

A

EPA (Environmental Protection Agency), 161, 176–77, 235
EVs (electronic vehicles), 164
EXIM (Export-Import), 56
exporters, 28, 91

F
Facebook, 19, 120, 123, 130, 199, 206
FDI. *See* foreign direct investment
firms, foreign, 66, 79–80, 125
FIRRMA (Foreign Investment Risk Review Modernization
Act), 92–93, 130
First Opium War, 31
fishing rights, 52, 193
floods, 50–51, 96, 175, 179
foreign direct investment (FDI), 14, 24, 148, 194
freedom, 19, 33, 61, 117, 173

G
Gates, Bill, 106
GDP (gross domestic product), 6, 74, 89, 101, 115, 141, 172,
179, 221, 225
GDP, global, 65, 90
GDP growth, 101
gene editing, 113–15
Germany, 25, 75, 89, 110, 120, 205
global economy, 4, 9, 35, 45, 71, 74–75, 77, 79, 99–101, 155,
191
globalization, 27, 70, 75, 77, 99, 101, 191, 195
  economic, 195
global leader, 112, 121, 180
global power, 3–4, 9, 40, 48, 64, 187, 201, 206
governance, good, 20, 196, 200
GPS (global positioning system), 152, 155
Great Recession, 25, 27, 32, 76–77, 86
Greece, 65, 67, 205
GSD (General Staff Department), 119
Gulf States, 58

H
HEU (highly enriched uranium), 143

investors, 48, 92, 126, 129, 194
Iran, 13, 53, 60, 98, 109
Iraq, 36, 60, 138, 141
Israel, 5, 46, 59, 67–69, 93, 105, 155, 205

J
Japan, 52, 60, 64, 75, 80, 110–11, 120, 155, 159, 193, 196
Jinping Thought, 196–97
Jinping, Xi (President), 5, 9, 13, 57, 62, 71
Jintao, Hu (President), 58

K
Kaduna, 143
Kenya, 5, 56, 184, 205
Khashoggi, Jamal, 34
Kissinger, Henry, 42
Korea, 32–33

L
lasers, 153, 158
  chemical, 153
  robot, 153
  satellite-killing, 153
Latin America, 4, 17, 44
law, 6–7, 11, 20–21, 63–64, 71, 92–93, 96, 152, 158, 195–97, 200–201
leaders, 18, 34, 39, 45, 48, 51, 100–101, 123, 127, 133, 146–47, 202
  world's, 3, 20, 123, 195, 200
leadership, 39, 49–50, 75–77, 100, 116, 159, 180, 197
leadership position, 180
liberalism, 6, 12
Los Alamos Club, the, 144-45

M
Made in China 2025, 29, 132
Malaysia, 184
Manila, 63–64
manufacturing, 14, 26, 82, 87, 102, 112, 121, 127, 155, 191
Mao Zedong, 31

Nicaragua, 169, 233
Nigeria, 5, 143, 205, 226
NIH (National Institutes of Health), 115–16
North American Free Trade Agreement, 172
NSF (National Science Foundation), 115–16

O
Obama, Barack (President), 26, 38, 132, 161, 173, 187, 203
Obama administration, 79, 107, 121, 130–32, 138
OFDI (outward foreign direct investment), 94–96, 98
ozone layer, 51

P
Pacific, 28–29, 65, 71, 87, 94, 186–87, 194, 202
Pakistan, 59, 165, 167, 184
Panama Canal, 169
Paracel Islands, 11, 38, 137–38, 193
Paris Climate Accord, 13, 49, 51, 77, 99, 161, 163, 166, 174, 176, 180
partnership, 97, 131, 168, 193
Peking University, 145
permafrost, 168
Persian Gulf, 61
Pew Research Center, 4, 25, 209
Philippines, 5–6, 45, 63–64, 72, 91, 110, 196, 205
PISA (Program for International Student Assessment), 116, 221
PLA (People's Liberation Army), 109, 119, 138, 140, 150, 152–53
plastics, 89
Poland, 110, 173–74, 205
policies
 aggressive, 51
 climate, 51
 disruptive, 45
 economic, 17, 96
 environmental, 187
 global, 197
 industrial, 127
 nationalistic, 46

Z
Zambia, 55–56, 184